The]
Companion:
Sewing

The Pattern Companion: Sewing

Edited by Cassandra Case

With material by
Anita Louise Crane, Arden Franklin,
Mary Jo Hiney, Sally McCann, Susan Mickey,
Mary Morris, and Joanne O'Sullivan

Sterling Publishing Co., Inc.
New York

Library of Congress Cataloging-in-Publication Data Available

2   4   6   8   10   9   7   5   3   1

Material in this collection was adapted from:
Every Sewer's Guide to the Perfect Fit, by Mary Morris & Sally McCann
© 1997, by Mary Morris & Sally McCann
Gifts for Baby, by Joanne O'Sullivan © 2003 by Lark Books
Sewing with Fabulous Vintage Fabrics, by Arden Franklin © 2004 by Arden Franklin
Sewing for the first time®, by Mary Jo Hiney © 2002 by Mary Jo Hiney
Sewing Vintage Style, by Mary Jo Hiney © 2003 by Mary Jo Hiney
Sewing Projects in an afternoon®, by Susan Mickey © 2004 by Susan Mickey
Two-Hour Dolls' Clothes by Anita Louise Crane © 1999 by Chapelle Ltd.
Two-Hour Teddy Bears by Anita Louise Crane © 1998 by Chapelle Ltd.
Two-Hour Vests by Mary Jo Hiney © 1998 by Chapelle Ltd.

Detailed rights information on page 192.

Book design by Alan Barnett

Published by Sterling Publishing Co., Inc.
387 Park Avenue South, New York, NY 10016
© 2004, Sterling Publishing Co., Inc.
Distributed in Canada by Sterling Publishing
c/o Canadian Manda Group, 165 Dufferin Street
Toronto, Ontario, Canada M6K 3H6
Distributed in Great Britain by Chrysallis Books Group PLC,
The Chrysalis Building, Bramley Road, London W10 6SP, England
Distributed in Australia by Capricorn Link (Australia) Pty. Ltd.
P.O. Box 704, Windsor, NSW 2756, Australia

Manufactured in China

Sterling ISBN 1-4027-1272-3

Contents

Introduction

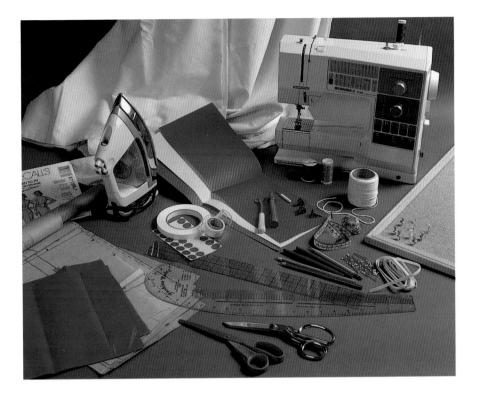

Anyone with sewing experience can find something in this book to instruct, delight, challenge, or inspire. Whether it's learning how to surmount a frustrating fitting problem, make a gift for someone, or utilize your collection of vintage linens, there are projects that will lead you through the basics and point you in the right direction to be innovative in your own right.

Because of size restrictions, most sewing patterns in this book will need to be enlarged. Enlarge patterns at any copy center, according to the percentage indicated, or to your own measurement needs. It may be necessary to move the page and copy several times in order to enlarge the entire pattern. You can then overlap and tape the enlarged pieces together, or request the copy center to use blueprint-sized paper. Other good papers for patterns can be found in the Glossary on page 188. Always use paper scissors to cut out the pattern, not your good fabric shears.

TOOLS FOR SEWING

Your **sewing machine** needs to have straight-stitch, zigzag, and buttonhole capabilities. Most serious sewers prefer a machine with metal parts—a simple machine without fancy stitches.

A **serger** or **overlock machine** that makes a professionally finished edge is a great new invention in home sewing. It is not absolutely necessary, but is fun and nonetheless useful to own.

Using good quality **thread,** which doesn't break or tangle easily, keeps frustration and cursing to a minimum. Thread has a shelf life, so beware—if you raid old Aunt Cynthia's stash of spools from the 30s, the thread will probably be rotten or weak.

Different **needles** do different things. You always need to use the appropriate needle for the weight of fabric you are using and the kind of stitch you want to make. This goes for hand-sewing needles as well as machine needles. Thin, fine needles are for lighter weight fabrics; heavier, larger needles are for heavier weight fabrics. Ball point needles are for knits and fabrics whose finely-woven fibers you don't want to shred when sewing.

You cannot sew without **straight pins** and a **pincushion** or magnetic pinholder of some sort. Pins with glass or plastic ball heads are great for basic sewing and are easy on the fingertips. Nickel-plated steel pins are rust and corrosion resistant and will stick to magnets.

Though it takes getting used to, a **thimble** will protect your fingertips from painful needle pricks.

Scissors are one of the most important tools a sewer will own. Spare no expense! Use fabric scissors specially made for the job of cutting fabric. When you buy a pair of scissors, hold them in your hand so that you can be sure the size and weight are right for you. Do not let anyone else use your scissors—cutting through something metal (even a pin!) can ruin a good pair. Constant thread clipping can dull a good pair of scissors, as can using them to cut paper or other non-fabric items.

You will also need a little pair of **snipping scissors** and/or **tailor's points** to keep at the machine for clipping, and a pair of **craft/paper scissors** for cutting out patterns and other non-fabric items. These can be inexpensive, and you can replace them often.

A **seam ripper**, or craft knife, is invaluable for un-doing seams and for cutting buttonholes.

A really good **iron** is most important—preferably heavy duty with strong steaming and pressing capabilities. Often the difference between something that looks

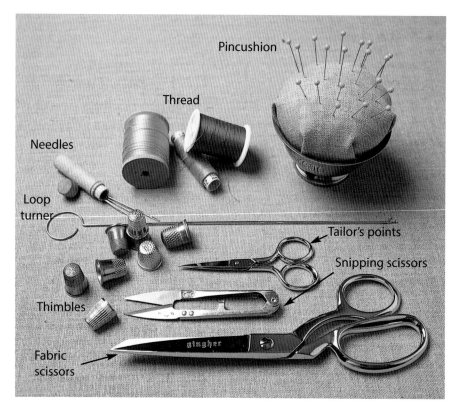

- Pincushion
- Thread
- Needles
- Loop turner
- Thimbles
- Fabric scissors
- Tailor's points
- Snipping scissors

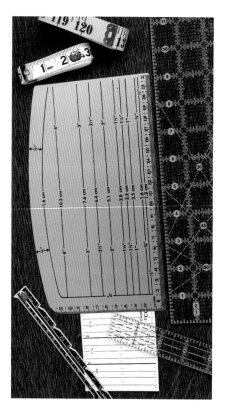

homemade and something that has a professional finish can be measured in the pressing of each step.

The sturdier your **ironing board,** the better. It should be large enough to easily press your project. You can make an ironing table with a little batting and muslin if you have room to keep something like that around. Otherwise, a collapsible one that folds away for storage is fine.

A **dressmaker's ham** is used for molding darts, curved seams, and sleeve caps.

A **presscloth** is an absolute must to protect fabrics when pressing.

A **seam roll** is used for pressing long seams and narrow areas. It eliminates the seam allowance "ridge marks."

A **sleeve board** is used for pressing sleeves and small, hard-to-reach areas.

The **easy hem gauge** is used for measuring while pressing a hem in place.

A **hem and trim measuring guide** is adhesive-backed and is made to be placed on your sewing machine.

A **sewing gauge** with a movable slider is great for measuring and marking hems, buttonholes, tucks, pleats, scallops, and other sequences.

A good fabric **tape measure** is a must. They are available in 60" lengths and 120" lengths, and have metric measurements on the reverse sides.

A **grid-lined ruler** is a transparent straight-edged ruler with imprinted grid lines, available in an assortment of sizes; it allows for checking the fabric grain line and markings. It is made from hard

plastic or from flexible plastic, and is useful when using a rotary cutter.

Special tools, called **French curves,** are made for altering curves on patterns.

The word "twin" in the name **Dual-purpose Twin Marking Pen** indicates that this pen has two ends. One end contains blue ink that can be removed with a damp cloth. The other end contains purple disappearing ink that is both air and water soluble.

A **dressmaker's marking pencil** is available with blue, pink, silver, and white lead. The marks can be removed with a damp cloth.

Tailor's chalk or a chalk wheel is used for marking construction details and alterations on fabrics.

A **smooth tracing wheel** is used to transfer pattern markings onto fabric and is used with wax-free tracing paper.

Used with a tracing wheel or ballpoint pen, **wax-free tracing paper** is used to transfer pattern markings and design lines for embroidery and/or needlework.

The **rotary cutter** is a tool that

looks and works like a pizza cutter, originally designed for quilt making. It has a round razor-type blade at the end of a handle, which can be covered when not in use. The blade is replaceable.

The rotary cutter must be used with a **grid-lined ruler** and a **cutting mat.** The cutting mat has a self-healing surface that absorbs the impact of the blade. Choose a mat with precise grid markings.

STITCHES

Some projects in this book call for special embroidery stitches.

BLANKET STITCH

Bring the needle out to your edge or hem. Make an upright stitch ¼" or more in from the edge, with the needle pointed down. Catch the thread under the point of the needle as you come out on the hem or edge. Repeat.

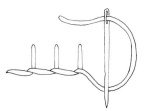

FRENCH KNOT

Bring the needle up from back of work. Wind the thread a few times around the needle tip, close to where it exits the fabric. Sew back into the fabric close to the exit hole. Pull the thread to tighten the knot.

SATIN STITCH

This stitch can be used to cover fabric entirely with stitches. Bring the needle up at the lower edge of the area you want to cover, and insert the needle directly across the area. Make each stitch touch the previous one.

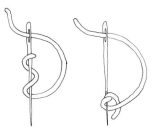

RUNNING STITCH

This is the simplest stitch and is often used for hand sewing. Bring the needle to the right side of your work and stitch from right to left.

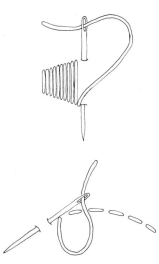

TOPSTITCH

A topstitch is used on the right side of the fabric, about ¼" in from the edge. It's essentially a Running Stitch and is used for decorative purposes. Topstitching can also be done by machine.

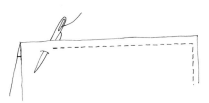

WHIPSTITCH

Insert the needle into the fabric, then bring the needle and thread over the fabric edge. Insert the needle again ⅛" to ¼" from the starting point and repeat. Used for a strong, secure bond.

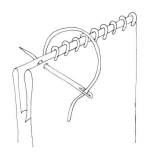

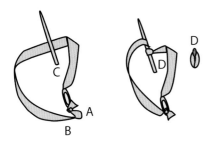

BULLION LAZY DAISY STITCH

Bring needle up through fabric at A. Keep ribbon flat, untwisted, and full. Go down at B. Come up at C, but do not pull needle through. Snugly wrap ribbon around needle tip one to three times. Holding finger over wrapped ribbon, pull needle through ribbon and put down through fabric at D.

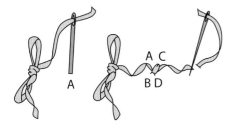

CASCADE STITCH

Thread ribbon on needle. Allow ribbon to twist. Go down at A. Come up at B and go down at C, making a small backstitch to hold cascade in place. Come up at D. Repeat at intervals for desired length.

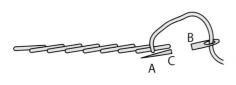

CORAL STITCH

Bring needle up through fabric at A. Hold ribbon loosely on surface of fabric with opposite thumb. Go over ribbon and down at B. Come up at C with point over ribbon again, forming a knot. Repeat.

Note: To alternate direction, change angles of B and C.

OUTLINE STITCH

Bring needle up through fabric at A. Keep floss to the right and above needle. Go down at B. Come up at C. Repeat.

STEM STITCH

Bring needle up through fabric at A. Keep floss to the left and below needle. Go down at B. Come up at C. Repeat

ABOUT BIAS

Cutting on the bias means to cut at a 45 degree angle to the grain line of a fabric. The bias is the diagonal between the straight grain and the cross grain.

FINDING THE BIAS

1. Pull on the opposite diagonals to straighten the fabric. (Sometimes fabric is pulled "off grain" during processing.)
2. Pull a thread on the cross grain to find the true straight-of-grain line. (See below.)

3. Take one corner of the cross grain edge and fold it over, lining the cross grain edge up to the selvage. The diagonal fold is the true bias. Use a straight edge marking tool parallel to the fold. *Option:* Position a gridded ruler along the cross grain and lengthwise grain (warp and weft) and draw a 2" square. Draw a line connecting the opposite corners and continue the line. (See below.)

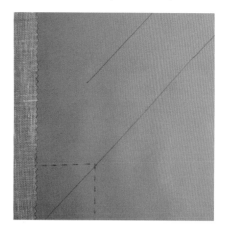

MAKING BIAS BINDING

Bias binding is made by cutting strips of fabric on the bias (45 degrees from the selvage edge) in straight lines. To determine how wide the bias strips need to be for the size binding you want, use this simple formula: Cut four times the finished width. For example, ½" visible finished binding is 2" cut width (½" x 4 = 2).

SEAMING BIAS

In order to seam bias strips, the short edges from two bias pieces must be angled identically, and the angle must be along a grainline. If necessary, trim bias edges to match grainline, then place edges, right sides together, and stitch a ¼" seam. Repeat until all strips have been seamed, but do not join the last piece to the first. Press seams open. (See below.)

CONTINUOUS BIAS

You can make a large amount of bias strips by piecing the fabric before cutting.

1. Draw the diagonal lines at a 45 degree angle from the selvage.
2. Join the shorter ends of marked fabric, right sides together, with one strip width extending beyond the edge at each side. Do not align the corners, but make sure one strip lines up with the next one over. (See Photo, center top.)
3. Stitch, using a ¼" seam allowance. Press seams open.
4. Cut apart on the marked lines to make one long strip.

BOB'S BIAS TAPE MAKER

You can easily make your own bias tape maker. This super trick is from Bob Trump, a tailor at The Rep Theatre of St. Louis:

1. On a stable piece of fabric, draw two parallel lines the distance between which will be the width of the bias.
2. Draw a set of three vertical lines to create two squares. The distance between these parallel lines is also the desired width of the bias.
3. Take a few hand stitches from point 1 to point 2, then a few more from point 3 to point 4, and next from point 5 to point 6. The stitches must be taken in this order—when you are finished you will have what looks like a Roman numeral XI.
4. Feed the strips of bias through the "X" and the "I" (in that order), positioning the strips so that the fabric folds into bias tape. (See below.) Press as you pull the bias binding tape along.

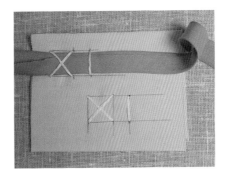

BIAS PIPING

You can buy readymade piping in fabric stores, but it's easy to make

your own—simply cover cord with bias strips. (Piping made this way is called cording.) The cord is available in a variety of diameters and is sold by the yard.

1. Cut bias strips of fabric, seaming as needed to get the length you need.
2. Place cord inside the fabric and wrap the cord, aligning the edges of the bias strip, wrong sides together.
3. Stitch along the cord as closely as possible, using the zipper foot of your machine. (See below.)

BIAS-COVERED CORD

Used for straps, belts, curtain tie-backs, and trim; to make your own, use simple round cotton cord in the desired diameter.

1. Cut and seam enough bias strips to cover the length of cord you need.
2. From the bias strips, seam a tube with a circumference that will accommodate the cord.
3. Attach a loop turner or bodkin to one end of the tube and pull it right side out.
4. Attach the bodkin to the end of the cord and thread it through the tube. (See below.)

FINE TOUCHES

FRENCH SEAM

This seam is finished on both sides and hides the raw edge.

1. Stitch fabric with wrong sides together using a ⅜" seam allowance.
2. Press seam flat and trim to ⅛".
3. With right sides together, stitch again using another ⅜" seam allowance, enclosing the previously made seam inside.
4. Press the seam allowance to one side.

SIMPLE MITERED CORNER

1. At the corner of the turned back seam allowance, make a diagonal fold. Press with an iron.
2. Open the fold and stitch along the crease line.
3. Closely trim the seam and press open.
4. Turn the hem under and stitch by hand or machine.

FABRICS

All fabric is composed of fiber. Fiber can be natural or man-made, and woven, knitted, or fused. Basic knowledge of fiber categories helps you choose a fabric with an idea of how its fiber content will impact how it will handle, wear, clean, and behave. Natural fibers are: Wool, silk, cotton, flax, and linen. Man-made fibers are: Acetate, acrylic, fleece, metallics, microfibers, nylon, polyester, rayon, spandex, tencel, and tri-acetate. When buying new fabric, look for content and care labels on the bolts, or ask the shop-keeper for this information.

WORKING WITH VINTAGE FABRICS

If you shop flea markets, garage sales, or thrift shops, look for table-cloths, handkerchiefs, curtains, antique petticoats, dresser scarves, bedspreads, napkins, table runners, and end-bolts of vintage upholstery fabrics, among other things. You can work around imperfections in vintage pieces, and use details like tucks and elaborate laces that will add character to a project with very little work from you.

LARGE TEXTILES

This category includes all table-cloths and sheets, as well as bed-spreads and quilts. The variety of tablecloths is endless—sheer, boldly patterned, embroidered, embel-lished with cutwork—both linen and cotton. Luxurious 100 percent cotton and linen sheets are also available. Chenille bedspreads and cutter quilts are great finds also.

What's a Cutter Quilt? A dam-aged quilt that has enough useable yardage is referred to as a cutter quilt. Never cut vintage quilts that are in good condition; fine antique handiwork should be preserved.

The most important thing about finding a large, intact linen is that it will usually give you enough fabric to make an entire garment. Pure linen and cotton sheets feel fabu-lous on the skin, and if they have embroidery, you can incorporate it into your design. Plain sheeting can be used for the body of dresses, for lin-ing, and to augment smaller pieces.

MEDIUM TEXTILES

Table runners, bridge cloths, dresser scarves, and place mats fall into this category, and you can often find lace pieces that are big enough to be considered a medium-sized linen.

What's a Bridge Cloth? A 36" x 36" square tablecloth made to cover a card table. The square size is stan-dard; large enough to make a child's dress or an entire pillow or purse. They can also be used for collars, cuffs, sleeves, and yokes, or applied to the bottom of a child's dress.

SMALL TEXTILES

These are handkerchiefs, hand tow-els, lace doilies, antimacassars, and small table linens like dinner or cocktail napkins. You can use these pieces on yokes and sleeves, or col-lars or cuffs, or as embellishment for a pocket. A sewn collage incor-porating scrap linens in a crazy-quilt style can even make large enough pieces of fabric to use in covering a chair or making a gar-ment or coverlet. Although a small fur piece isn't a textile, it fits in this category too, because it does make sumptuous cuffs and collars.

CLEANING VINTAGE TEXTILES

Often, the pieces you find will need a little tender loving care, i.e., a good cleaning. The chemical compound sodium perborate, a mild oxidizing agent, is best, but is sometimes hard to find in its pure state. A drug store may be able to order a small quantity of sodium perborate, but it's least expensive when bought in bulk. (Check the Internet or a swimming pool sup-ply store.) Some products contain-ing sodium perborate can be found in the grocery store, such as powdered bleaches that are safe for colors, or some general-purpose stain removers. Check the fine print to be sure that the product contains sodium perborate. If you can't find sodium perborate in pure form, use one of these products.

For cleaning and stain removal, soak the linens overnight in this solution: ½ cup of sodium perborate per gallon of warm water. (You'll need to use a larger quantity of the substitute products that contain sodium perborate.) If the stains don't come out to your satisfaction, try soaking them again in a fresh solution. After the stains have been removed, eliminate the chemical smell by washing the linens by hand or machine, using a mild detergent.

REPAIRING VINTAGE TEXTILES

Approach tears or holes two ways: Try to repair them, or cut around them. Although small holes aren't really that noticeable, you don't want them to continue to ravel, so you should darn all holes with a tight zigzag stitch. If you find a hole in a vintage linen that features cutwork, embroider around it and the hole will look like part of the cutwork.

Since you're cutting the linens anyway, you can avoid stains, holes, and tears when cutting out your project. The collage technique is a great way to use small remnants of linens and lace. Tight machine-zigzag edging keeps the remnants from raveling, just as it prevents a hole or tear from worsening.

LAYOUT ON VINTAGE FABRIC

Whether you use a purchased pattern or make your own custom pattern pieces, you will want to display the textile's design to the best advantage for your project. Think of the individual elements—pockets, sleeves, collar, cuffs, yoke—as you study your vintage fabric.

You will probably not be able

follow purchased pattern instructions for laying out the pieces. To best utilize design elements in vintage fabric, you may need to fold the fabric crosswise (generally not suggested in purchased pattern directions) or refold after cutting out each piece.

If you have rows of embroidery on a tablecloth, arrange the pattern pieces so the embroidery flows down the front and/or back of the garment. If your textile has stripes, remember to match them when laying out pattern pieces. Place patterns over clusters of flowers or fruit, embroidered designs, or cutwork, to feature them on your project. A pretty edge can be used as a hemline or the bottom edge of a sleeve, omitting a standard hem.

A common problem when working with vintage textiles is not having quite enough fabric. Piece fabric together. If you have a white linen with a lovely striped border to make a shirt, and want to have the stripes on the sleeves, too, but don't have enough fabric left to cut out the entire sleeve, cut the sleeve out of a matching white linen and apply the leftover striped fabric to the hem of the sleeve. (See page 154 for use of this solution.) You can always mix fabrics—adding a hem, or a cuff, or a collar from a contrasting fabric. This can lend a great deal of charm to your project.

MAKING A MUSLIN

A muslin is a simple prototype of a garment with no facings or linings. The name is taken from the inexpensive fabric from which they are often made.

The making of a muslin gives you a good idea of how a final garment will be constructed, and lets you know how the garment style looks on you and whether it needs fitting. It can save you much time, money, and frustration in the long run, especially when using expensive or one-of-a-kind fabrics. Any fabric store should have lightweight or medium-weight muslin. It is inexpensive and worth buying in bulk.

The next section in this book, *It's Only Fitting*, will demonstrate in detail how to measure yourself and alter a paper pattern to fit you perfectly. Use your altered paper pattern to cut a muslin prototype, transferring all markings, seamlines, darts, etc., to the muslin. Machine-baste only the basic garment pieces together, omitting facings or linings, and try the garment on to check the fit. When you are satisfied, you can take the basted muslin apart and use the pieces as your personal pattern. They will last much better than paper, and you can use your personal alterations to adjust other patterns, as well.

Personal Measurement Chart – 1

	Body Measurements	Wearing Ease	Total Body Measurements	½ Total Body Measurements	Pattern Measurements	Changes + or -
	1. High Bust					
	2. Full Bust					
	2A. Bust Point Width	0"				
	2B. Front Bust	+1"				
	2C. Back Bust	+1"				
	3. Total Waist					
	3A. Front Waist	+½"				
	3B. Back Waist	+½"				

Personal Measurement Chart – 2

	Body Measurements	Wearing Ease	Total Body Measurements	½ Total Body Measurements	Pattern Measurements	Changes + or -
	4. Total Hip					
	4A. High Front Hip	+¾"				
	4B. Low Back Hip	+1"				
	5. Bicep	+2"				
	6A. Nape of Neck to Bust Point	0"				
	6B. Bust Point to Center Front	0"				

Personal Measurement Chart – 3

	Body Measurements	Wearing Ease	Total Body Measurements	½ Total Body Measurements	Pattern Measurements	Changes + or -
	7. Center Back	0"				
	8A. Waistline to High Hipline	0"				
	8B. Hip Depth	0"				
	9. Waistline to Knee	0"				
	10. Shoulder to Elbow	0"				
	11. Elbow to Wrist	0"				

Pants Measurement Chart – 1

	Body Measurements	Wearing Ease	Total Body Measurements	½ Total Body Measurements	Pattern Measurements	Changes + or -
	3. Total Waist					
	3A. Front Waist	+½"				
	3B. Back Waist	+½"				
	4. Total Hip					
	4A. High Front Hip	+¾"				
	4B. Low Back Hip	+1"				

Pants Measurement Chart – 2

	Body Measurements	Wearing Ease	Total Body Measurements	½ Total Body Measurements	Pattern Measurements	Changes + or -
HIP BONE	**8A.** Waistline to High Hipline	0"				
HIP DEPTH 3"	**8B.** Hip Depth	0"				
CENTER POINT	**12.** Crotch Length	0"				
	13. Crotch Depth	0"				
	14. Thigh Circumference	3" or more for style				
WAIST TO ANKLE	**15.** Outseam	0"				

It's Only Fitting

DEFINITION

Good fit is characterized by a garment that follows the shape of the body with no indication of stress or wrinkling; the shoulder seam sits on the shoulder; the curves at neckline, armholes, hips, and waist follow the natural contours of the body without either binding or gapping; the length of sleeves and hems are smooth and consistent around the entire width and fall to the most flattering point.

Few things are as maddening as spending a great deal of money on fabric, then many hours on cutting, constructing, and finishing a garment, only to have it not fit.

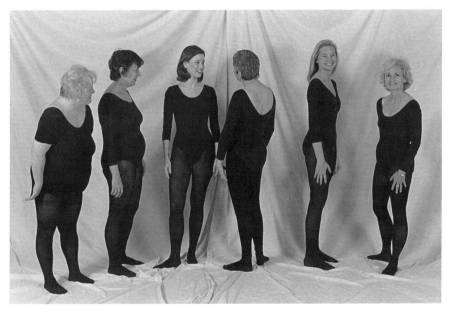

A book on sewing patterns can perhaps be most useful by showing you how to accurately fit your own body and how to personally tailor the many enticing patterns you can buy from established pattern companies.

Although a few supple individuals may manage to measure and fit themselves, it is highly recommended to recruit a sewing friend to be a fitting buddy. Not only will an extra set of hands and eyes prove invaluable, you can have a great deal of fun on the way to achieving great fitting clothes. If you do not have a friend who sews and might enjoy being your fitting buddy, consult your favorite fabric store or needlework shop. They may steer you to a group in your area that can introduce you to new sewing friends.

LOOK AT YOURSELF

Good fit begins in front of a full-length mirror. Get yourself into a leotard or form-fitting body suit (a bathing suit is not a good choice, as padding and form-correcting features can distort the truth). It is best to wear the foundation garments you will wear under your clothing covered by something like a leotard, or a snug T-shirt or camisole, and leggings. Now study yourself with an honest eye. Remember, this is a process of figure assessment, not of judgment. There is no good or bad here, simply reality. This is the first step toward understanding which styles, regardless of the dictates of fashion, will be most flattering for you.

Note the general shape of your body. Weight aside, is your body straight, with relatively little difference between your hip, bust, and waist measurements, or is it curvy, with a 10" or more difference between your waist and your bust and/or hips?

- Most pattern companies design for a woman who is 5' 6" tall. Are you taller or shorter than this?
- Do you have sloping or very rounded shoulders or are they unusually straight or broad?
- Is your back unusually straight? Do your shoulder blades protrude? Are you swaybacked?
- Do you have especially prominent curves, including one or more of the following: full bust, large abdomen, pronounced seat, or rounded upper back?
- Do you have either an unusually high or low bust or hip curve?
- Are clothes consistently too short or too long in the waist? In the sleeves?

TAKING MEASUREMENTS

The goal is not to achieve the smallest or largest number, but to record the actual circumference or length so that you can achieve the best fit. Well-fitting clothes can disguise "flaws" and will be the most flattering.

Measuring in the correct place is vital. Use strips of elastic at key spots on your body to serve as visual cues. Cut one piece of elastic at least 4" larger than your waist, two others at least 4" larger than you think your bust measurement is, and another piece at least 6" bigger than you think your hips are at their widest point. Tie each of these around the appropriate area

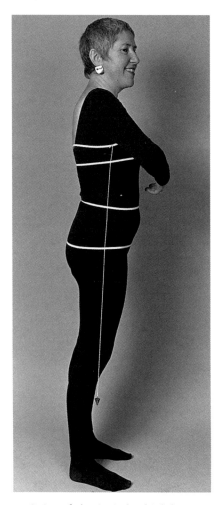

Strips of elastic tied at high bust, full bust, waist, and low hip; with a plumb line attached at the armhole point.

of your body, snug enough to stay in place but not so tightly as to cause distortion.

Around the upper chest and bust, the tape measure should be snug but cause no dents or distortion. Around the waist, you should be able to feel the tape measure, but without a sensation of either tightness or looseness. Around the fullest part of the hip, you should be able to hold the tape together at the appropriate number and easily move the tape up and down over the thighs, seat, and abdomen; you may need to loosen the tape a bit. The measured number may seem unusually large, but remember that it is infinitely easier to remove extra width from pattern and fabric than it is to add width after cutting.

Other key points are the neck point (N.P.); nape of the neck; shoulder point (SH.P.); bust point (B.P.); and wrist bone. If you wear a long-sleeved leotard or body suit, your fitting buddy can mark these points right on the leotard in chalk; or, she can use stick-on dots or masking tape along with a flow pen to mark exact points.

Measurement charts are supplied on pages 14–18. Photocopy the charts and use a pencil so that measurements can be revised, if needed.

Note: All measurements, whether on you or the pattern pieces, should be rounded up to the nearest ⅛". More precise adjustments can be made during and after fitting.

The first column, "Body Measurements," in the Personal Measurement Chart is for your measurements; the column, "Wearing Ease" indicates the preliminary amount of fitting ease, if any, for that area; "Total Body Measurements" is your body measurements *plus* fitting ease, if appropriate. In the column "½ Total Body Measurements," divide your circumference measurements in half, to correspond with those of

the pattern pieces, which represent half of any area. In the column "Pattern Measurements," enter the measurements of the pattern pieces at each designated point. The pattern already includes fitting ease. In the final column, "Changes," you will calculate the amount of change, if any, to make in each area, so that pattern pieces will equal your actual body measurements plus appropriate fitting ease. You can make adjustments during fittings if you feel more comfortable with either more or less ease.

DRESS MEASUREMENTS

Measurements #1, #2, #3, and #4, are total circumference measurements. Although these measurements are principally used for determining the proper size pattern to buy, the key measurement for determining correct dress pattern size (the high bust measurement) does not even appear on the pattern envelope. For example, a woman with a large bust does not necessarily have a broad back or wide shoulders, so she would have to make major back and shoulder adjustments to a pattern that was chosen for her actual bust measurement. On the other hand, a broad-shouldered woman with an A cup would find the neck and shoulders too constricting if she chose a pattern by her full bust measurement.

Measurement #1: High Bust—around the body, under the armpits, and above the breasts

Measurement #2: Full Bust—the circumference around your chest at the fullest point of the breast

Measurement #3: Total Waist—remember that it is actually a curve; *Note: It is important that the tape measure follow the curve as it actually appears on your body, as indicated by the elastic.*

Measurement #4: Total Hip—taken 7" below the waistline

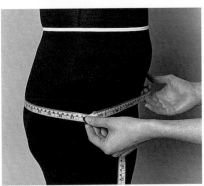

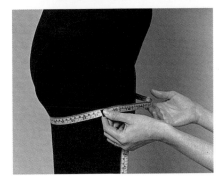

Take the hip measurements with the tape measure held loosely enough to slide easily over the abdomen (top), seat (center), and thighs (bottom).

After these measurements have been taken, your fitting buddy should pin a plumb line at each armhole point and observe from the side whether you tend to carry your weight to the front or to the back and if you have any unusual features such as a swayback, a protruding abdomen, buttocks, or shoulder blades. Make notes on your Personal Measurement Chart, as these characteristics affect how a garment hangs.

Next, following the plumb line, find the dividing points between your front and back at the High Bust, Full Bust, Waist, and High and Low Hiplines, and mark them on

Taking the high bust measurement.

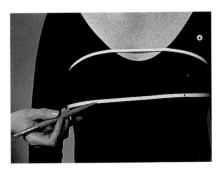

Marking the bust points on the elastic for reference.

the elastics. Since patterns are divided from front to back, you must take the circumference measurements in the same way so that alterations can be made in the segments where they are actually needed.

Measurement #2A: Bust Point Width—the distance between the right and left bust points

Measurement #2B: Front Bust—the total front bust measurement from side to side

Measurement #2C: Back Bust—across the back at the bustline, following the bustline elastic

Measurement #3A: Front Waist—from one side point to the other across the front

Measurement #3B: Back Waist—from one side point to the other across the back

There are two sets of hip measurements—the High Front Hip and Low Back Hip. Measuring these areas separately gives the actual maximum circumference of your

body below the waist, as well as the exact areas where adjustments need to be made.

Measurement #4A: High Front Hip—measured 3" below the waistline across the fullest part of the abdomen

Measurement #4B: Low Back Hip—taken at the widest part of the hip, not at the thighs or below the crotch level

Measurement #5: Bicep—taken just below the armhole point when your arm is relaxed; it corresponds, approximately, to the cap line on the pattern. *Note: The measurement should be taken with the arm slightly bent and the tape held close to the bicep, but not so tightly as to make a dent.*

Measurement #6A: Nape of Neck to Bust Point—shows if the bust point on your pattern needs to be raised or lowered

Measurement #6B: Bust Point to Center Front—to the waistline just above the navel; will identify if you are short- or long-waisted

Measurement #7: Center Back—from the nape of the neck to the waistline. *Note: Women with rounded upper backs, unusually developed back muscles, or protruding shoulder blades may need more length as well as width.*

Measurement #8A: Waistline to High Hip—the distance from your waist to the top of your hipbone curve. *Note: Patterns place the high hip at 3" to 3½" below the waist on the side seam.*

Measurement #8B: Hip Depth—distance from the waistline to the fullest part of the hip. *Note: Patterns place the hip depth at 8½" to 9" below the waist. #8A and #8B determine the shape of your hip curve, and indicate how to redraw the hip-curve lines for skirts and pants if they differ significantly from your pattern.*

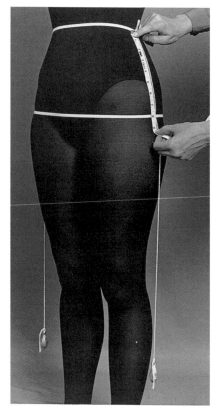

Measuring hip depth with elastic strips as reference for waist and low hipline. Plumb lines indicate the natural dividing lines of the body.

Measurement #9: Waist to Knee—from the side waist point to the middle of your knee; helpful as a reference for skirt length

Measurement #10: Shoulder Point to Elbow—taken with the elbow slightly bent, arm held slightly forward and raised to waist level (as if looking at your watch)

Measurement #11: Elbow to Wrist—taken with the arm in the same position as for #10. *Note: Both #10 and #11 are related to the length generally recommended for dress sleeves—to the bottom of the wrist bone. Jackets are a bit shorter and coats longer, but since these variations are built into patterns, expect to make the same modifications as to a dress sleeve pattern.*

PANTS MEASUREMENTS

The Pants Measurement Charts are found on pages 17-18. Keep the pieces of elastic around your waist and low hipline. The hip elastic should pass over the fullest back curve but should not be below the crotch in the front. Make sure the line it makes is parallel to the ground. Attach the plumb line(s) at your side, to determine the natural position for the side seam.

Transfer the following measurements to the Pants Measurement Chart:

#3 Total Waist, #3A Front Waist, #3B Back Waist, #4 Total Hip, #4A High Front Hip, #4B Low Back Hip, #8A Waistline to High Hip, #8B Hip Depth.

Measurement #12: Crotch Length—front: from crotch point to center front waistline; back: from crotch point to center back waistline

Tape together the beginning ends of two tape measures (see photo below) and tie a plumb line at that point. Position the plumb line so it falls straight toward your inner ankle bones. This determines both the placement of your crotch point and the location of your inseam. Hold the measuring tapes with enough ease for comfort.

Joining tape measures at their beginning ends for easier measurment of crotch length.

Measurement #13: Crotch Depth—sit on a firm surface (hard chair) and have your fitting buddy measure from the side waist point along the outseam to that surface

Measurement #14: Thigh Circumference—the thigh at the fullest point, usually right at the crotch line; also make a note whether there is a need for greater fullness at the front or the sides

Measurement #15: Outseam— the natural line indicated by the plumb lines from the side waist point to just below the outside ankle bone. *Note: You may not want your pants to end at your ankle, especially if you wear high-heeled shoes with pants, but it is a good reference point. If you and your fitting buddy have noted that one of your hips is higher than the other, take this measurement on both sides in case they differ.*

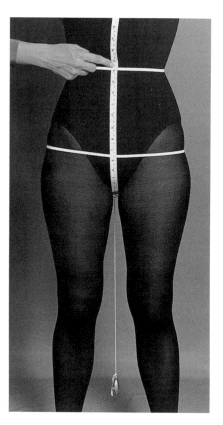

Measuring crotch length with two measuring tapes joined at their beginning ends. A plumb line is attached at the join.

FITTING A DRESS

You will probably find you need to buy a pattern at least one size larger, maybe more, than you wear in ready-to-wear. Regardless of the number on the envelope, choose the size that will need the fewest and least drastic changes.

The key measurement for tops or dresses is your High Bust or upper chest. If your bust measurement differs by 2" *or less* from your High Bust measurement, choose your pattern size according to your bust measurement. If the difference is *greater than* 2", choose the pattern size according to your High Bust measurement. Waist and hip changes to the dress are easier to make than upper chest, upper back, neck, and shoulder changes. If you are making a skirt or pants, however, the Hip measurement is more significant. The goal is to avoid making any adjustment of more than 4". This reduces the chance of distortion and also preserves the original lines of the garment.

PREPARING THE DRESS PATTERN

If your pattern is multi-sized, use a fine-tip colored flow pen to trace the size you will be cutting. If you are one size for the bust (determined by your High Bust measurement if you wear other than a B cup), another size for the waist, and yet another for the hip, trace the armhole, shoulder, and neck for the bust size. Next, choose the appropriate lines for your waist and hip, and blend the lines between sizes as you move with your flow pen from one area to the other. (See Figure 1.)

If there is only one cutting line for all the sizes on a multi-size pattern, but different stitching lines for each size, use the colored pen to mark the appropriate stitching line for your size. Then, rough-cut your pattern, allowing the greatest amount of extra tissue possible

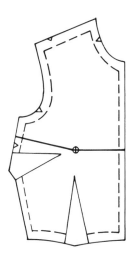

Figure 1 Marking the appropriate cutting line on a multi-sized pattern.

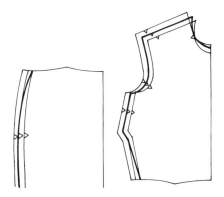

The flexible ruler, turned on its edge, is used to measure curved lines.

above the sleeve cap and, in particular, along side seam edges to allow for adjustments you may need to make. Use a warm dry iron and pressing cloth to carefully iron each piece, removing all fold lines and wrinkles. This is necessary because the machines that prepare patterns for the envelope cause creases that can make a pattern significantly smaller than the pattern-maker intended. Also iron the extra tissue paper provided so that it is wrinkle-free.

Draw a dashed line (if one is not already provided) to represent the stitching line ⅝" inside the original cutting line as provided by the manufacturer. If the seamline passes through a dart, do not draw anything between the two legs of the dart. (See Figure 2.)

If not already included, also add the following: bust point, bustline, hipline (just below the darts), low back hipline (at the widest point of the seat curve), and sleeve cap line

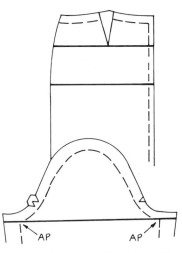

Figure 2 Drawing the bustline and stitching line, skipping over darts.

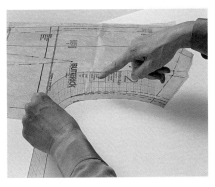

Figure 3 *(Top)* Drawing in the high hipline in the front and the low hipline in the back; *(Bottom)* drawing in the sleeve cap line.

(connecting the armhole points on each side of the sleeve). (See Figures 2 and 3.)

Measuring the pattern
Measure your pattern at each of the points you measured on yourself, along the line provided, skipping over seam allowances and darts. Since many of these measurements are along curved lines, turn the flexible ruler on its edge along the curved seamline and measure the total distance, excluding any darts, between seamlines. Record these numbers in the "Pattern Measurements" column on the Personal Measurement Chart.

Because each pattern piece covers only one quarter of the body, their combined measurements should correspond with the numbers you recorded in the "½ Total Body Measurements" column. In the final "Changes" column, calculate any correction (+ or -) you will need to make in that particular area of the pattern by comparing your ½ Total Body Measurements to those of the pattern.

Blending or "trueing" seamlines and cutting lines

When you make corrections, place the pattern pieces and extra tissue, if needed, on a cork or foam core mat. Pin one part of the pattern piece to the mat, leaving the other free to be manipulated.

To blend an altered seamline use a French curve, Fashion Ruler, hip curve, or straight ruler. For a straight seamline, use the transparent ruler or the straight edge of the Fashion Ruler to draw a new straight line that connects the beginning and ending points of the new seam. (See Figure 4.)

To blend a curved seamline is a bit trickier, as a "jog" or area of unevenness occurs in both the stitching and cutting lines. (See Figure 4.)

1. Locate the mid-point of the jog and mark it with a dot.
2. Blend through the dot along the seamline in both directions, back to the original line—above and below the alteration. The new seamline should be continuous and free of any waviness. To

guide you, use the French curve, hip curve, or the portion of the Fashion Ruler that most closely resembles the curve you are attempting to blend.
3. Make corrections to the seam allowance and cutting lines.

MINOR CORRECTIONS
Lengthening or shortening
Almost all commercial patterns come marked with lines to indicate where bodices, skirts, pants, sleeves, and hems can be shortened or lengthened.

1. Measure the amount you need to shorten above or below the lengthen/shorten line on the pattern and draw an alteration line parallel to the one provided on the pattern.
2. Draw a guideline at a right angle to the lengthen/shorten line, or extend the grainline.
3. Slash along the lengthen/shorten line, separating the pattern into two parts.
4. Overlap the pattern pieces to the alteration line. This is called the "slash and slide" method. An alternative method eliminates the need to cut the pattern in two—fold along the lengthen/shorten line, creating a tuck. (See Figure 5.)

5. Pin and tape the alteration into place. Blend seamlines and cutting lines, and redraw darts as necessary.

To lengthen a pattern, use a similar procedure:
1. Draw a guideline at a right angle to the lengthen/shorten line or extend the grainline.
2. Slash along the lengthen/shorten line.
3. Place the two pattern pieces over a fresh piece of tissue paper; pin and tape the cut edge of one pattern piece to the tissue.
4. Measure the amount you need to lengthen from the taped edge and draw an alteration line on the tissue, parallel to the cut edge; extend the guideline or grainline across the tissue.
5. Match the cut edge of the second pattern piece to the alteration line you drew, aligning seamlines and guideline or grainline. (See Figure 6.) Pin and tape in place. Blend seamlines and redraw darts as necessary.

Adjusting width at the side seams is called an "exterior correction."
1. Measure in or out from the side seam the required amount and mark. On the bodice, make marks to adjust for both bust and waist. On the skirt, mark to adjust for both waist and hip. To preserve the line of the skirt, also make a mark at the hemline the same distance from the seamline as the one you made at the hipline.
2. Fold any darts closed and redraw the seamlines, making straight lines for the side bodice seam and side skirt seam from hipline to hemline. (See Figure 7 on page 25.)

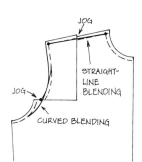

Figure 4 Blending straight and curved seamlines.

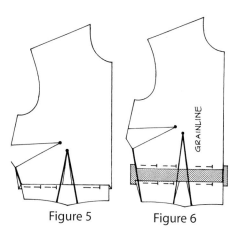

Figure 5   Figure 6

(Left) Shortening a pattern piece by folding along the lengthen/shorten line. *(Right)* Lengthening a pattern piece with the slash and slide method.

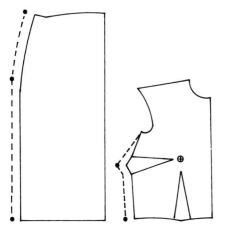

Figure 7 Adding width at the side seams.

3. Use the hip curve and/or Fashion Ruler to redraw the hip seamline. For a high hip curve, use the curvy end of the ruler; for a lower curve, use the flatter side of the ruler. Begin drawing the new curve at the waist and continue down the side of the skirt.

MAJOR ALTERATIONS
Adding or subtracting width
A second method for adding or subtracting width—folding a tuck or slashing/overlapping to subtract width, or spreading apart to add width—is similar to the slash and slide technique for length. The difference is that the slash or fold line is now vertical rather than horizontal. This method of width adjustment is called an "interior alteration." Because it affects two areas of the pattern, it is considered a major alteration.

For example, to alter a skirt front:
1. Draw a vertical slash or fold line from the waist seam to the hemline, about 1½" in from the side seam and parallel to the grain line; the line should not interfere with any darts. (See Figure 8.)
2. Draw a guideline at a right angle to the slash line or use the lengthen/shorten line as a guideline.

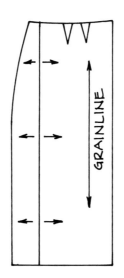

Figure 8 Adding or subtracting width along a slash line from waist to hem.

3. Determine the amount of width adjustment needed across the waist and hip of the skirt front.

A. To subtract width:
4a. Draw an alteration line the needed amount away from and parallel to the first line; again, this line should not interfere with any darts.
5a. Slash or fold along the first line; slide the edge over to the alteration line, and align the guideline.
6a. Pin and tape in place; blend waist seamline and hemline.

B. To add width:
4b. Cut along the first line and lay the two parts of the pattern over tissue on the cork or foam core mat; pin and tape one part in place.
5b. Measure and draw an alteration line on the tissue the needed distance away from, and parallel to, the taped cut edge. Slide the edge of the loose pattern piece out to the alteration line, matching guidelines to keep cut edges exactly parallel.
6b. Pin and tape the second pattern part to the tissue; blend waist seamline and hemline. Extend the hipline or guideline across the tissue.

Adjustments for curved areas
Alterations to prominent curves often involve more than one area of the body. For example, adjusting the armhole curve may affect the back, front, and shoulder areas. Three different methods can be used to alter curves; the one you choose will depend on the size of the adjustment and whether you need to adjust more than one area at a time.

The slash and pivot method
This method can be a minor alteration when used to alter the length of the shoulder seam. It can also be a major alteration if both length and width must be adjusted over a prominent curve, such as the bust, abdomen, back, and seat. This method requires slashing through darts and other lines, and spreading or overlapping the parts of the pattern.

The wedge slash and pivot method
This method is considered a minor alteration and is not used to adjust for prominent curves. Use it if you need to adjust only the length of the shoulder seam, leaving the chest area relatively unaffected. Follow these steps:
1. Make a mark on the shoulder seam 1½" in from the shoulder point.
2. Make a second mark on the armhole seam opposite the notches.
3. Draw a diagonal line between the two marks.
4. Slash along the line through the shoulder seam allowance to, but not through, the second mark at the armhole seam. (See Figure 9 on page 26.)
5. Clip through the armhole seam allowance to, but not through, the second mark, creating a hinge.
6. To shorten the shoulder seam, make a mark the needed distance toward the neckline from the diagonal slash. Pin the hinge to the cork or foam core mat and along the inside edge of the slash. Pivot the outer part of the

pattern until the slash overlaps and meets the mark. The overlapped correction will resemble a wedge. Pin and tape in place, keeping the pattern flat. Redraw a straight shoulder seamline.

7. To add length to the shoulder seam, draw and slash along the same line as described above. Pin the hinge to the cork or foam core mat and along the inside edge of the slash. Pivot the slash open. The needed addition will resemble a wedge; it will be widest at the shoulder and will taper to the armhole seam. (See Figure 10.) Add tissue; pin and

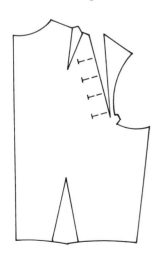

Figure 9 The wedge slash and pivot method to alter shoulder seam length.

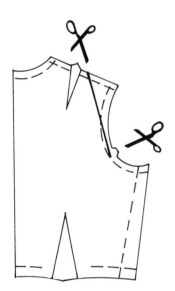

Figure 10 Shoulder seam is lengthened by opening wedge along slash to armhole hinge

tape in place; redraw a straight shoulder seamline.

The L-slash method

The L-slash method is used to alter two or more areas—such as shoulder seam length and chest width—that are in the vicinity of a curved seam, such as the armhole. Follow these steps:

1. Make a mark on the shoulder seam 1 to 1½" in from the armhole seam.
2. Draw a vertical slash line from this mark down to a level opposite the armhole notches.
3. Square a line from the end of the slash line over to the armhole edge.
4. Slash along both lines; draw the alteration line parallel to the vertical slash line.
5. Slide the L-section in or out, inserting tissue as needed. (See Figure 11.) If you need to move the position of the entire armhole, extend the vertical slash line down below the armhole and square the second line to the side seam. (See Figure 12.)
6. Blend shoulder and armhole seamlines and cutting lines as needed. Remember that whatever change you make to the front shoulder must also be made to the back shoulder.

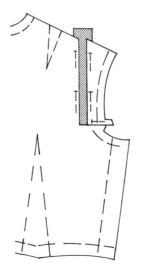

Figure 11 L-slash method to alter shoulder seam length and chest or back width.

You now have a choice between two methods of altering the shoulder seam: the wedge and pivot, which changes only shoulder length; or the L-slash, which alters the area below as well. Whichever you choose, the same alteration in shoulder length must be made to both the front and the back. You can, however, use the L-slash in front, if the chest also must be altered, and the wedge in back, if the upper back does not need any change.

The box method

Similar in technique to the L-slash, the box method is commonly used to correct one specific area. For example, to alter back width without affecting either the height of the armhole or the length or height of the shoulder seam, follow these steps:

1. Draw a horizontal line from the armhole seam at the notch 1½" to 2" into the interior of the pattern.
2. Draw a second line, parallel to the first and approximately 2" below the shoulder point.
3. Square a line to the two end points of the previous lines to form a box; the armhole seamline is the fourth side of the box.

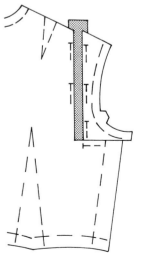

Figure 12 L-slash method to alter armhole position as well as shoulder seam length.

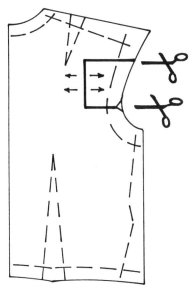

Figure 13 Box method to alter back width.

4. Cut along all three lines you drew. Draw the alteration line parallel to the vertical side of the box and slide the box in or out the necessary distance, adding tissue if needed. (See Figure 13.)

5. Blend armhole seamline and cutting line as needed.

MINOR ADJUSTMENTS TO THE BODICE

It is not recommended to make more than 1" additions to or subtractions from the side seams per pattern piece (for a total of 4" in extra circumference). Larger changes will result in distortion of the basic design. It is better to buy a larger pattern to begin with.

One exception to this general 1" rule is that, if you change either the bust or the waist at the side seam of the bodice, you may add that amount plus 1" to the other area. This exception also applies to waist/hip changes. For example, if you add ½" to the side seam at the bustline, you may add up to 1½" to the same seam at the waist. If you add 1" to the waist at the skirt side seam, you may add up to 2" to the hips. (See Figure 14.) But if you take in the bust by ½", you may only add ½" at the waist.

If only slight differences are needed, make minor additions to or subtractions from the darts, up to a maximum of ½" on each side of the dart legs at the base. Record each change you make, rounding up to the nearest ⅛", so that you can make it on all patterns you use.

With this rule in mind, re-measure the Front Bust circumference of the pattern and compare it to your personal Front Bust measurement (#2B). Do the same for the front waist of the pattern, comparing it with your personal Front Waist measurement (#3A). Once you have determined the amount of change needed at the side seams, use the flexible ruler to measure and mark the exact amount of addition or subtraction needed at the waist point and full bust.

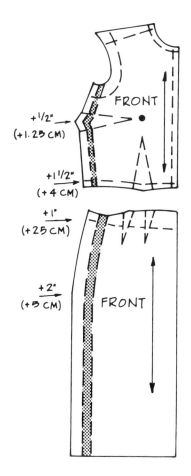

+½"
(+1.25 CM)

FRONT

+1½"
(+4 CM)

+1"
(+2.5 CM)

+2"
(+5 CM)

FRONT

Figure 14 Adding circumference at side seams.

MAJOR ALTERATIONS TO THE BODICE FRONT

Bust cup adjustments

For women who wear a C cup or larger, not only will binding across the bust be eliminated with this alteration, but the side seam, armhole, and even neckline will fit more smoothly.

Compare your Full Bust and High Bust measurements. If your Bustline measurement is 2" larger than your High Bust, you probably wear a B cup and need no adjustment. Skip ahead to Bust Point and Dart Corrections. Those with less than 1½" difference wear an A cup or smaller and usually can wear the B cup bodice without adjustment; although, if you usually get vertical folds over your bust area, you may wish to reduce the fullness. (You will be using the same slashes as for a C cup, but overlap pattern segments instead of spreading them to attain your correct measurement.) For a C cup, there is about 3" difference between the full bust and high bust.

Rule of thumb: The difference between the Full Bust and High Bust measurements, minus the B cup allowance of 2", divided by 2 equals the amount of correction needed to the front pattern piece.

So, if the difference between your high bust and full bust is 3", you will add ½" more in width to the bustline area on each side of the bodice front and approximately the same in length by doing a bust cup correction.

If you need to make a total correction of more than 1", you wear larger than a D cup. In that case, make two corrections: Method 1 to add the first 1" in width and some of the extra length you require, and Method 2 to provide any additional correction needed. If you try to make the entire D cup correction with Method 1 alone, the darts will be too pointy and the armhole seam will become distorted. On the other hand, if you use Method 2 alone, you will not get the additional length you need, so you may add width to the chest area that you do not want. If after following both methods you still need correction, add width at the side seams.

Method 1
Bust cup corrections
This adds up to 2" additional width to the entire front bodice and approximately 1" more in length to the bust area without affecting the upper chest or shoulder. It can cause some armhole distortion, so should not be used to make more than a 1" correction on the front pattern piece.

1. Extend mid-line of waist dart up to center of the bust point symbol. (If no symbol is provided, extend mid-lines of bust dart and waist dart until they converge—this is the bust point.)
2. Draw a dot on the armhole seamline opposite the single notch.
3. Clip through the seam allowance to, but not through, the dot.
4. Draw a second line at an angle from the bust point up to the dot.
5. Draw a third line through the center of the bust dart to the bust point. (See Figure 15.)
6. Slash through center of the waist dart to the bust point, then at an angle out to, but not through, the dot on the armhole seam, creating a hinge at the seamline.
7. Cut through center of the bust dart up to meet slashes at the bust point, creating another hinge there.
8. Carefully place the pattern over extra tissue on the cork or foam core mat.
9. Pin along the inside edge of the waist dart slash and the slash to armhole up to the hinge; place a pin through the hinge.

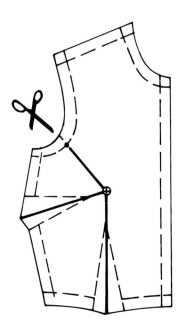

Figure 15 Slash lines for bust cup correction.

10. Gently pull the rest of the pattern down and out, spreading open a rectangle along the waist dart slash—½" wide for a C cup, and up to 1" for larger sizes. (If you need more, make 1" correction here, then use Method 2 for more width.) Pin, then tape securely in place with removable tape.
11. A triangular insertion will open at the bust dart and another along the slash to the armhole. (See Figure 15.) See that the tissue overlaps at the clip in the armhole seam allowance so the pattern lies flat; pin this in place to keep it flat while taping.
12. The bodice will now be uneven at the waist. To adjust, draw a horizontal line from the bust point through the center front seam allowance. (See Figure 16.)
13. Slash along this line and, over tissue, slide the lower center front down until it lines up at the waistline. Pin and then tape in place. (See Figure 17.)

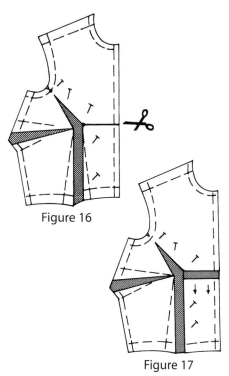

Figure 16

Figure 17

(Top) Bust cup correction with slash line for lengthening center front. *(Bottom)* Bust cup and front waistline correction.

Method 2
Bust cup corrections
For those who wear a double D cup or larger, this adds up to another 1" of width to the front pattern piece beyond the previous method. It also gives more width to the upper chest area without either adding to the shoulder, or significantly altering the armhole shape or length of the pattern.

1. Extend the mid-line of the new waist dart to the shoulder seamline; make a dot where the line meets the shoulder seamline.
2. Clip through the shoulder seam allowance to the dot, creating a hinge.
3. Extend the mid-line of the bust dart to the bust point or until it intersects the waist dart mid-line. (See Figure 18 on page 29.)
4. Slash up the center of the waist dart to, but not through, the dot on the shoulder seamline.
5. Slash through the center of the bust dart to, but not through, the bust point or extended waist dart mid-line.

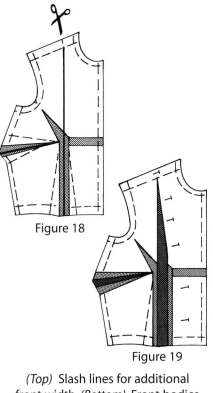

Figure 18

Figure 19

(Top) Slash lines for additional front width. *(Bottom)* Front bodice corrected for bust cup and additional width.

6. Choose a second color of tissue to distinguish this correction from the Method 1 correction and carefully place the pattern over the new tissue on the cork or foam core mat.

7. Pin along inside edge of the waist dart slash and through the hinge at the shoulder seamline.

8. Gently pull out the pattern, spreading open another rectangle along the waist dart, until its width equals the amount you need to add, up to an additional 1". (See Figure 19.) Tape securely. This adds a triangular insertion above the bust line with no bulge at the shoulder line; width in the chest area; and spreads the bust dart open a bit more. If you still need additional width, add it at the side seams.

Bust point and dart corrections

Whether or not you make the bust cup change, you must check that the bust point on the pattern is in the correct position. If you don't

need a bust cup correction, do these corrections first. If you make a bust cup correction, make these adjustments next.

Lay the front and back bodice patterns out with shoulder seamlines overlapping and neck points (where shoulder seamlines meet the neck seamline) matched. With the flexible ruler on its edge, measure around the neck seamline from the center back, through the neck point, and down to the bust point. (See Figure 20.) Compare this measurement to #6A on your Personal Measurement Chart. If needed, mark the pattern at the correct level. Now check #2A on your chart. Measure this distance from the center front to the bust point mark you made for #6A. Adjust and redraw the bust point symbol, if needed. Once you have determined the correct position of the bust point on the pattern, be sure that both darts are pointing to the bust point. If not, one or both darts may need to be moved.

Box method—moving bust and waist darts

1. If not already indicated, draw the mid-line of the dart(s) to be moved. If waist dart has a rectangle of new tissue because of a bust cup correction, draw the line vertically through the middle of the new tissue, parallel to the grainline or center front.

2. Draw two more lines exactly parallel to the first; each line runs through the point where a dart leg intersects the seamline.

3. Square a line through the dart point that connects the three lines you drew in steps 1 and 2 and form a box around the dart. (See Figure 21.)

4. Cut the box and move the entire dart, adding tissue as needed. The waist dart point should be directly below the bust point; the bust dart point should be opposite the bust point. (See Figure 22.)

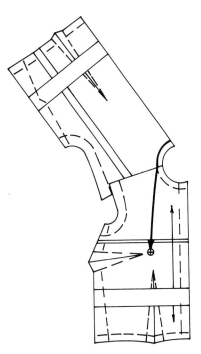

Figure 20 Overlapping front and back bodice pieces to re-measure distance from nape of neck to bust point (measurement #6A)

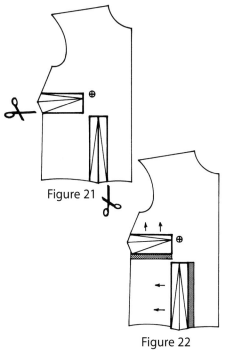

Figure 21

Figure 22

(Top) Drawing boxes for moving darts. *(Bottom)* Moving bust and waist darts.

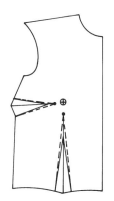

Figure 23 Redrawing darts after moving.

Redrawing the darts

After moving darts, the ends of the darts may need to be redrawn. To redraw the darts:

1. Extend the mid-line of the waist dart to the bust point and mark a new dart point 1" below it. Extend the bust dart mid-line to the bust point and mark a new dart point 1 to 1½" away. *Note: You may have to adjust these new dart points again during fittings.*

2. Redraw the dart legs. (See Figure 23.) For the bust dart, the legs should intersect the side seamline at the original points. If you have made a bust cup correction, this dart will have become either deeper or narrower. For the waist dart, the legs should intersect with the original points on the waistline. This dart may also have become either wider or narrower as a result of a bust cup correction. If the waist dart base is too wide, it may cause stress lines. If so, reduce dart base to add circumference at the front waist.

MINOR ADJUSTMENTS TO BODICE BACK

Lengthening or shortening

To keep the front side seam and the back side seam the same length, use either the front measurement as a guide or divide the difference between the two in half; then, add to one and subtract from

the other. If you make a prominent back curve alteration, lengthen or shorten the lower back to coordinate the front and back side seams.

If your pattern offers two options for lengthening and shortening the back bodice, be aware that any correction at the upper lengthen/shorten line, which runs into the armhole, would make the armhole bigger or smaller and require redrawing the armhole. Therefore, use only the lower set of lines to make the needed length correction, following the slash and spread or overlap procedure described on page 24. Tape all changes securely.

Shoulder adjustments

Evaluate the front chest and across the back for extra folds of tissue or signs of stress—these would indicate the need for an alteration. If the shoulder seam needs to be lengthened or shortened, if the length of the shoulder seam is within ½" of the length on you between the neck and shoulder points, use the wedge slash and pivot method described on pages 25-26 to make the adjustment. If both the shoulder seam and chest need correction, use the L-slash method to make the adjustment.

It is possible that the shoulder area needs a wedge slash correction in the front and an L-slash correction in the back, or the other way around. Keep in mind, however, that the same amount of correction must be made to both the front and back shoulder seam, so that the two seams will be the same length when sewn together. Also, bear in mind that the prominent upper back curve alteration may have widened the shoulder dart or created a dart if none had existed. If this is the case, the back shoulder seam will need to be eased or darted into the front shoulder seam. The back alteration at the shoulder seam, however, must still equal any correction made to the front.

Sloping or square shoulder adjustments

If you have sloping or square shoulders, you can redraw the shoulder seams up to ¼" lower or higher at both the front and back shoulder points. (See Figure 24.) This small amount will not have a significant effect on the length of the armhole. If, however, the armhole seam will be changed by more than ¼", use the L-slash method to make the adjustment. (See Figure 25.)

Forward shoulder adjustments

The neck point should be in line with the ear lobe; the shoulder point at the end of the shoulder seam should be positioned at the center of the upper arm. There are two common shoulder seam alteration options. The first is, if the entire seam falls further back, it

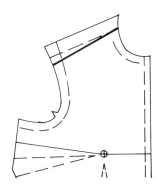

Figure 24 Adjusting for sloping shoulders.

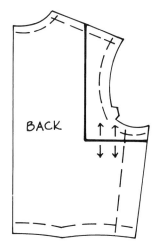

Figure 25 L-slash alteration for sloping or square shoulders.

must be redrawn in a more forward position. Move the seam down in front until it falls in the proper place; add the same amount in the back. This will shift the entire seam so it centers on your shoulder. Use the second option if the neck point is in the proper position, but the shoulder point must be moved forward. Re-pin the seam until you have achieved the proper alignment. Then redraw the seamline, making it a straight line between the original neck point and the new shoulder point on both front and back.

Note: If the shoulder point has been moved forward, you will also have to move the circle at the top of the sleeve cap forward an equivalent amount.

Bodice back dart adjustments

Deepening the back waist darts at their base will compensate for the greater curve of a swayback or slightly rounded upper back. Remember that any waist circumference you eliminate here must be added at the side seam. Deepening the base of the shoulder dart might also help accommodate a moderately rounded back, but you must compensate for any reduction in the shoulder seamline by lengthening it at the shoulder point until it matches the front when the dart is pinned closed, and then redrawing the armhole as needed. Every time you change the width of a dart, you must adjust and redraw it, and compare it to its matching seam to be certain that both are still the same length.

Neckline Adjustments

If you need to lower the neckline in front because you hold your head in a forward position or have unusually broad or straight shoulders, deepen the neckline clips in the tissue until they reach the collar bones and then redraw a lower stitching line. (See Figure 13.) You will need to likewise adjust any facings or collars to compensate.

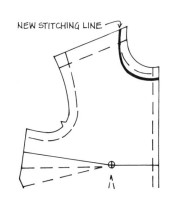

Figure 26. Lowering the front neckline.

MAJOR ALTERATIONS TO BODICE BACK

Individual bone structure, varying shoulder slopes, differences in muscle development, spinal curvatures, and shoulder blade characteristics, combined with a greater need for fitting ease, all call for alterations to accommodate this hard-working part of the body. Almost no one matches the statistical average for which commercial patterns are designed.

1. If a line is not already provided, draw an angled horizontal line across the upper back; from the center back through the shoulder dart point and then up to the shoulder point.
2. Draw a second line through the middle of the shoulder dart. If there is no dart, draw a slightly angled line down from the middle of the shoulder to the horizontal line. (See Figure 27.)
3. Slash along the horizontal line to, but not through, the shoulder point; clip the seam allowance to create a hinge at this point.
4. Slash along the dart or diagonal line to, but not through, the horizontal line, to create a hinge at this point.
5. Carefully place the pattern over tissue on the cork or foam core mat.
6. Pin along the lower edge of the horizontal slash and at the shoulder hinge.

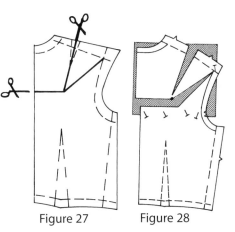

Figure 27   Figure 28

(Left) Slash lines for prominent back curve alteration. *(Right)* Finished alteration for prominent upper back curve.

7. Gently spread the pattern up. A rectangle will form above the horizontal slash, from ½" to 1" wide; the shoulder dart will open wider or, if there was no shoulder dart, a new one will form. (See Figure 28.)

Note: This extra width can be eased into the shoulder seam if you do not want to create a dart.

8. Pin and then tape the alteration securely in place.
9. Blend all seamlines and cutting lines, and redraw darts if necessary. The center back seamline or fold line should be extended down to remain a straight line.

MINOR ADJUSTMENTS TO SLEEVE

Common fitting problems in long set-in sleeves are length and width, especially of the upper arm. Make needed length alterations at the lines provided, rather than at the bottom of the sleeve. Referring to the Personal Measurement Chart, compare your Shoulder to Elbow (#10) and Elbow to Wrist (#11) measurements to those of the pattern. Make any needed length adjustments. It is not uncommon to have to lengthen or shorten above the elbow, but do the opposite below the elbow, to position an elbow dart correctly.

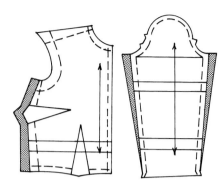

Figure 29 Adding circumference to underarm, to equal bodice circumference addition.

A minor bicep circumference alteration can be made to the underarm seam, but only if an alteration was made to the bodice side seams. The distance between the armhole point and the notches must match on both the sleeve and the bodice. If you make an adjustment to the bodice side seams at the armhole point, you must now add or subtract the same amount to the underarm seams of the sleeve at the armhole point. (See Figure 29.) Unless you need to do the major bicep alteration, fold closed the elbow dart (if there is one) and blend and true the seamlines from the new armhole point to the original wrist line. When redrawing the underarm seam, remember to add enough seam allowance.

Compare your bicep circumference (#5 on the Personal Measurement Chart) with that of the pattern. If your Bicep measurement plus the required ease approximates that of your pattern once you have made any underarm corrections, no further adjustment is needed at this point.

MAJOR ADJUSTMENTS TO SLEEVE

Bicep circumference adjustments

If your biceps need more room or are thin, the sleeve will either pull and strain, especially when the arms are in a forward position, or it

will hang limply and look empty. There are two methods to correct problems of bicep circumference. Both are major adjustments because they cause more than one area to change—the shape of the armhole seam and the width of the sleeve at the bicep.

Method 1
for adding width

If you need to change 1" or less in the sleeve width at the bicep or cap line, make these interior alterations:

1. Draw a line down the center of the sleeve from the shoulder point to the hemline, parallel to the grainline.

2. Clip the seam allowances opposite the ends of the line you just drew, creating hinges at the shoulder point and hem; also clip the seam allowances to, but not through, the armhole point on either side.

3. Beginning at the center, slash horizontally along the bicep line to, but not through, the armhole point on either side; then, from the center, slash down the line you drew to the hemline and up to the shoulder point, leaving hinges at both ends.

4. The pattern is now very fragile, held together by four tiny hinges—at the shoulder point, hemline, and armhole points; place it carefully over tissue on the cork or foam core mat, putting a pin through the hemline hinge.

5. To add width up to 1" at the bicep or cap line, pull the pattern apart to create an opening along the center slash. The edges of the bicep slash will overlap and the sleeve cap will shorten. (See Figure 30.) Pin and tape in place.

6. To reduce width, gently overlap the edges of the center slash up to 1". In this case, the bicep slash will open up and the sleeve cap will become taller. (See Figure 31.) Pin and tape in place.

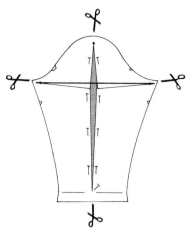

Figure 30 Adding circumference to bicep.

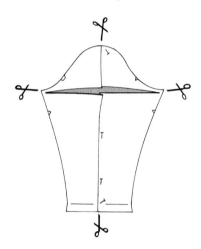

Figure 31 Reducing bicep circumference.

After this adjustment, the sleeve cap height will be altered; therefore, the original height must be restored.

1. Measure the total armhole seam length around the sleeve and around the armhole of the front and back bodice. Compare the measurements; there should be approximately 1" additional ease in the sleeve cap. Restoring the sleeve cap height will also add to or subtract from the cap ease. Take care when adding here, because the bicep adjustment below also adds to the sleeve cap ease.

2. If you need more or less length around the sleeve cap, draw a horizontal line through the sleeve cap about halfway

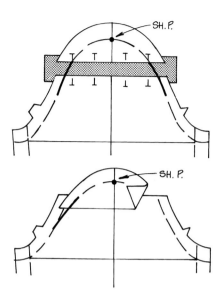

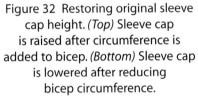

Figure 32 Restoring original sleeve cap height. *(Top)* Sleeve cap is raised after circumference is added to bicep. *(Bottom)* Sleeve cap is lowered after reducing bicep circumference.

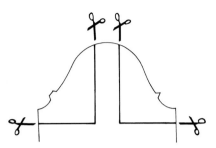

Figure 33 L-slash cutting lines for bicep circumference alteration.

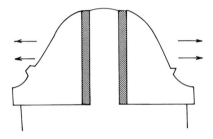

Figure 34 L-slash sections are moved out to add circumference at bicep.

between the notches on either side and the shoulder point; slash along this line.

3. If you have added fullness to the sleeve at the bicep, place the pattern over extra tissue on the cork or foam core mat and spread the two parts the amount the horizontal bicep line overlapped, or to add up to 2" of ease. If you have decreased fullness, overlap the two parts the same distance that the edges of the horizontal cap line slash spread apart or the amount of necessary additional ease up to 1". (See Figure 32.)
4. Pin and tape in place; blend and true the sleeve cap stitching line.

Method 2
For adding width
If, after completing Method 1, you still need more width, follow this method, which is used when more than 1" must be added. This method is a variation of the L-slash; follow these steps:

1. Draw two parallel lines on either side of the center line of the sleeve and about 2" apart. These lines should extend from

the cutting line of the sleeve cap to 1" below the bicep or cap line.
2. From the bottom of each line, square a line and extend it to the underarm seamline, forming an "L" on each side of the sleeve; slash along each "L." (See Figure 33.) *Note: Do not use the bicep line for this purpose.*
3. Place the pattern pieces over tissue and pin the center section to the cork or foam core mat.
4. To add width, spread each L-section away from the center one-half of the total needed distance, keeping the slashed edges parallel to the center line. (See Figure 34.)
5. Pin and tape all sections in place; blend and true all seamlines and cutting lines as necessary.
6. Re-measure the bicep line to be sure you have added the correct amount.

MINOR ALTERATIONS TO SKIRT

There are three methods to achieve the proper circumference at the waist: minor exterior adjustment, minor dart adjustment, and major

interior correction.

Method 1
Exterior adjustments
As with the side seams of the bodice, you can add up to 1" at the side seam to each pattern piece, for a total of 4". Begin by adding to or subtracting from each side seam at the waist exactly what you added to or subtracted from the side seam of the bodice at the waist point. (See Figures 7 and 8 on page 25.)

Note: If you need more than 1" (total of 4") and cannot coordinate Method 1 with needed hip alterations for Method 3, proceed to Method 2.

Method 2
Dart adjustments
You can add or subtract to the skirt waist dart(s) the equivalent of any additions or subtractions that were made to the bodice waist darts. You may take a dart out entirely or change a too-wide dart that pokes out into two smaller darts. Consider using this method in combination with Method 1 or 3.

Remember that to retain the darts' original relationship to one another and to the center lines, the distance at the waistline from the center to the closest dart leg should be the same in both the bodice and the skirt. If the distance is not the same, the skirt dart must be moved. If there are two front skirt darts, the inside leg of the inside dart should line up with the inside leg of the bodice waist dart. (See Figure 35 on page 34.)

If the skirt dart or darts must be moved:
1. Draw a box around both darts. The vertical sides of the box are parallel to the center line, and the horizontal bottom of the box is drawn just under the longest dart. (See Figure 36 on page 34.)
2. Slash along all three sides of the box.

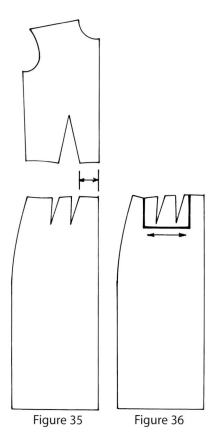

Figure 35   Figure 36

(Left) Alignment of bodice and skirt waist darts. *(Right)* Moving skirt darts.

3. Over tissue on the cork or foam core mat, slide the box to the right or left until the dart nearest the center front matches up with the bodice waist dart.
4. Pin and tape in place.
5. Pin or tape the skirt front darts closed and blend the waistline seam as needed.

MAJOR ALTERATIONS TO SKIRT

Method 3
Interior corrections
If you need to add or subtract more circumference to the waist than can be achieved by either of the two methods described above, use an interior correction.

This correction is especially effective for a very slim individual who needs to subtract circumference. It can also be used to adjust for a flat seat or to compensate for full hips or thighs.

Referring to your Personal Measurement Chart, locate the alteration measurement for the following areas: High Front Hip (#4A) and Low Back Hip (#4B).

The interior alteration will be "even"—opened up or overlapped equally. For example, if you need to make a total change of 2" at the front waist and 2½" at the high front hip, you can make an even interior change of 2" to alter the waist and most of the hip; then add the remaining ½" needed at the hip with an exterior change. If you have a prominent tummy or seat curve, you could alternatively make an interior correction for the entire 2½" and then enlarge the waist darts to absorb the additional ½".

If, in the back, you need to subtract 1" at the waist and 2" at the low hip, you can make an even interior adjustment that subtracts 1" from both areas and then subtract the remaining 1" from the hip with an exterior change. If you have a flat seat, you could alternatively make the larger 2" adjustment to the hip and make the waist darts smaller.

To review how to make this alteration, see Major Alterations, Adding or Subtracting Width, on page 25.

Redrawing waistline curves
Make sure any changes to the skirt have been well taped. Fold and tape the darts closed with removable tape. Pin the side seam, wrong sides together, seam allowances to the outside. Attach the pattern waistline to the elastic around your waist with pins, or slip it under the elastic. Check to see that the hem falls evenly. If you have made the corrections accurately, it should.

If the hem does not fall evenly, have your fitting buddy pull down on the front hem until it is even. This will bring the pattern waistline down past your natural waistline. If the gap created is ½" or more, you will need to make the major abdomen curve adjustment. If the gap is less than ½", slip extra tissue under the waist of the pattern and redraw the front waistline as described below.

If the problem with the hemline is in back, your fitting buddy should pull down on the back hem until it is even. Again, to add ½" or more, make the major seat curve adjustment. If it is less than ½", redraw the back waistline as described below.

If you have to pull the back waist up above the natural waistline to make the hem horizontal and sides vertical, the waist seamline and cutting lines will have to be redrawn to accurately reflect this figure variation. Keep in mind that while pulling the hemline up or down, try to keep it exactly horizontal to the ground and the side seamlines perpendicular to the ground. The waistline seam, however, may not remain horizontal; instead, it will follow the natural line of your body.

To raise the waistline:
1. At the center front, measure up to the natural waistline and make a mark on the extra tissue.
2. Unpin the pattern pieces and lay them flat.
3. Use the curved ruler to connect the side waist point, which has remained unchanged, with the new mark at center front. Make the curve as gentle as possible. (See Figure 37 on page 35.)
4. Correct seam allowance and trim away any excess tissue before re-opening the darts.

To lower the waistline:
1. With tissue pinned on, adjust the hemline so it is horizontal to the ground. At the center back, measure down to the natural waistline and re-mark the waistline.
2. Take tissue off, keeping the darts closed.
3. Use a curved ruler to connect the side waist point, which has remained unchanged, and blend the waistline with the new mark at center back. Be sure not to

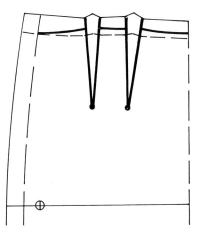

Figure 37 Raising the waistline.

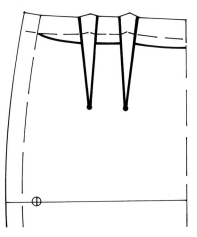

Figure 38 Lowering the waistline.

make the new waistline too scooped; the back waist is usually a very subtle curve. (See Figure 38.)

4. Correct the seam allowance and trim away any excess tissue before re-opening the darts.

Curved abdomen corrections

This provides both additional length and width to cover a larger curve than the pattern-maker anticipated. Proper adjustment for a prominent raised abdomen actually makes the abdomen appear less prominent because of added length and width where needed.

1. Draw a horizontal line from the center front to just below the point of the nearest dart. If there is a second dart, continue the line to the point of this dart. If

the second dart is longer or shorter than the first, angle this section of the line slightly to arrive at the dart point.

2. Continue the line diagonally up to the side waist point.
3. Extend the mid-line of each dart to, but not through, each dart point.
4. From the center front, slash along the horizontal line and then along the diagonal line up to, but not through, the side waist point.
5. Clip the seam allowance to create a hinge at the side waist point.
6. Slash along the lines through the center of each dart to, but not through, the dart point, creating a hinge at each dart point.
7. Place the pattern over tissue on the cork or foam core mat, pinning along the lower edge of the horizontal slash and at the waist point hinge.
8. Gently spread the pattern piece up at the waistline to raise the center front up to 1", to accommodate the abdomen curve. The darts open up and a V-shaped opening appears along the diagonal slash to the waist point. (See Figure 39.)
9. Be sure that the two edges of the horizontal slash are exactly parallel and the proper distance apart to make the needed correction. Pin and tape all pieces securely.
10. Because this correction moves the center front out, extend the center front all the way to the hemline, adding tissue. This step provides extra width, just as moving the waistline up provided extra length.

Seat curve corrections

For many individuals, a prominent seat curve is an area of concern. Symptoms of fitting problems in this area include a sensation of tightness in the back, horizontal wrinkles across the back, S-curved side seams, pocket gapping, and

hiked-up hemline in the back. The steps described at left for the prominent abdomen adjustment can also be performed on the skirt back pattern to correct for a similar problem in back. (See Figure 40.) After completing the correction, record all changes on the Personal Measurement Chart and the pattern pieces.

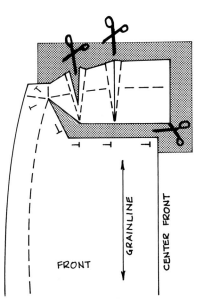

Figure 39 Abdomen curve alteration provides additional length and width to front.

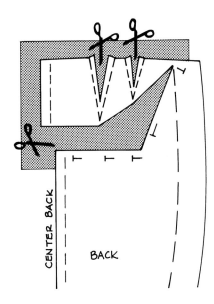

Figure 40 Seat curve alteration provides additional length and width to back.

FITTING PANTS

PREPARING THE PATTERN

The key measurement for choosing a pants pattern is your full hip measurement. Your pants pattern size can be as much as one, two, or even more sizes away from your dress size—this is not unusual! If you are making a pant suit or pants and top, you may need to buy two different size patterns or a multi-size pattern with the proper range of sizes. It is no reflection on your personal worth, it simply means that you have your own distinctive proportions, and they must be taken into account when fitting your clothes.

As with the dress pattern, rough-cut the pattern leaving as much extra tissue as possible. Use a barely warm dry iron to smooth away wrinkles. If you have a multi-size pattern, use a colored flow pen to mark the proper cutting line for your size, then use a flexible ruler to draw in all stitching lines (if not already provided), high front and low back hiplines (the hip point is often indicated on patterns with the same symbol used to indicate the bust point), and crotch line.

Measuring the pattern

Consult your Pants Measurement Chart and measure all corresponding areas on the pattern pieces. Record the results in the "Pattern Measurement" column. If using a pattern with pleats, fold the pleats all the way to a point below the crotch line, to get accurate measurements. If your pattern has slant pockets, include the pattern piece for the back of the pocket, match it to all of the appropriate symbols, then tape the pocket in place for measurements and fittings.

In the "Changes" column, calculate any adjustment you will have to make. Keep in mind what you and your fitting buddy noted about your shape and also how ready-to-

wear pants tend to fit you; they are valuable hints about corrections you need to make.

MINOR ADJUSTMENTS TO PANTS

A common complaint about pants is that the crotch is either unattractively loose or too uncomfortably high and tight. Comparing your body measurements to those of the pattern may at first be very confusing. You may find that you need to increase one, such as crotch length, and decrease the other, such as crotch depth, which at first seems impossible. Remember that every action causes a reaction—lengthening or shortening crotch depth also changes crotch length.

Crotch depth

Begin your alterations by correcting the crotch depth in both the front and back. The good news is that, if you need a change of 1" or less in the crotch depth, or if the crotch depth conflicts with apparent changes you need to make in crotch length, you do nothing. You may find that other needed changes will also correct the crotch depth problem.

If the needed crotch depth change is between 1" and 2" and does not conflict with an apparent crotch length change, alter the pattern in this area by adjusting the lengthen/shorten lines on both the front and back. Cut or fold along the parallel lines and, if necessary, add tissue. (See Figure 41.) If you think you need an adjustment of more than 2", make half of the adjustment now and test it during the tissue fit.

Back crotch length

Once you have made any crotch depth adjustment, re-measure the back crotch length on the pattern—from crotch point to center back at the waistline—and determine how much additional change you need. Then redraw the crotch

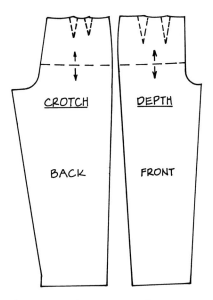

Figure 41 Adjusting crotch depth at lengthen/shorten lines.

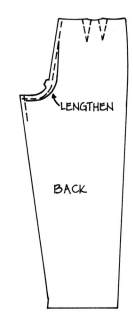

Figure 42 Adjusting back crotch length. In this case, back crotch is lengthened by drawing a deeper curve.

curve—less curve to shorten and more curve to lengthen. (See Figure 42.) For a moderate adjustment, you can shorten by re-curving in to a maximum of ¼" inside the original line, or lengthen the curve by drawing a new line ¼" outside the original line. For a larger adjustment, you can re-curve up to 1" outside the original curve.

The deeper back curve, while providing more length, will also eliminate some bagginess in the seat area. Some low hip circumference will be lost, but it is usually not significant and can be adjusted for in the side seam.

Back crotch length wedge adjustment

If, after making the changes on the previous page, you still need up to 1" additional crotch length in the back, you may be able to achieve good fit with a wedge adjustment.

Note: This alteration is not recommended for the front; only for the back. You cannot use this adjustment for a change of more than 1".

The center back seam functions like a dart, shaping the back curve from waist to hip. The wedge adjustment performed in the back angles this "dart" more acutely, resulting in a much better fit for those who have a relatively small waist and a seat curve that is both low and pronounced, or for those who have a swayback posture. On the other hand, overlapping the wedge compensates for the relatively flat seat common in older figures; it straightens out and reduces the dart-like angle of the center back seam.

To make the wedge adjustment:

1. Make a horizontal slash through the center back seam allowance and seamline, perpendicular to the grainline, all the way across to, but not through, the side seamline. If you have not already used the lengthen/shorten lines to adjust for crotch depth, make the slash along one of these lines. If you have already used them, draw another horizontal line either a little above or slightly below the lengthen/shorten lines and slash along it.
2. Clip the side seam allowance, leaving a hinge at the seamline.

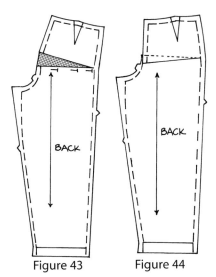

Figure 43   Figure 44

(Left) Wedge adjustment, with slashed edges spread apart to lengthen back crotch.
(Right) Wedge adjustment, with slashed edges overlapped to shorten back crotch.

3. If you need to lengthen the crotch, place the pattern over extra tissue on the cork or foam core mat, pin along the lower slash line, and spread the upper piece up to a total of 1" at the center seamline. (See Figure 43.)
4. If you need to shorten the crotch to adjust for a flat seat, overlap the two slashed edges up to 1" at the crotch curve, thus removing a wedge-shaped section of pattern at the center. (See Figure 44.)
5. Blend and true seamline and cutting lines.

If you still need a bit more change in the crotch length, and you need more width in the thigh than has been provided, lengthen the crotch extension slightly, up to 1". If you need less length and have thin thighs, you may be able to shorten the extension slightly, again up to 1". (See Figure 45.) Begin with a ½" change for the tissue fit. After any change to the crotch extension, blend the inseam and cutting lines to the knee area.

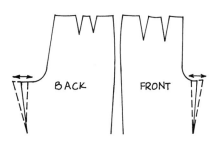

4Figure 5 Lengthening or shortening crotch length by adding to or subtracting from crotch extensions.

Front crotch length

If a crotch depth change was made, re-measure the front crotch length. If you need further adjustment, there are three methods: First, you can either raise or lower the waistline up to ½", as you did on the skirt. Second, you can add or subtract from the crotch point; begin with a ½" correction and re-fit. Third, you can make the same major abdominal correction as you did on the skirt.

Note: The front crotch curve is rarely re-curved. However, slight bagginess in front can be eliminated by deepening the curve up to ¼" or less. Wait until after fitting to see if this correction is really necessary. It is better to eliminate any such bagginess by reducing width at the crotch point.

Re-evaluate after the tissue fit since the interrelationship of crotch length, crotch curve, crotch depth, and thigh width is so complex. Your goal is to achieve a smooth comfortable fit, with no points of undue stress and no wrinkles or folds. (Horizontal wrinkles indicate tightness and vertical ones indicate shortness; vertical folds indicate excess width and horizontal folds indicate excess length.) If you cannot make the needed adjustments in back crotch length using the wedge method, you will need to consider the major adjustment described on page 38.

MAJOR ADJUSTMENTS TO PANTS

Abdomen or seat curve adjustments

If you have an especially prominent curve in the seat or the abdomen, use the major correction for abdomen and seat curves described in corrections for dress skirt on page 35. The mechanical steps are the same, but are applied to the pants pattern pieces. (See Figures 46 and 47.) Choose this alteration if you do not have a swayback and the line from your waist to the hip is relatively straight but full.

Pin and tape everything firmly in place; redraw the center seamline and cutting lines or the zipper extension.

Note: It is important that the center front seamline remain parallel to the grainline. Otherwise, it will not lie properly over the abdomen. To keep the center front seamline parallel to the grainline, the waistline may actually become smaller. Therefore, make any further adjustments at the darts or side seam to maintain needed waist circumference.

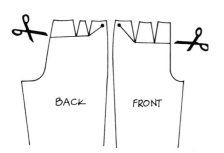

Figure 46 Slash lines for major curve adjustment.

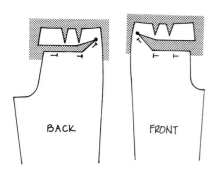

Figure 47 Adjusting for curvy abdomen in front and curvy seat in back.

Waist circumference adjustments

Once the crotch depth, curve, and length in both the front and back have been corrected, you can make needed circumference changes, including the relatively minor adjustments of side seams and waist darts. Re-measure the front and back waistlines and high and low hiplines to determine if you need to add or subtract width at any of these points. (See Figure 48.) As you did in the skirt, you can add up to 1" at the side seam for additional width at the waist or hip. If you are making corrections in both areas, you may add or subtract more, so long as there is no more than 1" difference between the two corrections. For example, if you have added 1" at the waist, you may add up to 2" at the hip. To make any greater changes, use the interior width adjustment described at right. Once any changes have been made at the side seams, blend and redraw seamlines and cutting lines to the original hemline.

The waist circumference can also be adjusted slightly by either widening or narrowing the darts. However, try not to widen a dart by more than a total of ½" or it may poke out when sewn. To prevent this, a single dart can be divided into two smaller darts or you can curve the darts, using a Fashion Ruler or hip curve to follow the contours of the body where the dart ends become narrower. (See

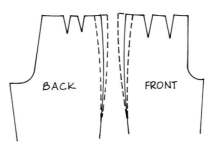

Figure 48 Adjusting waist circumference by adding to or subtracting from side seams.

Figure 49.) If dart corrections, along with side seam adjustments, are insufficient, you will have to consider the interior change below.

Interior width adjustments

Adding or subtracting width to pants—over and above what can be accomplished through the major correction and side seam and dart corrections described above—can be accomplished through interior alteration. This alteration actually involves four areas—waist circumference, hip, thigh, and hem. Interior alteration is effective when used to compensate for a large front thigh, because the adjustment is balanced throughout the front leg and therefore does not overemphasize the thigh and hip.

To calculate how much alteration is needed, check your waist and hip measurements. Subtract the smaller measurement from the larger to determine how much to accomplish with the interior alteration. For example, if you need to add 2" at the waist and 1" at the hip, make a 1" interior alteration in both areas, and add the remaining 1" waist correction at the side seam.

1. Just outside the waist dart nearest the side seam, measure and draw a slash line parallel to the grain line and extend it the entire length of the pattern piece you are adjusting. (See Figure 50 on page 39.)

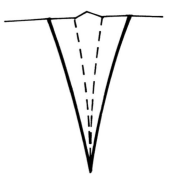

Figure 49 Adjusting waist circumference by making darts wider or narrower.

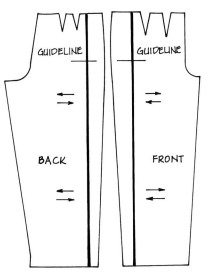

Figure 50 Even interior alteration to add or subtract width.

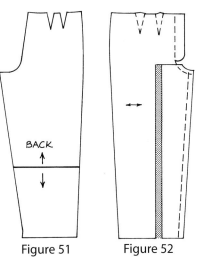

Figure 51   Figure 52

(Left) Adjusting for length at lengthen/shorten lines, rather than hemline; this prevents changing the taper of the pant leg. *(Right)* L-slash alteration to add width at front thigh.

2. Follow the procedure described for a skirt on page 25. Pin and tape in place. *Note: The interior alteration does change the taper of the lower leg, but it does so while retaining the proportion necessary for that pattern piece.*

3. Re-measure the waist, hip, and thigh and make any needed adjustments. Because the waistband is the easiest piece to adjust and alteration depends on the final waist dimensions of the pants, corrections can wait until after all other adjustments are completed.

Lengthening or shortening

After you have made all other corrections, compare your outseam measurements to those of the corrected pattern and make any needed adjustments at the lengthen/shorten lines on the leg. If no line is indicated, draw one perpendicular to the grain line just below the knee area, running all the way across from inseam to outseam. (See Figure 51, also Methods for Lengthening or Shortening on page 24.) As you have with other pattern pieces, cut or fold along the line or lines, and overlap or spread apart over tissue to make the needed changes. It is best not to make length adjustments at the hemline because it will change the taper of the leg.

Front thigh adjustments

If you notice excessive tightness in the front thigh area, a fitting problem found in young athletes with highly developed thigh muscles, perform the following L-slash alteration:

1. Draw a vertical line from the hem up the center of the front pant leg to a point opposite and just below the bottom of the fly; take care to keep this line parallel to the grain line.

2. Square a line to the front crotch, just below the fly.

3. Cut up through the hem, along both lines, and through the seam allowance.

4. Place the pattern over tissue and make an even internal correction by spreading the two vertical cut edges up to ½" apart, keeping the cut edges parallel. (See Figure 52.)

5. Tape in place; blend and redraw the front crotch line.

This alteration, which is a variation on the more common full interior correction already discussed in this section, relieves the tightness across the front of the thighs without causing the pant leg to gap at the hip or side seams. *Note: This alteration is appropriate only for a relatively slender individual with well-developed thighs.*

SECTION I

Accessories

Eyeglasses Case

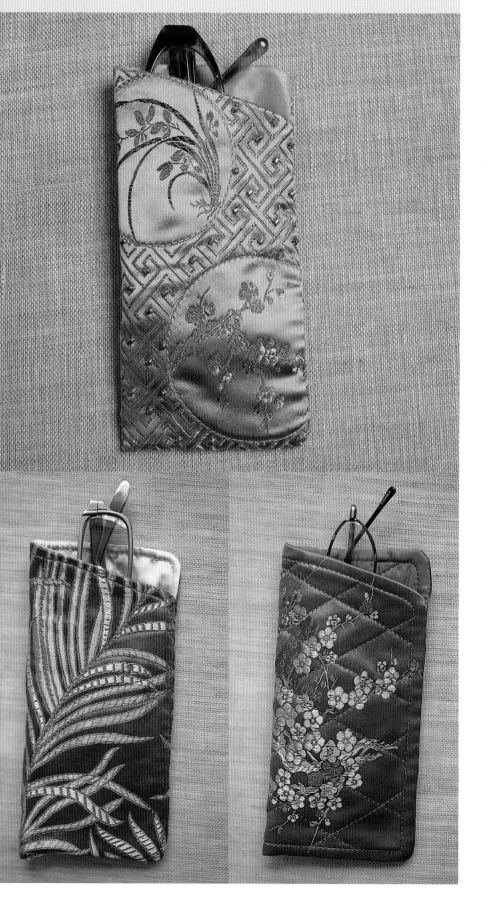

MATERIALS

⅛ yd. fashion fabric
⅛ yd. lining

⅛ yd. baby flannel (for interlining)
Thread to match fashion fabric
Paper for pattern

CUTTING & CONSTRUCTION

1. Trace or photocopy the pattern provided on page 44. When cutting out the pattern from the fashion fabric and flannel, the slanted edge should be on the upper left corner. Flip the pattern to cut the lining. Cut out on the solid lines; a ¼" seam allowance is included.

2. Place the fashion fabric and lining with right sides together. Place the flannel interlining with its right side to the wrong side of the fashion fabric. Pin all the layers together. Sew the pieces together leaving a 2" opening for turning. Clip the corner seam allowances. (See Photo 1.)

3. Holding the flannel and fashion fabric together, turn right side out. Slipstitch the opening closed and press.

4. Fold case in half. Pin along the side and bottom. Leaving the angled end open, slipstitch the bottom and sides together.

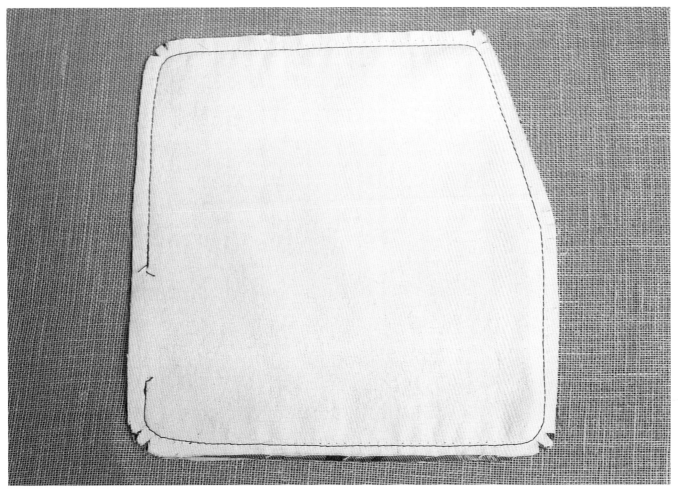

1. This shows the fabric layers, stitched together with the corners clipped.
The flannel interlining is on top.

QUILTED CASE VARIATION

1. Cut out fabrics.
2. Place the flannel interlining on the wrong side of the fashion fabric. Pin the layers together.
3. On the interlining, lightly mark a quilting pattern or use the fabric design to guide the quilting. Machine-quilt the layers together.
4. Pin the lining to the quilted fashion fabric, right sides together. Stitch the case, following steps 2 through 4, of the eyeglass case instructions given previously.

BEADED CASE VARIATION

1. Cut out fabrics.
2. Place the fashion fabric and lining with right sides together. Place the flannel interlining with its right side to the wrong side of the fashion fabric. Pin all the layers together.
3. Sew the pieces together leaving a 2" opening for turning. Clip the corner seam allowances. (See Photo 1.)
4. Holding the flannel and fashion fabric together, turn right side out. Slipstitch the opening closed and press.
5. Bead the case, either using the fabric design as a guide, or sewing beads randomly on the outside of the case. Be sure to only stitch the fashion fabric as you sew on the beads.
6. Fold it in half. Pin along the side and bottom. Leaving the angled end open, slipstitch the bottom and sides together.

Pattern for Eyeglasses Case

(Actual Size)

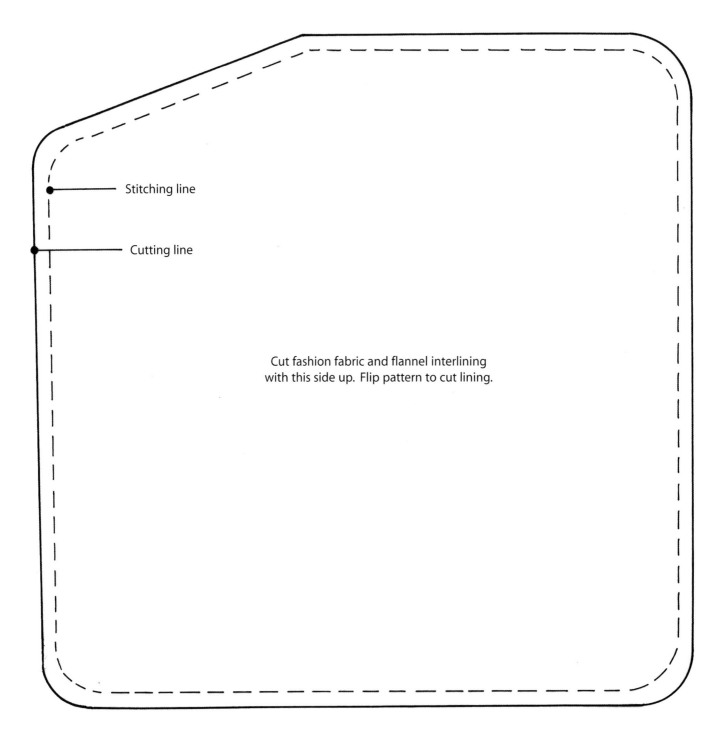

Stitching line

Cutting line

Cut fashion fabric and flannel interlining
with this side up. Flip pattern to cut lining.

Neck Pillow and Sleep Mask

MATERIALS

Recommended Fabrics
Silk brocade
Silk dupioni
Washable fleece
Terrycloth
Velvet

Neck Pillow

½ yd. fabric
Polyester stuffing
Matching or contrast piping
Thread

Additional Materials for Relaxation Pillow Variation

9" zipper
½ yd. muslin

Lavender, buckwheat hulls,
  or millet or a combination
  (for filling)

Sleep Mask

¼ yd. fabric (for top)
¼ baby flannel or soft cotton
  (for lining)
24" of ½" (purchased or homemade) bias tape in a contrast
  fabric
2 pieces of ¼" wide elastic, each
  14" long
Optional: Tightly woven dark
  cotton (for interlining)

NECK PILLOW

CUTTING & CONSTRUCTION

1. Using the pattern provided on page 48, cut two pieces.
2. Baste piping ¼" from edge of one piece. With right sides together, stitch pieces together using a ¼" seam allowance. Leave an unstitched opening between the notches for turning and stuffing. Clip the curves and the seam allowance as needed. (See Photo 1.)
3. Turn right side out; stuff to desired firmness; slipstitch the opening closed.

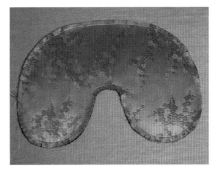

1. Neck pillow with sewn seam and an opening for stuffing.

RELAXATION PILLOW VARIATION

1. Using the pattern provided, cut out two pieces from muslin and two pieces from the fabric.
2. With right sides together, stitch muslin pieces together using a ¼" seam allowance. Leave an unstitched opening between the notches for turning and stuffing. Clip the curves and the seam allowance as needed. Turn right side out.
3. Stuff to desired firmness with lavender or buckwheat hulls, or millet or a combination; slip-stitch the opening closed.
4. Baste piping ¼" from edge of one piece of cover fabric.
5. Set a zipper between the notches of the covering fabric, using a ¼" seam allowance and following the package instructions. Open the zipper.
6. Pin the seam, with right sides of fabric together. Stitch the pillow seam, using a ¼" seam allowance. Turn right side out through the zipper.
7. Insert the filled muslin pillow. (See Photo 2.)

2. Neck pillow variation with zipper inserted.

SLEEP MASK

CUTTING & CONSTRUCTION

1. Copy the mask pattern on page 47.
2. Cut one mask pattern from the top fabric and one from the lining fabric. *Option:* Cut a third piece from dark woven cotton.
3. With wrong sides together, pin together the layers of fabric, and stitch around the edge using a ¼" seam allowance. Trim the seam allowance to ⅛". (See Photo 1.)

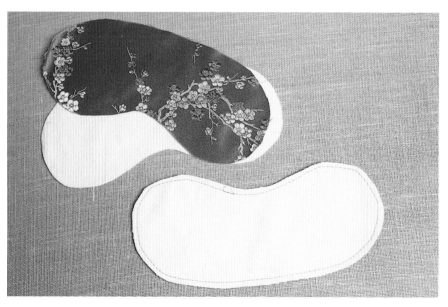

1. The pieces of the sleep mask, separately *top,* and stitched together with lining on top, *bottom.*

4. Mark the strap attachment points on the back piece. Pin the elastic straps at these points so the straps are parallel across the back of the mask. Make sure the ends of the elastic face the seam allowance. Tack the straps by machine on the stitching line. (See Photo 2.)

5. Bind the edges of the mask with the bias tape, covering the stitching ¼" from the edge. *Note: It works best to press the bias binding around the curves as you pin.*

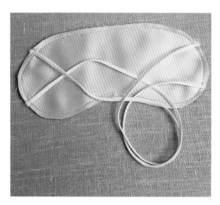

2. The elastic straps are pinned in place before the bias binding is attached.

VARIATIONS

- Bead or embroider the fashion fabric side.
- Use a quilted fashion fabric or machine quilt the fabric you've chosen.
- Use a sheer fabric or lace for the top fashion layer and a second solid fashion fabric for the middle layer.

Pattern for Sleep Mask

(Actual Size)

Attach straps

Straight of grain

Attach straps

Pattern for Neck Pillow

Enlarge at 175% for actual size

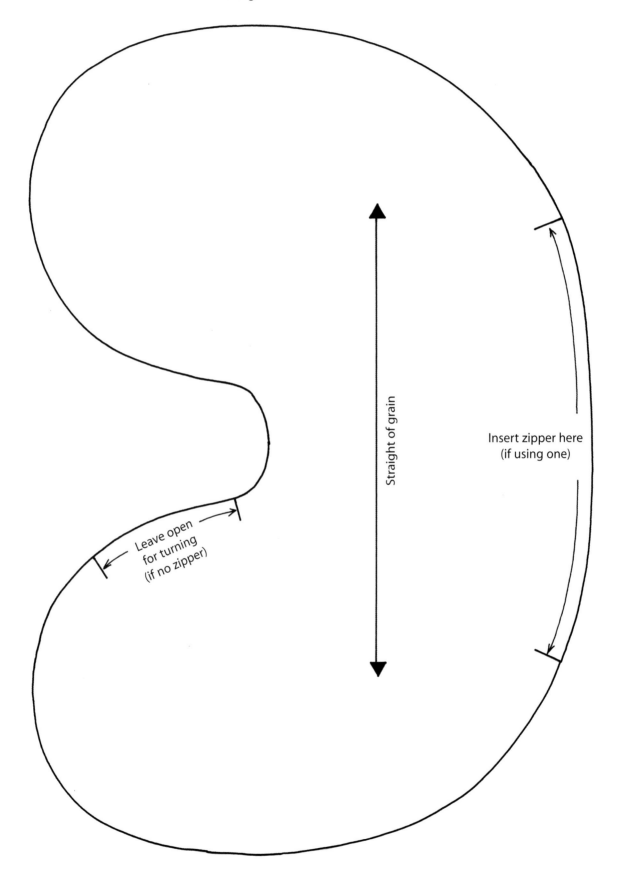

Straight of grain

Insert zipper here
(if using one)

Leave open
for turning
(if no zipper)

Tooth Fairy Pillow

MATERIALS

¼ yd. each of two contrasting fabrics or scraps
¾ yd. lace, ½" to ¾" wide

Thread to match fabric
Chalk
Pillow stuffing
Optional: Small shank button

This tiny pillow holds first the tooth, then the gift of the fairy. The pieced top requires very little fabric.

CUTTING & CONSTRUCTION

1. Cut a 6" square (pillow bottom) and a 4" square (pillow top) from fabric #1, following the diagrams in Figure 1.
2. Cut a 6" square from fabric #2 (triangles on pillow top).
3. Using chalk, draw diagonal lines from opposite corners to divide the 6" square from fabric #2 into four triangles. Cut on the chalked lines.
4. Cut a 4" square from fabric #2 for the pocket.
5. Fold the 4" pocket square into a triangle and press. Set aside.
6. With right sides together, using a ¼" seam allowance, stitch the long edges of two triangles to opposite sides of the 4" square of fabric #1. (See Figure 2.) Press seam allowances toward the triangles. (See Photo 1.)

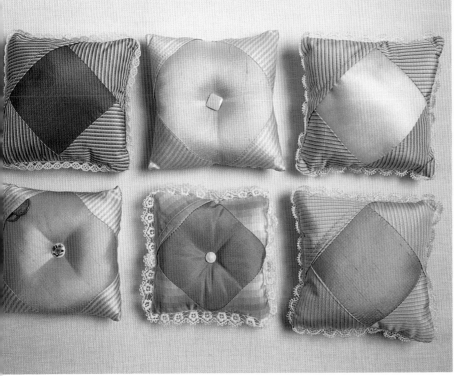

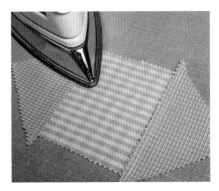

1. Pressing the triangles after stitching.

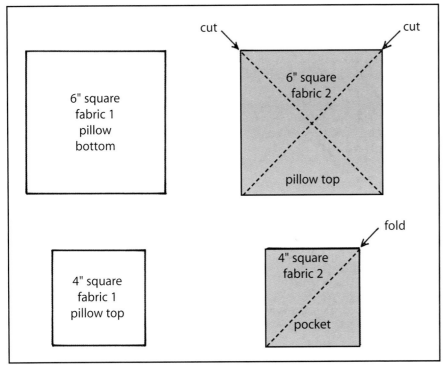

Figure 1

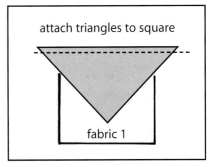

Figure 2

49

7. With right sides together, using a ¼" seam allowance, stitch the remaining two triangles to the remaining sides of the square, stitching across other triangle to end of pieces. Press seam allowances toward the triangles.

8. Place the pressed pocket triangle over the right side of one triangle on the pieced block. Line up the folded edge of the pocket with the seam of the triangle of the center square. Stitch the two unhemmed edges to secure. (See Photo 2.) This piece is the pillow top. True it back into a square, if necessary, by pressing and trimming. (Be sure to leave a ¼" seam allowance.)

9. Pin the lace along the stitching line on the right side of the trued top with the finished lace edge to the inside.

10. Stack the top and bottom with right sides together. (The bottom may be slightly bigger than your trued top. If it is, trim it to match for easier sewing.) Using a ¼" seam allowance, stitch the top to the bottom catching the lace between the layers. (See Photo 3.) Leave a 1" opening at the top for turning.

11. Trim corners and seams. Turn pillow right side out and stuff until firm. Slipstitch opening closed.

Option: With a hand needle and a double strand of thread, stitch through the center of pillow and add a button.

2. Stitching the pocket over one corner.

3. Sewing the seam with lace inserted.

Pajama Bag

MATERIALS

⅛ yd. cotton fabric, 44" wide
(for bottom section)

¼ yd. cotton fabric, 44" wide
(for middle section)

⅜ yd. cotton fabric, 44" wide
(for top section and lining)

1½ yds. ribbon, ½" wide

Child's socks, 1 pair

Polyester stuffing

CUTTING & CONSTRUCTION

1. Cut the fabric for the bottom section front/back (hereafter referred to as A) 4" wide x 13" long as shown in Figure 1 on page 52.

2. Cut the fabric for the middle section front/back (hereafter referred to as B) 5" wide x 13" long as shown in Figure 2 on page 52.

3. Cut the fabric for the top section/lining front/back (hereafter referred to as C) 23" wide x 13" long as shown in Figure 3 on page 52.

4. Using a fabric-marking pen or pencil, mark the fold line and the casing stitch line placements on C as shown in Figure 3.

5. Pin the long edges of A and B fronts with straight pins placed vertically, right sides together, aligning the edges.

6. Backstitch to lock the stitches. Stitch the long edges together, using a ¼" seam allowance. Press the seam allowance open.

7. Repeat steps 5 and 6 above to sew A and B backs, and the long edges of B and C fronts and backs together.

Note: This will form the pajama bag front with a self-lining.

8. Pin the front to the back, right sides together, matching the seams at the sides. Stitch the side seam lines, using a ⅜" seam allowance. Openings must be left for turning the pajama bag right side out and for the drawstring; discontinue the stitching for a 4" space along one side seam and for ½" space on both side seams as shown in Figure 3 on page 52. Press the seam allowances open.

9. Stuff the socks with polyester stuffing and pin the socks

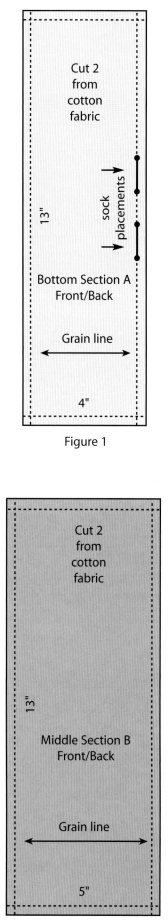

Cut 2
from
cotton
fabric

sock
placements

13"

Bottom Section A
Front/Back

Grain line

4"

Figure 1

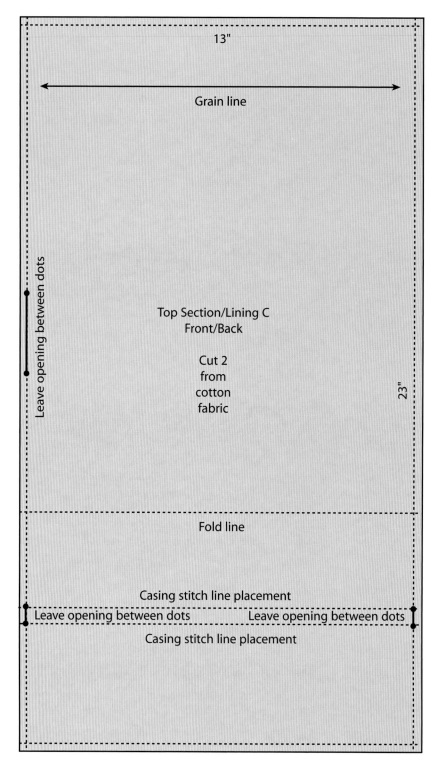

13"

Grain line

Leave opening between dots

Top Section/Lining C
Front/Back

Cut 2
from
cotton
fabric

23"

Fold line

Casing stitch line placement

Leave opening between dots   Leave opening between dots

Casing stitch line placement

Figure 3

Cut 2
from
cotton
fabric

13"

Middle Section B
Front/Back

Grain line

5"

Figure 2

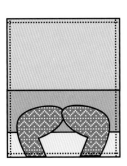

Figure 4

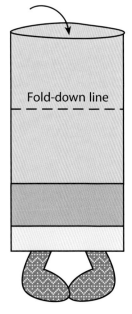

Fold-down line

Figure 5

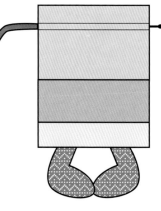

Figure 6

together along the ankle edges. Pin the top sides of the socks at the ankle edges to the bottom edge of "A" on the right side of the front as marked in Figure 1 and shown in Figure 4.

10. Machine-baste the socks in place, using a ¼" seam allowance.

11. Pin the front to the back, right sides together, aligning the bottom edges. Stitch the bottom seam line, using a ⅜" seam allowance, making certain to sew the socks into the seam. Press the seam allowance open.

12. Clip the bulk from each corner. Turn the pajama bag right side out through the opening along the side. Using a point turner, accentuate each corner. Slipstitch the opening closed.

13. Fold the lining portion of the fabric to the inside of the pajama bag along the fold line as shown in Figure 3 on page 52 and in Figure 5 above and press.

14. Pin the lining in place. Stitch both casing stitch lines from the outer side of the fabric, beginning at one of the side seams. Press.

15. Cut the ribbon into two equal lengths. Thread one length of ribbon through the eye of a ballpoint bodkin. Beginning with the left side seam casing opening, slip the bodkin and the ribbon through the casing, exiting at the right side seam opening as shown in Figure 6. Repeat for the right side with the remaining length of ribbon. Tie the ends of the ribbon at each side together. If desired, apply fray preventative to the ends of the ribbons. Pull on both ribbons to close the top of the pajama bag.

Note: Smaller versions may be made, as shown in the photo on page 51, by reducing the overall measurements and cutting out small feet shapes instead of using socks.

Fancy Felt Pincushions

MATERIALS

Wool-blend felts (20% wool–80% rayon or 35% wool–65% rayon), 7–10 assorted shades
Polyester filling
Stranded embroidery flosses: rayon, assorted shades (5)
Cardboard
Chenille embroidery needle: size 18–20
Fabric scissors
Straight pins
Tape measure
Tracing paper

PREPARE THE FELT

1. Before making the felt rose or purse pincushion, fleece the felt. Wet felt completely with warm water in a sink or basin. Do not rub or agitate. Wash colors separately, as some may bleed. The felt will shrink.

2. Squeeze by hand to remove as much water as possible. Avoid wringing felt. Place in clothes dryer on regular setting until felt is nearly dry, approximately 35 minutes. Do not over-dry.

3. Lay flat to dry completely, gently smoothing fabric by hand.

CUTTING & CONSTRUCTION
Rose Pincushion

1. Trace or photocopy patterns A and B below. Cut several shades of fleeced felt using Pattern A (petal); cut two shades of fleeced felt using Pattern B (leaf).

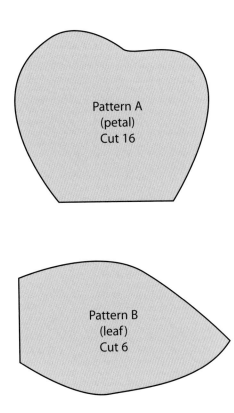

Pattern A
(petal)
Cut 16

Pattern B
(leaf)
Cut 6

2. Overlap and offset two petals. Refer to Stitches on pages 9–10. Using needle and decorative Straight Stitches, stitch two petals together with three strands of rayon floss. Lightly stuff petal with polyester filling, then gather-stitch ends closed. Repeat with each of eight sets of petals. Do not stuff center petal layer.

3. Join five bottom petals together with doubled thread at gathered edges. Pull thread as tightly as possible and secure thread. Join first petal to last.

4. Stitch remaining two petals onto top of joined five petals.

5. Roll center petal and secure roll at overlap. Stitch rolled petal to center of petals.

6. With needle threaded with two strands of embroidery floss, push up through bottom center of rose to top side of any petal, burying thread end inside petal. Using Straight Stitches, embroider a star. Stitch through petal about ½" and stitch another star. Stitch back through bottom center, then back up to top side of another petal. Continue to stitch stars on each petal.

7. Offset leaves and stitch together as for petals using decorative Straight Stitches. Secure leaves to underside of petals.

Parti-colored side of Purse Pincushion

Purse Pincushion

1. Using Patterns C–K on pages 56–57, cut purse pieces from different shades of fleeced felt.

2. For parti-colored side of purse, machine-stitch the left and right Ds together, and stitch the left and right Es together, using a ¼" seam allowance. Press seams open. Stitch D to E, matching the center front seams and using a ¼" seam allowance. Press seam open.

3. Center and pin circle H on joined segments. Pin moon I over top-left side of circle. Pin flower G and flower center F on top of circle. Using needle and two strands of rayon floss in assorted shades, appliqué moon, circle, flower, and flower center to parti-colored side with decorative Straight Stitches.

4. Pin remaining moon to center of single-color side. Pin second flower and center and appliqué each to purse in same manner as for parti-colored side.

5. Machine-stitch J to first side, right sides together, matching fold line of J to center seam at bottom edge center and taking a ¼" seam allowance. Stitch opposite side of J to C.

6. Turn purse right side out. Using decorative Straight Stitches, stitch over front and back seams at sides with three strands of rayon floss.

7. Cut a 1" x 5" strip from contrasting felt for top band. Using decorative Straight Stitches, hand-stitch top band to purse with three strands of rayon floss.

8. Cut three pieces of cardboard to fit inside purse bottom. Glue cardboard together. Place inside purse. Stuff purse firmly with polyester filling.

9. Using decorative Straight Stitches, hand-stitch open side of top band to purse C with three strands of rayon floss.

10. Fold one handle K in half, matching long edges. Beginning and ending 1" from each end, machine-stitch handle ⅛" from fold. Trim excess fabric from machine-stitched edges. Trim each end into a small circle. Repeat for second handle.

11. Using Crisscross Stitches, appliqué handles to both sides of purse at each circle with two strands of rayon floss.

Patterns for Purse Pincushion

(Actual size)

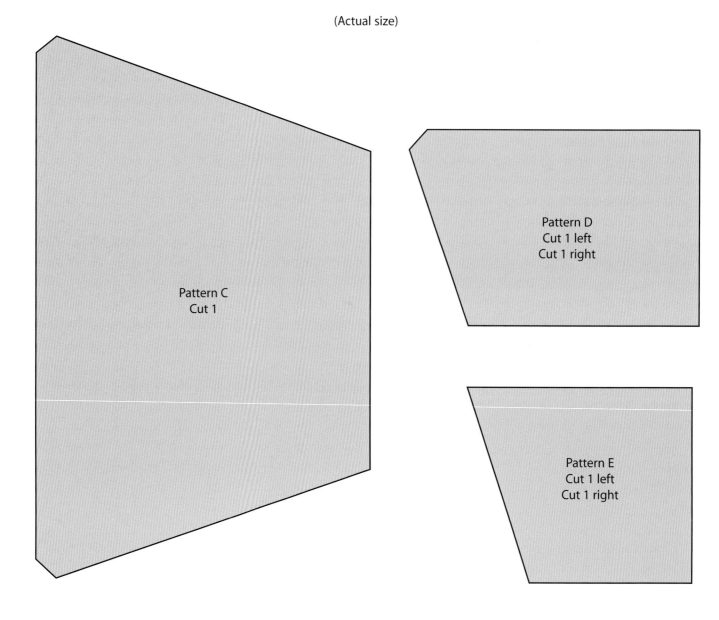

Pattern C
Cut 1

Pattern D
Cut 1 left
Cut 1 right

Pattern E
Cut 1 left
Cut 1 right

Patterns for Purse Pincushion

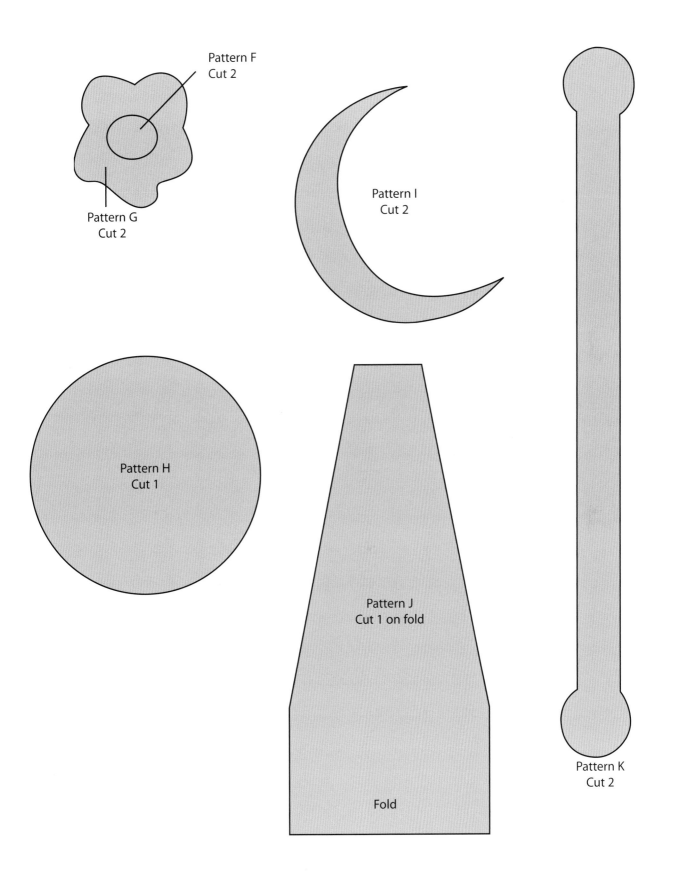

Pattern F
Cut 2

Pattern G
Cut 2

Pattern I
Cut 2

Pattern H
Cut 1

Pattern J
Cut 1 on fold

Fold

Pattern K
Cut 2

Monogrammed Memory Album

MATERIALS

Edge or corners of vintage
   embroidered piece
¾ yd. linen, 44" to 54" wide, lt.
   olive green
12" x 15" piece linen, natural
Silk ribbons:
   ½ yd. silk ribbon, ⅝" wide, lt.
     olive
   ½ yd. silk ribbon, ¼" wide, ivory
   ½ yd. silk ribbon, 4 mm wide,
     taupe
Standard binder with 2½" spine
Corded embroidery floss: dusty
   aqua for sprays and flourish

Stranded embroidery floss:
   pale aqua cotton for spray
   stems and flourish detail
   pale green rayon, for lettering
½ yd. vintage lace trim, ½" wide
Embroidery hoop
Embroidery needle: size 3
Light-box
Permanent-ink gel pen: lt. blue
   or green
Press cloth
Small fabric scissors
Straight pins
Tracing paper

MONOGRAM EMBROIDERY

In monogramming etiquette, promi-
nence is always given to the letter of
the surname. The surname initial is
sized larger and placed in the center.
It is flanked by smaller letters for
first and middle names, or a couple's
first initials. If the letters are all the
same size, they should follow the
regular rotation of the first, middle
(or maiden), and last names. When
the letters in a monogram entwine,
determine which of the cross-lines
should be brought forward to
emphasize the surname initial.

The simplest letters can be
enhanced with auxiliary stitches
and finely executed embroidery
designs. Once the fabric to be
monogrammed is secured in a
frame for embroidering, it can be
enriched with ornamental scrolls,
and a variety of stitches to break
each letter into light and shadow.

CUTTING & CONSTRUCTION

1. Using a light-box and gel pen,
   trace desired initials from
   Alphabet and Monogram Design
   on pages 59–61 onto center of
   linen. Using iron, heat-set ink
   after design has been traced.
2. Refer to Stitches on pages 9–10.
   Using Satin Stitch, work lettering with two strands of the
   rayon floss.

3. Using Stem Stitch, work stem sprays with three strands of cotton floss.

4. Using Bullion Lazy Daisy Stitch, work sprays with two strands of corded floss.

Note: The floss is wrapped two times around the needle.

5. Using Coral Stitch, work flourish with two strands of corded floss.

6. Using Outline Stitch, work flourish detail with cotton floss. Fill flourish's open space with cotton and rayon flosses. Once embroidery is completed, using press cloth, press work from wrong side.

7. Cut fabric for binder cover. Trim monogrammed piece to 11½" x 12¾". Cut 12¾" x 15⅗" piece from light olive green linen for spine/back. Cut two 11½" x 12¾" pieces from light olive green linen for pockets. Cut 12¾" x 26¼" piece from light olive green linen for lining.

8. Stitch spine/back piece to front, aligning 12¾" edges, taking a ½" seam allowance. Press seam allowance open. Overlap ribbon onto lace and stitch over seam along right edge of ribbon. Press.

Note: This is the outer cover.

9. Stitch a narrow hem along one 12¾" edge of each pocket, press. Pin opposite edge of each pocket to left and right edges of outer cover, right sides facing. Pin pockets to upper and lower edges of outer cover as well. Layer lining on top of cover/pockets, right sides facing, and pin.

10. Taking a ½" seam allowance and leaving a 4" opening along the back bottom edge, stitch all these layers together. Clip bulk from corners and edge-press seam allowances open. Turn right side out through opening. Push out corners and press well, with steam and spray starch, if necessary.

11. Slip binder into cover pockets.

12. Loop ¼" ribbon and tack to the center of the light olive green ribbon, using 4 mm ribbon. Using Cascade Stitch, stitch ends of 4 mm ribbon.

Monogram Design

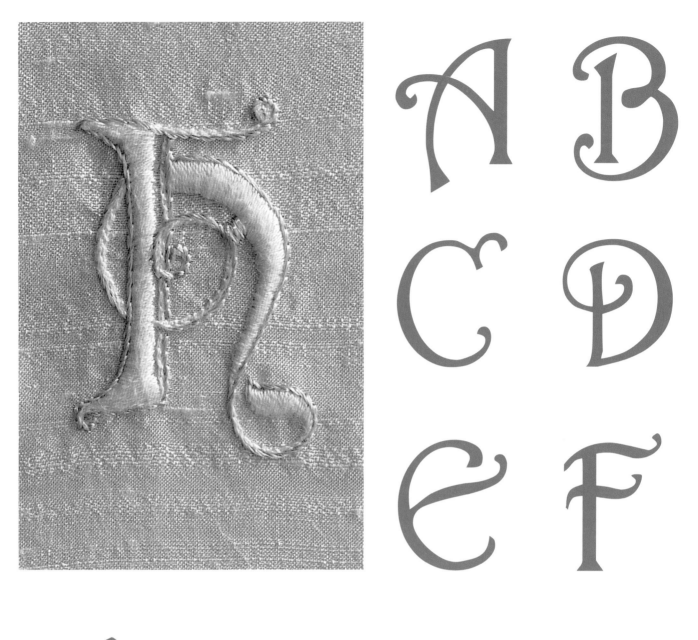

A B
C D
E F
G H I J K

L M N O

P Q R S

T U V W

X Y Z

Hanging Organizer

MATERIALS

½ yd. quilted muslin fabric,
  54" wide (for front)
½ yd. canvas fabric, 54" wide
  (for back)
¼ yd. chenille fabric, 60" wide
  (for pocket)

½ yd. striped cotton fabric,
  44" wide (for bias binding)
9" scrap of lace (for top corner)
2 yds. ribbon, ¼" wide
1 yd. ribbon, ½" wide
3 buttons with shanks, ⅝"
1 plastic ring, ¾" diameter
  (for hanger)

CUTTING & CONSTRUCTION

1. Enlarge the front/back pattern on page 63 to 300%. Cut out the pattern.
2. Position the pattern on the quilted fabric, aligning the grain line pattern marking with the selvage edges. Pin the pattern to the quilted muslin fabric.
3. Using scissors, cut the pattern piece from the quilted muslin fabric for the front of the organizer.
4. Repeat steps 2 through 3 with the canvas fabric for the back of the organizer.
5. Cut the chenille fabric for the pocket, 8" wide x 20" long. (See Figure 1.) You will need extremely sharp scissors, or a rotary cutter.
6. Mark the stitch line placements as shown in Figure 1 and on the front/back pattern onto the quilted front and the chenille pocket, using a fabric-marking pen or pencil.
7. Mark the dots on the front at the seam allowance for the ribbon placement as shown on the front/back pattern.

Making Bias Binding

1. Find the true bias of the cotton fabric by folding a corner of the cotton fabric down so the selvage edge meets the cut fabric edge on the crosswise grain, forming a 45° angle. Pin with straight pins to secure.
2. Cut along the fold, then fold the bias cut over on itself. Cut four 1½" wide bias strips. As you are working with a piece of fabric that is 18" long, the bias-cut lengths should be about 24".

Note: A rotary cutter is very helpful for cutting on the bias.

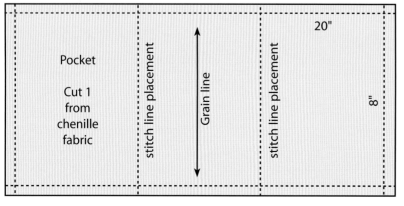

Pocket

Cut 1
from
chenille
fabric

stitch line placement

Grain line

stitch line placement

20"

8"

Figure 1

Pattern for Front/Back of Organizer

Enlarge pattern 300%

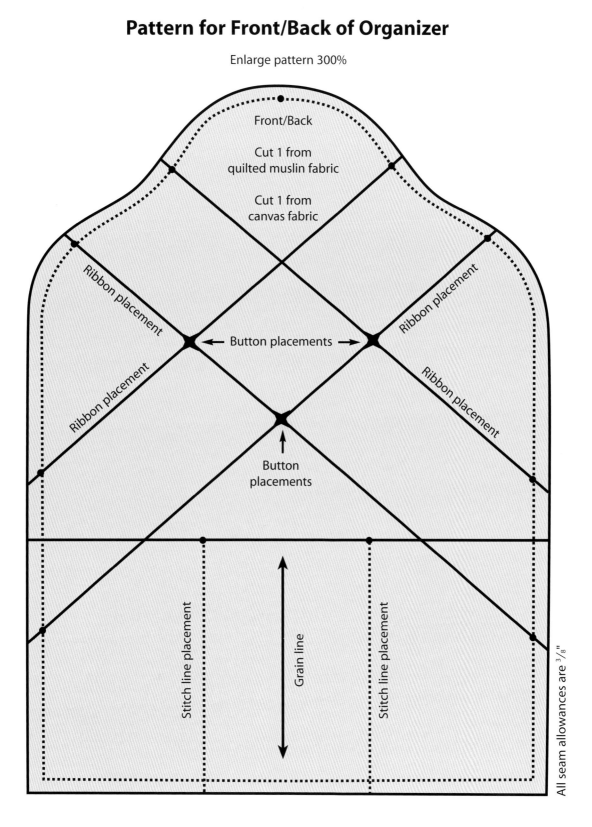

Front/Back

Cut 1 from
quilted muslin fabric

Cut 1 from
canvas fabric

Ribbon placement

Ribbon placement

Ribbon placement

Ribbon placement

← Button placements →

Button
placements

Stitch line placement

Grain line

Stitch line placement

All seam allowances are $^3/_8$"

Embellishing the Front

1. Pin the lace corner to the top of the front with straight pins placed vertically.
2. Topstitch the lacy edge of the lace corner, removing the pins as you stitch.

3. Machine baste the outer edges of the lace corner, using a ¼" seam allowance.
4. Pin the ¼" wide ribbon onto the front as shown on the front/back pattern. Baste in place.

5. Place the front over the back, wrong sides together, aligning all edges and pin the two layers together. Baste, using a ¼" seam allowance, and press.

Pockets

1. Working with one bias strip, pin and stitch the bias binding to the top edge of the pocket, right sides together, using a ⅜" seam allowance. (See Photo 1, below.)

Photo 1

2. Press the seam allowance toward the bias binding.

3. With the pocket wrong side up, press the remaining edge of the bias binding down ½" to the wrong side. Fold the bias binding over the top edge of the pocket seam, encasing the seam, and pin in place. (See photo 2, below.)

Photo 2

4. Working from the right side, edge-stitch the bias binding through all thicknesses just to the inside of the seam, making certain to catch the turned-under edge on the wrong side of the pocket. Press. (See Photo 3, at right.)

5. Matching the stitch lines on the front to the stitch lines on the pocket, pin the pocket to the front and stitch the pockets in place at the stitch lines.

6. Align both side edges of the pocket to those of the front and pin in place. Fold the extra fabric of the pockets to meet the dotted lines, forming inverted box pleats. Pin the pleats in place along the bottom edge and baste-stitch around the three sides, anchoring the pocket to the front.

Finishing

1. Working with a 3" scrap of bias binding, press under the bias edges ½", then press in half. Slip the pressed bias binding through the plastic ring. Pin the ends together.

2. Pin and baste-stitch the edges of the bias binding to the right side of the back at the center top. The ring will be hanging downwards at this point.

3. Stitch together the remaining strips of bias binding. The short edges from two bias pieces must have a 45° angle along the grain line. (See Figure 2.) If necessary, trim the short bias edges to match the grain line, then place right sides together and stitch, using a ¼" seam allowance. Press the seam allowances open.

4. Working from the front, pin and stitch the bias binding to the sides and top of the organizer through all thicknesses, using a ⅜" seam allowance.

Photo 3

5. Press the seam allowances toward the bias binding. With the back side up, press the remaining edge of the bias binding down ½" to the wrong side. Fold the bias binding over the edges of the organizer, encasing the seam, and pin in place.

6. Edge-stitch the bias binding through all thicknesses just to the inside of the seam. Make certain to catch the turned-under edge on the back side of the organizer and press.

7. Stitch the bias to the bottom edge of the organizer, leaving a ½" seam allowance of bias binding at the beginning and the ending of the bottom edge. Before pinning in place, fold in the side edges of the bias binding even with the finished side edge. Fold the bias binding again to encase the seam. Pin and edge-stitch from the front side.

8. Fold up the hanger ring and slipstitch the fabric edges of the hanger to the back at the center top.

9. Knot the ribbon at both ends. Slip the ½"-wide ribbon through the plastic ring and tie into a small bow.

10. Add the buttons as shown on the Front/Back Pattern.

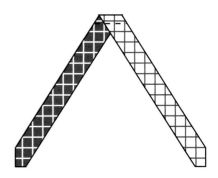

Figure 2

Flower Pot Purse

MATERIALS

25" bias-covered cord,
 ½" diameter
1 yd. bias piping, ¼" diameter
¼ yd. fashion fabric
¼ yd. lining

Medium weight sew-in
 interfacing
Heavy weight fusible interfacing
Paper for pattern
Thread in coordinating color

The bag is trimmed with bias-covered piping and the handles are bias-covered cord. You can use a contrasting or matching fabric to make the cord and piping. For a review of making piping and covered cord, see page 11.

CUTTING & CONSTRUCTION

1. Copy the patterns on pages 67-69, or enlarge to make the desired bag size. Cut out the pattern pieces.

Note: All pattern pieces include seam allowance.

2. Lay out patterns and cut fashion fabric; cut two sides and one bottom. From lining fabric, cut two sides, one bottom, and two pockets.
3. Fuse four layers of the heavy weight interfacing, placing the glue side up on the bottom layer and glue side down on all other layers. (See Photo 1.)
4. From the fused interfacing layers, cut one interfacing bottom.

5. From medium weight interfacing, cut two sides.
6. To make the inside lining pocket, stitch the two pocket pieces, right sides together, using a ¼" seam allowance. Leave about 1" open on one long side for turning. (See Photo 2.) Press and clip the corners. Turn to the right side and press again, turning the raw edges inside.
7. Pin the pocket to the right side of one lining piece, centering the pocket on the lining about a third of the way down and placing the turning opening on the bottom. (See Photo 3.) Topstitch. Make sure that the turning opening is caught in the topstitching.
8. Stitch the medium interfacing to the wrong sides of the fashion fabric side pieces, using a ½" seam allowance.
9. With right sides together, stitch the side seams in the fashion fabric side pieces. This creates a tube-like shape.
10. With right sides together, stitch both sides of lining side seams, using a ½" seam allowance.
11. Place the two bottom pieces, wrong sides together. Sandwich the interfacing bottom piece between these two pieces, centering it. Pin to hold. Stitch around bottom, close to the interfacing through all layers, using a zipper or cording foot. Leave an even 1" seam allowance all around. (See Photo 4.)
12. Trim the seam allowance on all bottom layers to ½".
13. Pin the stitching line of the piping at the stitching line on the fashion fabric bottom. Clip the seam allowance of the piping to ease around the curves. Stitch. (See Photo 5.)
14. Stitch piping to the top edge of the fashion fabric sides, using a ½" seam allowance.

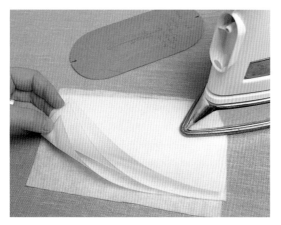

1. Fusing the stacked interfacing layers for the bottom piece.

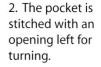

2. The pocket is stitched with an opening left for turning.

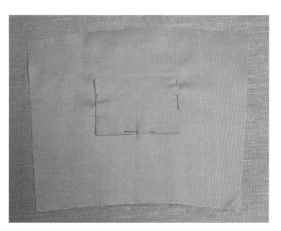

3. The pocket is pinned to one lining piece.

4. Stitching the layers together for the bottom of the bag.

5. The bag bottom with the piping in place.

6. Covered cord handles are pinned in place.

15. Cut 25" of covered cord in half (for handles). Pin handle ends between notches in the seam allowance at the top of the fashion fabric sides. Keep both ends of each handle on the same side. (See Photo 6.)

16. Pin and stitch the right side of the lining to the right side of the fashion fabric sides, using ½" seam allowance. (The handles are sandwiched between them.) All seam allowances should face the same way.

17. Stitch the bottom of the fashion fabric sides to the bag bottom, right sides together.

18. Turn the bag inside out. By hand, stitch the lining of the body to the lining of the bottom.

Patterns for Flower Pot Bag

(Actual Size)

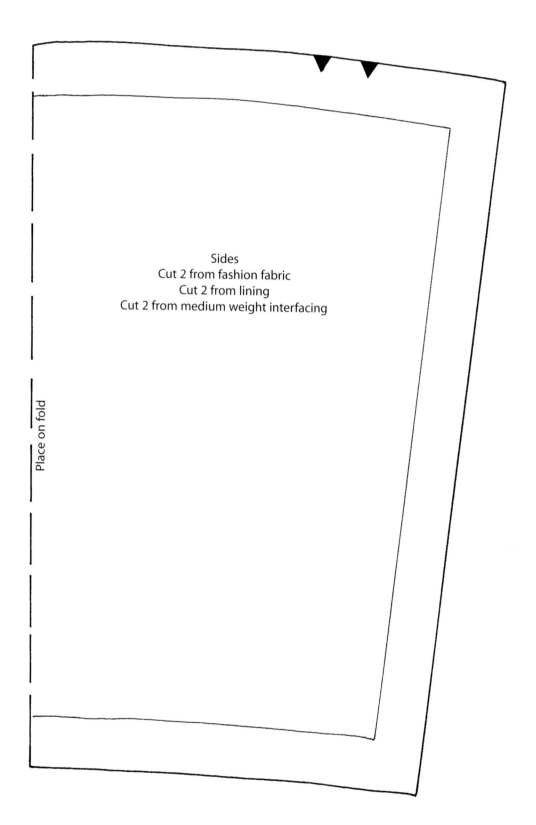

Sides
Cut 2 from fashion fabric
Cut 2 from lining
Cut 2 from medium weight interfacing

Place on fold

Patterns for Flower Pot Bag

(Actual Size)

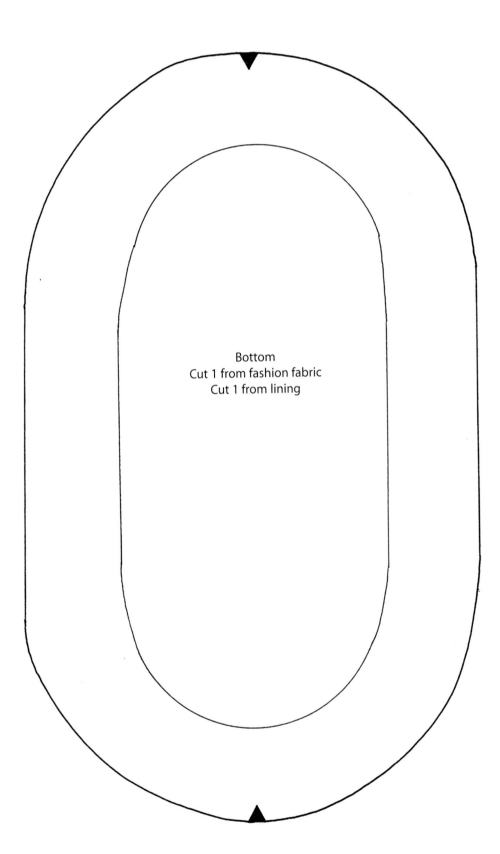

Bottom
Cut 1 from fashion fabric
Cut 1 from lining

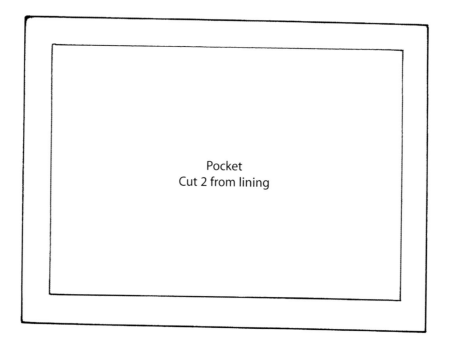

Pocket
Cut 2 from lining

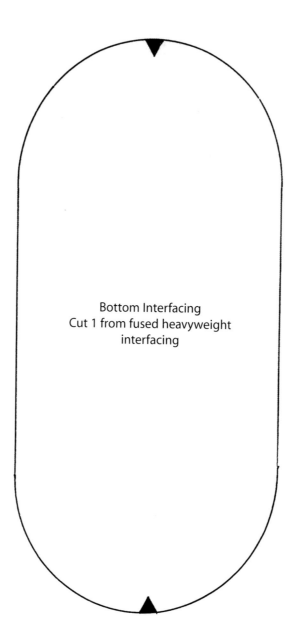

Bottom Interfacing
Cut 1 from fused heavyweight
interfacing

Zippered Pouch

MATERIALS

½ yd. fancy braid trim, 2" wide
  (for front and back)
½ yd. fancy braid trim, 4½" wide
  (for front and back)

1 yd. cording, ¼" wide
  for handle
1 nylon zipper, 7" to 9"
⅛ yd. beaded fringe, 2" to 4" long
⅓ yd. silk ribbon, 4 mm wide

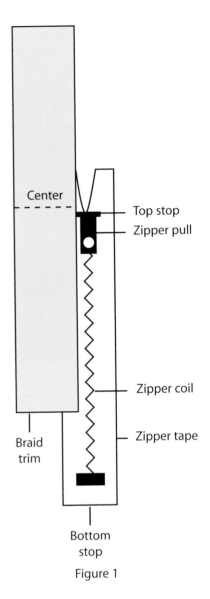

Center

Top stop

Zipper pull

Zipper coil

Zipper tape

Braid trim

Bottom stop

Figure 1

CUTTING & CONSTRUCTION

1. Cut the braid trims into 14½" lengths.
2. Beginning with the narrower of the two braid trims, fold in half and mark the center with a straight pin.
3. Place the zipper's top stop ¼" from the center mark so the edge of the braid trim lies against the coil edge. (See Figure 1.) Pin the braid trim to the zipper tape with straight pins placed vertically.

4. Replace the standard sewing machine foot with the zipper foot and move the position of the needle to the far right. Stitch the braid trim to the zipper tape, beginning at the center mark and place the stitches as close to the braid trim's selvage edge as possible. Make certain not to stitch into the zipper's top stop. Remove the pins as you stitch.
5. Fold the remaining braid trim in half and mark the center with a straight pin. Align the center and end of the wider braid trim with the center and end of the narrower braid trim. Pin the wider braid to the opposite edge of the zipper tape. Make certain the edge lies against the zipper coil.

6. With the position of the needle still to the far right, rotate the piece 180° in order to stitch the wider braid trim to the zipper tape as shown below.

7. If the zipper needs to be short-ened, beginning ⅜" from the end of the braid trim, whip-stitch tightly across the zipper coil 8–10 times, forming a new bottom stop. (See figure 2.) Trim the excess zipper even with the braid trim.

8. At the upper end, tuck the zipper tabs to the inside at a 45° angle, hand-stitching the tabs in place so they are hidden from the outer side. (See Figure 3.)

9. Beginning at the center marks, whipstitch the remainder of the braid trim's selvage edges together. (See Figure 4.)

10. Fold the braid trims in half, right sides together, matching the raw ends. (See Figure 5.) Using a ½" seam allowance, stitch the raw ends, easing the front to fit the back. Press the seam allowances open, turn the pouch right side out and press flat.

TIPS

- Fabric-basting glue is great for placing the zipper in the seam before stitching. Test fabric for staining before applying glue.
- Lapped zippers are used for side seams and often for back seams of garments.
- Take care not to touch the zip-per teeth of nylon zippers with a hot iron—they can melt.
- Some zippers are designed to not blend in with the project, but rather to become a design accent for it.

Finishing

1. Slip the cord handle ends within the top braid trim and pin to the upper edge, having ½" of braid trim within the pouch and placing the handle ends at the side folds. (See Figure 6.)

2. Zigzag-stitch the top braid trim edges together, catching in the handle ends. Zigzag-stitch the bottom braid trim edges together.

3. Tightly roll the tape at the top of the beaded fringe. Hand-stitch the "roll" to secure it; bind the roll with silk ribbon and stitch the beaded fringe roll to the zipper pull.

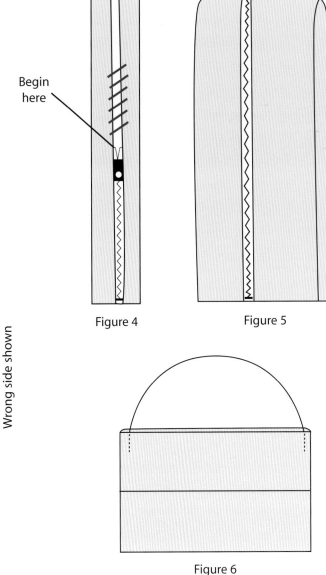

Begin here

Figure 4

Figure 5

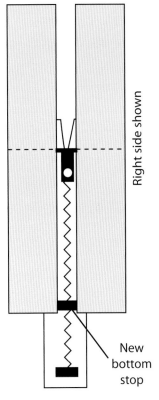

Right side shown

New bottom stop

Figure 2

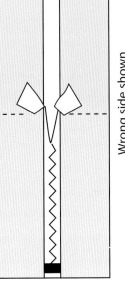

Wrong side shown

Figure 3

Figure 6

Cinch Knapsack

MATERIALS

1⅓ yds. fabric #1 (for front and back)

¼ yd. fabric #2 (for sides)

⅜ yd. fabric #3 (for bottom, pocket, casing, and straps)

¼ yd. fusible interfacing

⅓ yd. lining

60" cord, covered with bias strips cut from fabric #3

Thread

Paper for pattern

CUTTING & CONSTRUCTION

1. Make patterns for the bag from your choice of paper, using the templates in Figure 1. For the bottom, cut a rectangle 4½" x 9"; for the front and back, cut a 10" x 10" square; for the sides, cut a rectangle 5½" x 10".

Note: All pieces include a ½" seam allowance.

2. Using the bottom pattern, cut six layers of fusible interfacing without the ½" seam allowance (9" x 4½").

3. Using the front and back pattern, cut two from fabric #1.

4. Using the side pattern, cut two from fabric #2.

5. Using the bottom pattern, cut one from fabric #3.

6. For the casing, cut a strip of fabric #3 that measures 28" x 4".

7. From the lining fabric, cut one bottom piece and one piece 28" x 10" for the body lining.

8. Decide what size pocket you want for the outside of your bag. Cut two pieces this size plus ¼" seam allowance all the way around from the #3 fabric.

9. Fuse bottom layers of interfacing together with bottom layer glue side up and the rest glue side down. (See Photo 1.)

1. Fusing the stacked interfacing layers for the bottom piece.

2. Stitching the layers together for the bottom of the bag.

72

10. Sandwich the fused interfacing between the wrong sides of bottom lining and bottom fabric pieces. Stitch closely around the interfacing, using a zipper or cording foot to snuggle up close to the interfacing. (See Photo 2.)

11. Pin right sides of pocket together. Stitch around three sides with a ¼" seam allowance, leaving what will be the top of the pocket open for turning. Turn right side out. Press in the ¼" seam along the top. Topstitch the top edge closed ⅛" from edge.

12. Position the pocket on the right side of the front. Topstitch the sides and bottom ⅛" from the edge to secure.

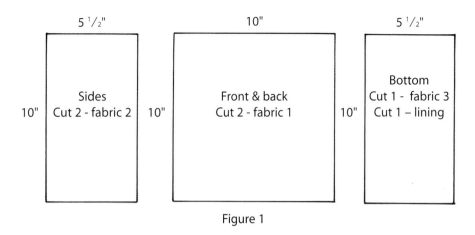

Figure 1

5 ½"	10"	5 ½"
10" Sides Cut 2 - fabric 2 10"	Front & back Cut 2 - fabric 1	10" Bottom Cut 1 - fabric 3 Cut 1 – lining 10"

3. Stitching the front, back, and sides to the bottom.

4. Pinning the bag lining to the bottom.

13. With right sides together, stitch the sides to the front, using a ½" seam allowance. Then stitch the sides to the back, making a tube. Press all seams open.

14. With right sides together, stitch the bottom piece to the bottom of all four sides of the bag, using a ½" seam allowance. (See Photo 3.)

Note: It may be easier if you pin and stitch one side at a time.

15. Stitch the body of the lining, using a ½" seam allowance to make a tube.

16. Pin the bag lining to the bottom with the right side of the lining to the lining side of the bottom. (See Photo 4.) Stitch, using a ½" seam allowance. Turn the bag right side out.

5. Pinning the casing to the top of the bag.

17. Line up the top of the lining with the top of the bag, wrong sides together. Stitch together ½" from the top.

18. Fold and press in ¼" each short side of the 28" x 4" strip of fabric #3. Fold over and press again. (This is the casing.) Topstitch to hem these ends.

19. Starting at the center of the back panel, with right sides together, pin the casing around the top of the bag. (See Photo 5.) Stitch, using a ½" seam allowance. Press the seam up. Fold under the other side of the casing ½" and press.

20. Fold the pressed edge ¼" below the line where the casing is stitched to the bag. Pin and stitch in the ditch from the right side.

21. Tack the opening of the casing closed ½" above the attachment line.

22. Thread the 60" of covered cord through the casing. Line up the ends of the cord and pull to even up inside the casing.

23. Stitch the end of the cord coming out of the right side to the right bottom back corner through all layers of the bag with the raw edge facing up. Fold long cord over raw edge and stitch ½" up to finish the end. Repeat for the end of the cord coming from the left.

Duvet Cover

MATERIALS

2 flat sheets, each 102" x 90" (queen size, or as desired)

2½ yds. fashion fabric (recommended: cotton, washable brocade, linen)

2½ yds. contrasting fabric

9 buttons

Thread in coordinating colors

1. Topstitching the hem on the long edge of the fashion fabric.

2. Seaming the fashion and contrasting fabrics.

CUTTING & CONSTRUCTION

1. Cut 23" off the bottom of the sheet for the top of the duvet cover.
2. Cut 6" off the bottom of the sheet for the bottom of the duvet cover.
3. Cut a 17½" wide strip of contrasting fabric 92" long.
4. Cut a 20" wide strip of fashion fabric 92" long. (See Figure 1.)
5. With right sides together, stitch together the long sides of contrasting fabric and fashion fabric, using a ½" seam allowance. Trim and finish the seams with either a zigzag stitch or an overlocked edge.
6. Turn under a scant ½" on the sides of the joined fashion fabric/contrasting fabric piece. (See Figure 2.) Topstitch.
7. To begin the buttonhole flap, turn under 3" on the long edge of the fashion fabric. Press. Turn this hem back to front, wrong sides together, and stitch a side seam at either end of the 3" hem. Turn the hem right side out. Topstitch along the pressed long edge. (See Photo 1.)
8. Mark the buttonholes across the top edge of the fashion fabric, spacing them evenly and leaving 2" on each side for the seams.

Note: Test the spacing with pins. The start of the buttonhole should be ⅛" + half the width of the button. For example, a buttonhole for a 1" button would start ⅝" away from the folded edge.

9. Make the buttonholes. (The three layers of fabric will stabilize the buttonholes.)
10. With right sides together, stitch the fashion and contrast fabrics to the top of the back sheet, using a ½" seam allowance. (See Photo 2 and Figure 3.)
11. With the right sides together, stitch the front and back sheets together along the bottom edge, using a ½" seam allowance.

12. With right sides together, stitch the sides of the front and back, using a ½" seam allowance. (The back of the duvet cover is longer than the front to allow for the buttoned foldover.) Turn right side out.

13. On the sides of the added piece (fashion fabric/contrasting fabric piece), turn under ½" hem so that edges of this piece are even with the edge of the back sheet piece. Topstitch.

14. Mark the placement of the buttons to match up with the buttonholes. Sew the buttons by hand.

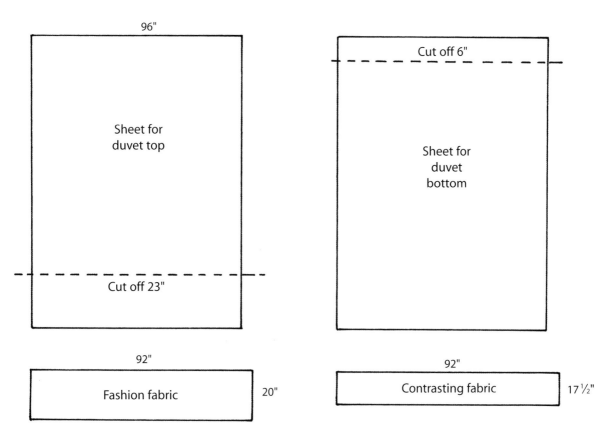

Figure 1

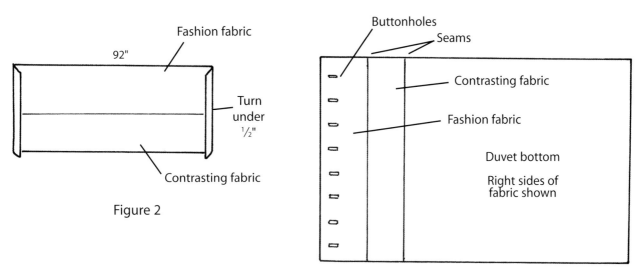

Figure 2

Figure 3

SECTION II

Baby Gifts & Toys

Nursing and Play Pillow

MATERIALS

1 yd. cotton print fabric
Straight pins
Paper for pattern

Polyester filling
Sewing needle
Thread
Scissors

This simple pillow will quickly become the favorite accessory of a new mom. It fits around her waist to make nursing or bottle feeding more comfortable. You can customize it for the new mom's size. When baby gets a little bigger, but can't quite sit up, parents can prop the child in the middle of the pillow for playtime.

CUTTING & CONSTRUCTION

1. Copy the pattern on page 79; enlarge it to the size needed, and modify the opening, if necessary, to fit the desired size. Cut out the pattern.
2. Fold the fabric in half. Place the pattern on the fabric, lining it up on the folded edge.
3. Pin the pattern and cut out the fabric.

Note: Do not cut along the folded edge.

4. Layer the two pieces of fabric with right sides together, and machine-stitch, leaving a 4" opening.
5. Trim the seams. Snip the seams at the curves. Turn the fabric right-side out and press.
6. Stuff with polyester fiber filling, and Whipstitch (see page 9) the opening closed.

Pattern for Nursing and Play Pillow

Enlarge to desired size

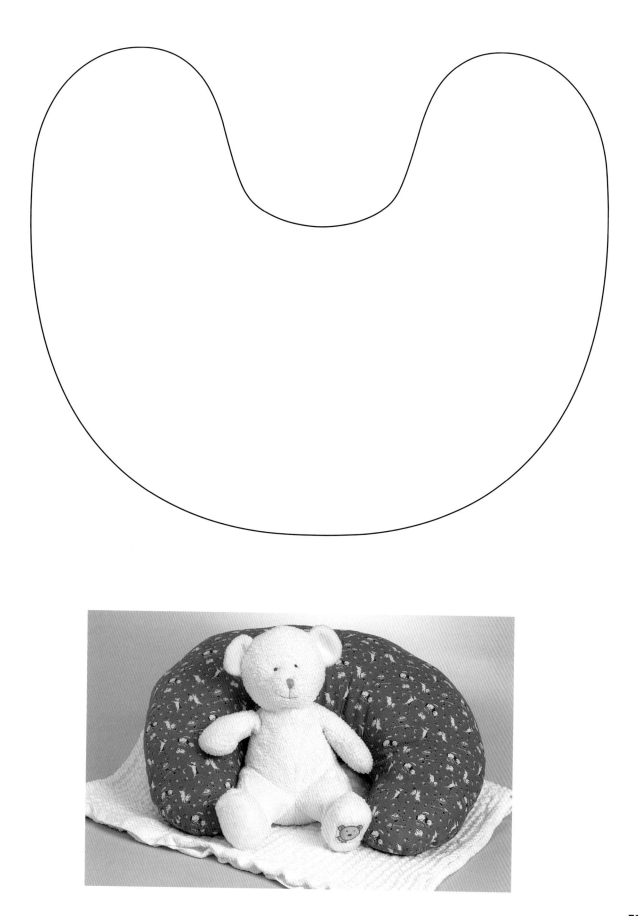

Soft Blocks and Ball

MATERIALS

1 yd. each of 3 coordinating fabrics
Measuring tape
Scissors

Coordinating thread
Large bells or other noisemakers
Polyester filling
Sewing needle

CUTTING & CONSTRUCTION

Blocks

1. The blocks can be made in three different sizes: 6", 9", or 12" squares. Cut two squares of fabric in each of the three colors, for a total of six squares of fabric.
2. Arrange fabric according to the diagram. (See Figure 1.)
3. Sew sides C-A-C together with right sides facing. Press seams open.
4. Sew side A1-B together with right sides facing, then sew to C-A-C. (See Figure 1.) Press seams open.
5. Sew side B1 on to the rest of the figure last, with right sides facing.
6. Pin right sides together and sew.

7. Pin top A1 down, leaving a 2" opening for filling.
8. Trim the seams to ¼" and turn right side out.
9. Stuff the block with fiber filling, add a bell or other noisemaker. Whipstitch (see page 9) closed.

Ball

1. Copy the pattern on page 81. Lay or pin the template on a piece of the first fabric and trace and cut around it. Cut two pieces of the first fabric. Repeat, cutting two pieces in each of the two additional contrasting fabrics.
2. With right sides facing, sew together two pieces in contrasting fabrics, using a ⅜" seam allowance. Add an additional piece cut out of the third fabric. Repeating the same order of the pattern, sew together the additional three pieces. Trim the seams. Snip around the curves of the inside edges to relax the seams and press.
3. With right sides facing, sew together the two three-piece panels of fabric. Leave a 2" opening for stuffing.
4. Turn the ball right side out. Stuff with polyester fiber filling. Add a bell and hand-stitch the opening closed.

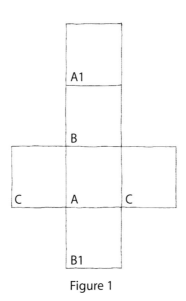

Figure 1

Pattern for Soft Ball

Enlarge to desired size

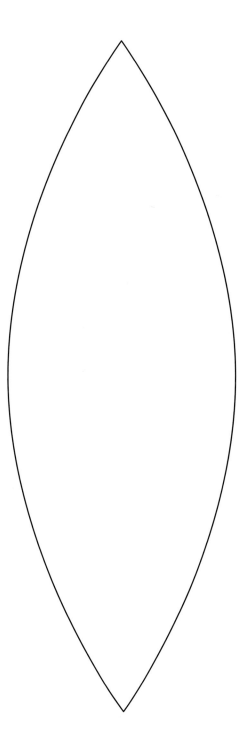

MATERIALS

Felt squares in 8 different
  colors
Polyester or cotton filling
Strong thread or embroidery floss

Bell or other noisemaker
Scissors
Straight pins
Sewing needle
Pencil or knitting needle

This rattle is bright, soft, and safe. It's also very simple to make; you can hand-sew it in minutes—just make sure you use strong thread so it will stand up to frequent use.

CUTTING & CONSTRUCTION

1. Photocopy the pattern on page 83, enlarging it to desired size.
2. Pin the pattern to your first piece of felt and cut around it. Repeat for each of the remaining seven colors of felt.
3. Thread the needle with a doubled length of thread. Hand-sew one side of two felt pieces together with a simple Running Stitch (see page 9). The seam should not be much wider than ⅛". Knot the thread at the end of each row of stitching.
4. Continue to add a felt piece to the previously joined pieces. When you sew the very last piece joining the rattle, leave a couple of inches unsewn.
5. Stuff the rattle with fiber filling, using a pencil or a knitting needle to pack it tightly. Add one or more bells to the filling well inside the rattle.
6. Hand-sew the opening closed.

Pattern for Color-Slice Felt Rattle

Enlarge to desired size

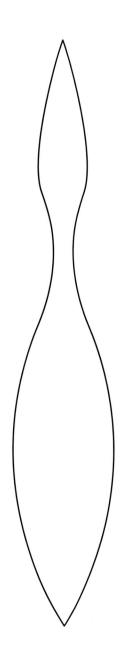

Stuffed Scottie Dog

MATERIALS

¼ yd. gingham fabric
¼ yd. upholstery fabric remnant
Polyester filling
1 yd. of ribbon, ¾" wide
White thread
Straight pins

Needle
Scissors
Pencil or knitting needle
Button for eye
Optional: lavender or chamomile
   for stuffing

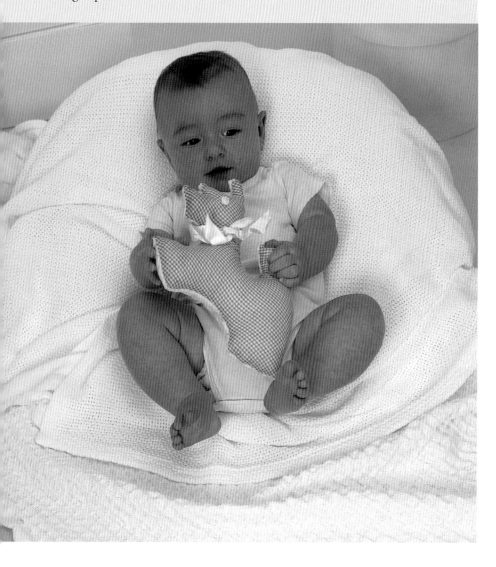

The scottie dog is easy to make and can even be sewn by hand. As an alternative, stuff the dog with lavender, chamomile, or another fragrant, calming herb.

CUTTING & CONSTRUCTION

1. Copy the pattern on page 85, enlarging it to the desired size, and cut it out.
2. Place gingham fabric and the upholstery fabric right sides together, pin the pattern on top of the fabrics, and cut out.
3. Pin the two cut fabric shapes right sides together. Machine-stitch together using a ¼" seam allowance all the way around the dog, leaving 1½" open near the rear foot.
4. Clip the curves and trim the corners.
5. Turn the dog right side out and push out all the edges using a pencil or knitting needle.
6. Starting at the head, use a pencil or knitting needle to tightly pack pieces of fiber filling into the dog.
7. Keep filling, working your way back from the head to the back leg opening.
8. Fold in the fabric at the bottom of the leg and hand-stitch closed.
9. Double your thread and stitch on the button eye. Be sure it's well attached.
10. Tie a bow with the ribbon at the dog's neck and hand-stitch in place.

Pattern for Stuffed Scottie Dog

Enlarge to desired size

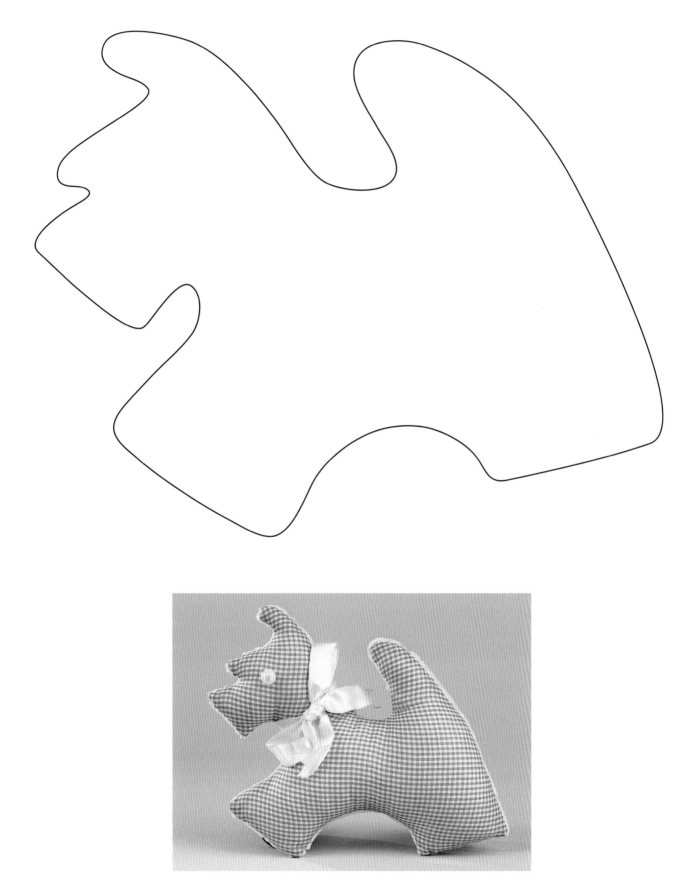

Fuzzy Ducky

MATERIALS

¼ yd. sherpa fabric, 54" wide
Wool felt scraps
1⅛ yd. ribbon, 1½" wide

Embroidery floss
Polyester filling
Optional: Feathers for tail and
  top of head

2. Using scissors or a rotary cutter, cut the pattern piece from the sherpa fabric, simultaneously cutting one body front and one body back.

3. Cut two beaks, two eyes, and two eyeballs from the felt scraps.

4. Position one beak on the body front as shown on the Fuzzy Ducky Pattern and one beak on the body back. Whipstitch (see page 9) the beaks in place along the inner edge, using two strands of embroidery floss. Whipstitch around the outside edges of the beaks, using two strands of embroidery floss.

5. Place each eyeball over each eye, then position on the body front as shown on the Fuzzy Ducky Pattern. Whipstitch in place, using two strands of embroidery floss.

6. Pin the body front and the body back, wrong sides together. *Optional:* Slip a feather between the layers at the top of the head and pin in place. Slip another feather between the layers at the tail and pin in place.

7. Zigzag-stitch the seam line, using a ⅛" seam allowance, leaving an opening on one of the seams as marked on the pattern.

8. Firmly stuff the duck with polyester stuffing through the opening. Zigzag-stitch the opening closed.

9. Knot ribbon at each end. Tie the ribbon into a bow around the neck of the duck.

Fleece is widely available with different depths and textured piles. This fleece is known as sherpa, as it has a lamb-like quality to its pile.

This fabric does not require a seam finish; however, because the fabric is thick, the seams must be trimmed to ¼", then overcast or topstitched to eliminate the bulk.

CUTTING & CONSTRUCTION

1. Enlarge the pattern on page 87; cut out the pattern and pin it on the sherpa fabric.

Note: Fleece has a nap. Make certain to lay pattern pieces so the nap runs one way, up or down for all pieces. If not laid this way, there will be a difference in the color of the pieces.

Pattern for Fuzzy Ducky

Enlarge pattern 150%

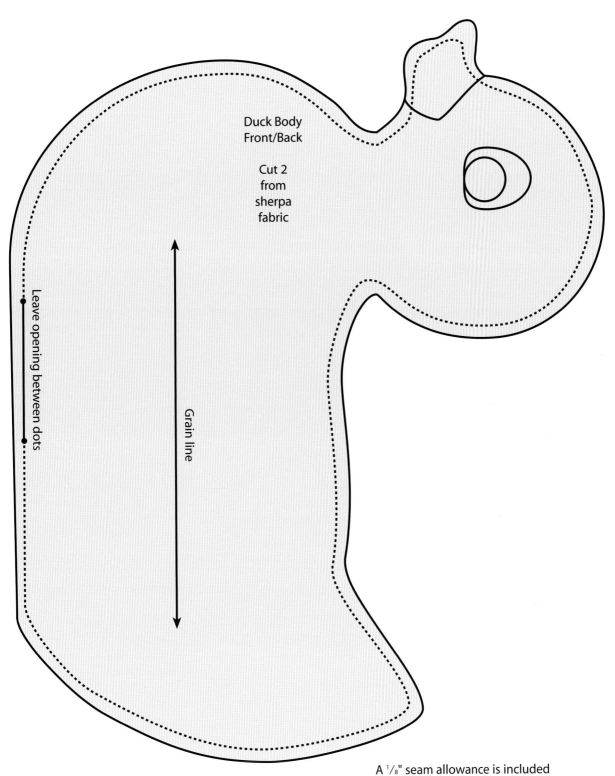

Duck Body
Front/Back

Cut 2
from
sherpa
fabric

Grain line

Leave opening between dots

A ⅛" seam allowance is included

Snuggle Bunny

MATERIALS

½ yd. each in 3 colors of velour
  terry cloth
Polyester filling
Thread in 3 colors
Embroidery thread in 3 colors

Large-eye and sewing needles
Straight pins
Pattern paper or graph paper
Pencil
Scissors
Ruler or measuring tape

This colorful, cuddly bunny is made from terry cloth, so it's soft, washable, and easy to chew on!

CUTTING & CONSTRUCTION
Bunny

1. Copy the pattern on page 89 onto pattern paper, adjusting to the desired size and using a ½" seam allowance all around. Cut out the pattern.
2. Fold ½ yd. of the velour terry cloth fabric in the desired color for the bunny's body. Pin the Snuggle Bunny Pattern to the fabric and cut out, starting at the fold.

Note: You'll have two identical bunny pieces.

3. On the right side of one of the bunny pieces, stitch the nose, lips, and eyes using contrasting colors of embroidery thread and a large-eye needle. Use French Knots for the eyes, Satin Stitch for the nose, and Running Stitch for the mouth. (See page of 9 for review all stitches.)
4. Pin the two bunny pieces right sides together. Machine-stitch all the way around using a ½" seam allowance. Leave a 3" opening on the bunny's side. Clip the curves and turn the bunny right side out, poking the legs, arms, and ears out with a pencil.
5. Stuff the bunny with polyester filling, starting at the far end, and working back to the 3" hole. Hand-stitch closed.
6. Use embroidery thread and a large-eye needle to stitch the fingers and toes.

Shirt

1. Copy the shirt pattern on page 89 onto pattern paper (adjusting to desired size) and cut out. Fold ¼ yard of terry cloth in a contrasting color. Pin the shirt pattern to the fabric and cut it out.

Patterns for Snuggle Bunny

Enlarge as desired
Note: Add desired seam allowance to pattern

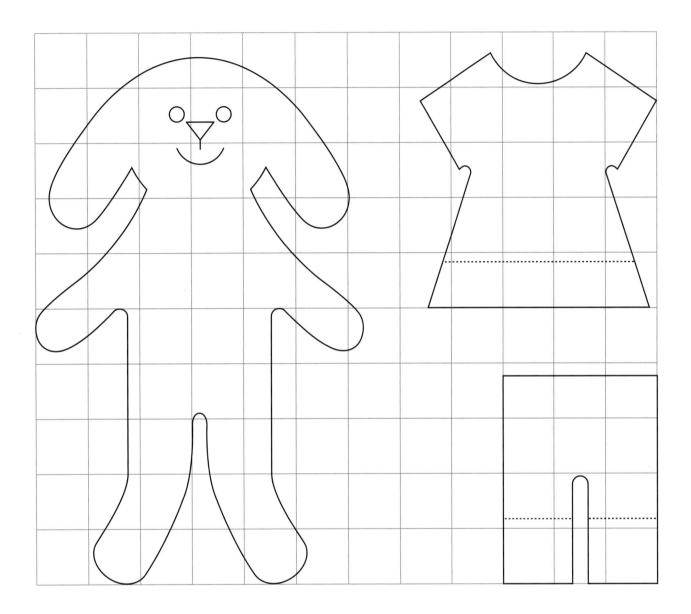

2. With the right sides together, machine-stitch the shoulder and side seams together using a ½" seam allowance.
3. Fold under a ½" hem at the neck and arms. Machine-stitch together.
4. Work Blanket Stitch (see page 9) around the neck, arms, and bottom.

Pants

1. Copy the pants pattern above, adjusting to desired size. Fold ¼ yard of terry cloth fabric in the third and final color, and pin on the pants pattern. Starting at the fold, cut out the pants.
2. With right sides together, machine-stitch the side seams and leg seams together using a ½" seam allowance.

3. Fold ½" of the fabric under at the bottom of each pant leg, and hem in place.
4. Work Blanket Stitch around the leg openings with embroidery thread.

Bear Necessities

For making the bears and some of the other projects in this section, you may find that in addition to the contents of the usual sewing basket, the following supplies will be helpful:

TOOLS

Awl for punching holes for safety eyes

Cardboard for creating sturdy pattern templates

Craft scissors for cutting paper and cardboard

Doll needle (5" or longer) for stitching all the way through head and body

Dressmaker pins with large beaded tops; best because they are more visible in fur

Fabric marker for transferring pattern markings onto fabric (*Note: Disappearing ink is good.*)

Kitchen funnel for placing plastic pellets into body

Mustache trimmer for trimming snouts

Pliers for pulling needles and thread through thick areas

Stuffing stick for pushing stuffing into toy (*Note: many prepackaged stuffing materials contain a stuffing stick.*)

MATERIALS

Embroidery floss for attaching arms and legs, and for stitching nose and mouth

Glass eyes for eyes; have a wire loop for attaching. NOT considered safe for small children's toys; use only on toys made for adult collectors

Heavy thread for attaching head, arms, and legs (carpet, upholstery, or quilting thread)

Plastic pellets for weighting toys to sit or stand on their own

Polyester stuffing for stuffing; also available in a heavier-weight stuffing called hard pack; safe and allergy proof

Safety eyes for eyes; have a locking disc that holds them in place. Considered safe for children's toys

SAFETY

When sewing a toy for a baby or small child, make sure fabrics meet safety requirements and that the eyes on a stuffed toy are safety-locked or embroidered. Buttons, ribbons, and small, detachable parts (i.e. any small part that might come off and be a choking hazard) are also not safe for little ones.

FABRICS

Felt for body and nose (does not fray)

Fuzzy felt for body; looks like plush fur, but is inexpensive and easy to work with

Low-loft quilt batting for body; can be dyed with coffee or tea for a darker color

Mohair for body; wonderful for creating a traditional bear, although expensive because it is imported

Synthetic fur for body; has a tendency to stretch, which works well for sculpting and molding faces

Plastic pellets for stuffing

Different types of fur: ½" mohair, short mohair, sparse mohair, and alpaca low-nap wool, *top row;* felt, low-loft quilt batting, synthetic long-nap fur, and fuzzy felt, *bottom row*

PATTERN & CUTTING TIPS

1. Trace the patterns onto tracing paper; cut out and glue or trace them onto cardboard, then cut out sturdy cardboard templates. Using fabric marker, transfer all markings onto templates, such as openings, eye and ear placement, fold lines, etc.

2. When laying out template pieces on fur, pay attention to the direction of nap. To determine nap direction, smooth your hand across fur to see which way the fur lies.

Note: Nap should go in the same direction (either up or down) on every section you cut for a project made of napped fabric. If not, the color and texture of the sections will appear to be different in the finished product.

3. Lay out templates or pattern pieces on the back of fur or felt fabric, checking carefully for nap directions. Using fabric marker, trace pattern onto fabric. (It helps to mark an arrow on back of fur in direction of nap.)

4. Using the tips of your fabric scissors, make little snips, cutting only the backing of the fur fabric, then gently pull the sections to separate the strands of fur.

SEWING TIPS

1. Sew all darts first. Use a small stitch on your machine so that going around curves will be easier. Setting your needle to stop down in the fabric also makes turning pieces simpler.

2. Pin two head pieces, right sides together. Sew from nose to bottom of neck. Sew from nose around head to bottom edge, leaving open at bottom. Trim close but not too close to seam at nose area. Remove pins. Turn right side out.

3. On body pieces, sew from top to bottom of front.

4. Pin front section to back section with right sides facing, matching side seams. Starting at top, sew all the way around.

Pattern pieces after being sewn

A sewn section that is ready
to be stuffed with plastic pellets
and polyester stuffing

STUFFING TIPS

1. The body in most projects has plastic pellets inserted first, then the top is filled with polyester filling. A kitchen funnel can be used to fill body with pellets.
2. Stuff hard-to-reach parts first.
3. For a soft toy, stuff paw and feet hard and then lighten up as you move up limb.
4. For a huggable bear, test firmness of each section before sewing that section closed.
5. For an even-looking bear, stuff all parts firmly and evenly.
6. For emergency repairs, stuff fur scraps in body of bear so that fur will be available.

Bear head in tea cup
for placement marking

DESIGNING THE FACE

Patterns have markings for location of eyes and ears. However, you can experiment for the look you prefer. Have fun personalizing your creation. Try moving pins around, using larger or smaller nose and even using a larger and smaller eye.

1. Methodically stuff head from neck opening with little pieces of polyester stuffing, using stuffing stick. Stuff nose firmly and sculpt head by shaping as you stuff.
2. Using embroidery needle, plump up cheeks and bottom of nose.
3. Place stuffed head in tea cup to hold upright. Use pins to mark eye placement. Choose desired eye color. Safety eyes are inserted before stuffing; glass eyes are attached after head is completely stuffed.
4. When embroidering over felt nose with embroidery floss and Satin Stitch, keep tension even and tight and untwist threads as you go. If you are not satisfied with the appearance, snip embroidered pieces and pull out thread, using pliers. Keep cutting and restitching until you like the appearance of nose and mouth.

INSERTING SAFETY EYES

1. Using fabric marker, mark placement for eyes.
2. Using an awl, make small hole on mark. Push safety eye through and from inside of head; press safety lock onto eye shank. Press very tightly until lock disc goes all the way down.
3. Repeat for other eye. Head is now ready to stuff.

INSERTING GLASS EYES

1. Cut 12" length of heavy thread. Thread through eye loop, then thread doll needle with both tails of thread. Crimp loop flat with pliers.

2. Insert needle into eye placement marked with pin, going all the way through head with needle and out back seam near neck. Repeat for other side coming out on opposite seam ½" from other threads.
3. Pull threads tightly to indent eyes into fur and tie into double knot. Rethread doll needle with all tails of threads and pull into head. Trim.

EARS TO HEAD

1. See Ladder Stitch on opposite page. Using embroidery needle, sew ear to head with heavy thread and Ladder Stitch, where marked, curving ears as you stitch.
2. Knot thread and pull ends of thread into head. Cut off excess thread. Repeat for other ear.

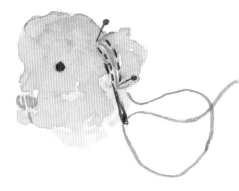

ARMS & LEGS TO BODY

1. Using doll needle with heavy thread, doubled about 3' long, take needle through arm, through body where indicated on pattern for arm position, and through second arm. (Pliers can help pull thread through thick areas.)
2. Thread on a button, then take needle back through arm, body, and first arm.

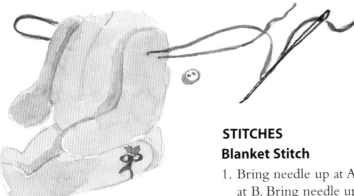

A jointed arm joined with a button, *at left;* a bear whose nose is being embroidered has arms that are joined with knotted strong thread only, *at right.*

3. Thread on another button with needle and thread ending up between button and arm. Pull threads tightly. Wrap thread around button and knot. Pull ends of thread into body. Repeat for legs. (See arms of bears above and in photo top right.) If making this toy for a very small child, the buttons can be omitted. Just make one or two more rounds of stitches to strengthen the joint, then tie thread ends in a strong knot and pull the ends back into the body with a doll needle.

HEAD TO BODY

1. See Ladder Stitch at right. Using embroidery needle, sew head to body with heavy thread and Ladder Stitch, lining up center of head and body.
2. Sew around neck twice to insure head is firmly attached.
3. Pull knot and ends of thread into body.

STITCHES
Blanket Stitch

1. Bring needle up at A; go down at B. Bring needle up again at C, keeping thread under needle. Go down at D and repeat.
2. Make all stitches equal in size and shape.

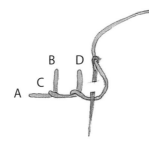

Ladder Stitch

1. Knot thread. Go in first edge at A and out ¼" at B. Drop down to next joining edge and out at C. Go in ¼" at D, and back up to other edge at E.
2. Repeat and pull tightly as needed.

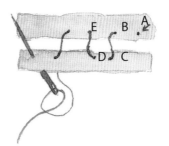

Satin Stitch

1. Keep thread smooth and flat. Bring needle up at A; go down at B, forming a straight stitch. Bring needle up again at C. Go down at D, forming another straight stitch next to the first.
2. Repeat to fill design area.

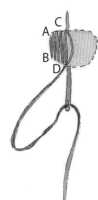

NOSE & MOUTH PATTERNS

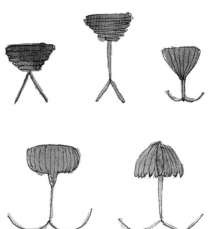

Breadloaf Bunny or Bear

MATERIALS

¼ yd. low-nap, plush, or synthetic
fur (for ears, head, body,
and tail)
Square felt scrap (for nose)
⅔ cup plastic pellets
Small bag polyester filling
Heavy Thread for sewing,
coordinating color of choice
Embroidery floss: pink

8 mm glass or safety eyes
Doll needles (5" or longer)
Sewing and embroidery needles
Pins
Craft and fabric scissors
Stuffing stick
Tracing paper
Cardboard
Fabric marker
Pencil

This pattern can make a bunny or
a bear. Use a different type of fur,
different ears and facial embroidery
to make the one you want.

CUTTING & CONSTRUCTION

1. Refer to Bear Necessities on
   pages 90-93. Copy pattern
   pieces on pages 95-96.
2. Place patterns on back of fabric.
   Using fabric marker, trace patterns. Using fabric scissors, cut
   out fabric pieces.
3. Sew head and ear pieces, with
   right sides together, leaving
   open where marked.
4. Sew body pieces with right sides
   together, leaving open where
   marked. Check all seams. Turn
   all sewn pieces right side out.

*Note: If using glass eyes, stuff head
first. If using safety eyes, insert eyes first
and then stuff head.*

5. Using stuffing stick, stuff head
   firmly with polyester filling.
6. Using pins, mark eye placement.
   Pull eyes onto face with doll
   needle and heavy thread.
7. Pin ears onto head where
   marked on pattern. With
   embroidery needle and heavy
   thread, sew ears to head, curving
   ears as you stitch, using Ladder
   Stitch. (See page 93.)
8. Trace desired nose pattern from
   page 93 onto tracing paper; cut
   out template. Using fabric
   marker, trace template onto felt.
   Cut out felt nose and pin onto
   face. Embroider over felt nose
   with embroidery floss and Satin
   Stitch. (Review Stitches on
   pages 9 and 93.) Embroider
   mouth.

9. Stuff arms and feet, leaving space between each paw and arm, and each foot and leg. Fill bottom of body with plastic pellets, then stuff body lightly to top with polyester filling. Gather-stitch around opening on body with heavy thread, leaving slightly open to fit base of head.

10. Sew across stitching lines where arms and legs meet body.

11. Align center seams of head and body and sew head onto body with heavy thread, using Ladder Stitch. Sew around neck twice to ensure that head is firmly attached. Pull knot and ends of thread into body.

12. Fold arms and legs to front of body; tack to secure with sewing thread.

13. For bunny: gather-stitch around tail with heavy thread; stuff tail and pull, gathering threads on tail to close. Sew tail onto back of bunny with embroidery floss using Ladder Stitch.

Patterns for Breadloaf Bunny or Bear

(Stands 8½" tall, patterns actual size)

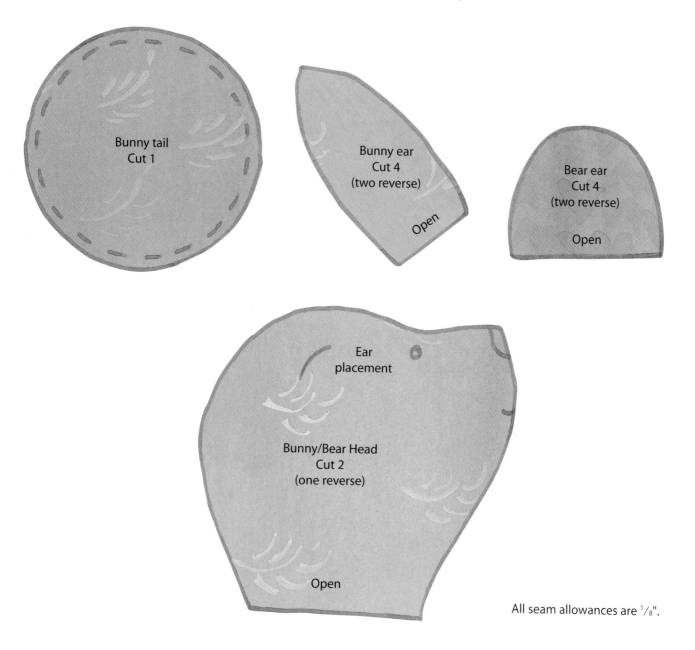

Bunny tail
Cut 1

Bunny ear
Cut 4
(two reverse)

Open

Bear ear
Cut 4
(two reverse)

Open

Ear placement

Bunny/Bear Head
Cut 2
(one reverse)

Open

All seam allowances are ⅛".

Patterns for Breadloaf Bunny or Bear

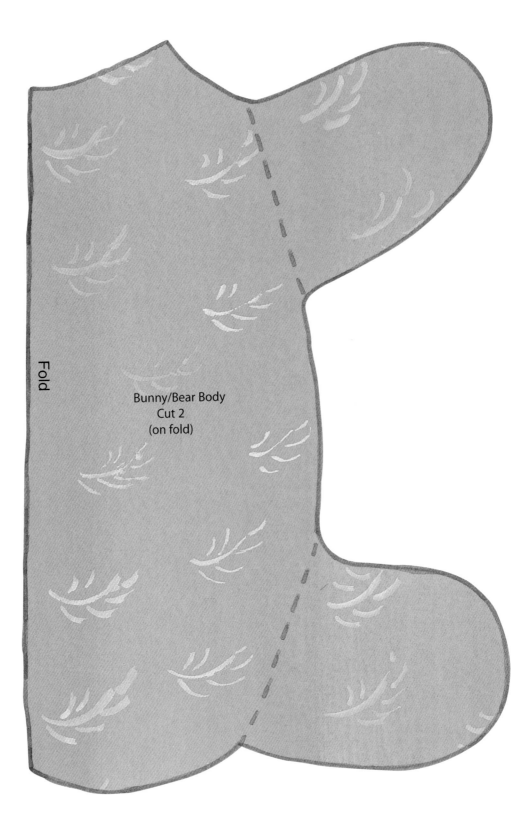

Fold

Bunny/Bear Body
Cut 2
(on fold)

Jointed Teddy Bear

MATERIALS

¼ yd. mohair or synthetic fur (for arms, ears, body, head, and legs)
Square felt scrap (for nose)
8 mm glass or safety eyes: black
1 cup plastic pellets
Small bag polyester filling

Embroidery floss: brown
4 medium buttons, antique or wood
½ yd. ribbon, width of choice, coordinating color of choice
Heavy thread for sewing; coordinating color of choice

A jointed bear's arms and legs are jointed like a doll's, with thread and buttons. This bear can wear the jacket on page 112.

CUTTING & CONSTRUCTION

1. Refer to Bear Necessities on pages 90-93. Copy pattern pieces on pages 98-100. Place patterns on back of fabric, trace them, and cut out fabric pieces.
2. Sew darts in head. Sew head pieces, with right sides together, from front top of chin to front bottom of neck. Place gusset, centering nose end at top of chin seam. Pin in place. Sew along one side from nose end, over top of head, to back bottom of neck. Repeat for other side.
3. Sew ear and arm pieces, with right sides together, leaving open where marked.
4. Fold leg pieces over, with right sides together. Sew around pieces, leaving open where marked.
5. Sew body darts. Sew body pieces, with right sides together, leaving open where marked. Check all seams. Turn all sewn pieces right side out.

Note: If using glass eyes, stuff head first. If using safety eyes, insert eyes first and then stuff head.

6. Stuff head firmly with polyester filling, using stuffing stick. Stuff arms and legs. Fill bottom of body with plastic pellets, then stuff body firmly to the top with polyester filling.
7. Using pins, mark eye placement; insert glass eyes onto face with doll needle and heavy thread.
8. Pin ears onto head where marked on pattern. Sew ears onto head, curving ears as you stitch, using heavy thread and Ladder Stitch. (See page 93.)

9. Trace desired nose pattern from Bear Necessities (page 93) onto tracing paper, creating template. Cut out template and trace template onto felt. Cut out felt nose; pin onto face and embroider over felt nose with embroidery floss using Satin Stitch. Embroider mouth.

10. Gather-stitch around opening on body with heavy thread, leaving slightly open to fit base of head. Sew arms and legs closed.

11. Using doll needle, sew arms and legs onto body with heavy thread and buttons.

12. Align center seams of head and body. Using Ladder Stitch, sew head onto body with heavy thread, turning while stitching. Sew around neck twice for strength. Pull knot and ends of thread into body. Tie ribbon around neck for tie.

Patterns for Jointed Teddy Bear

Stands 12" tall.

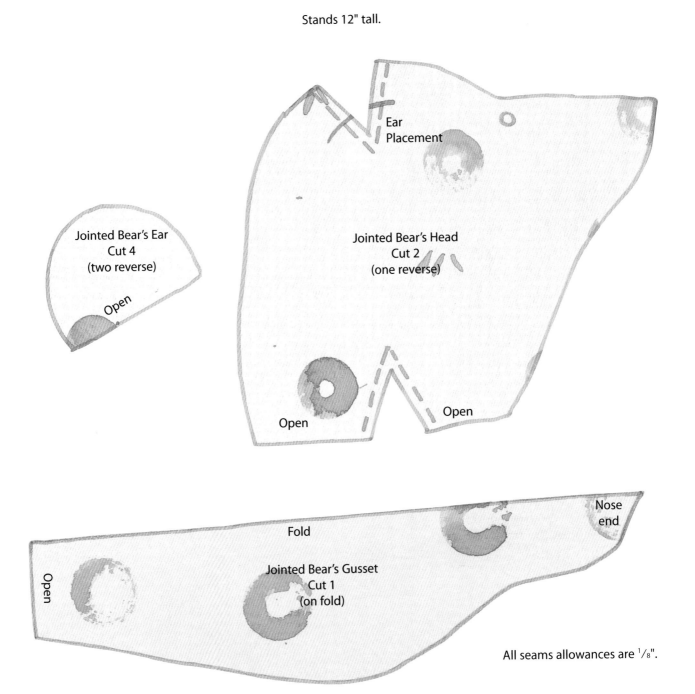

Jointed Bear's Ear
Cut 4
(two reverse)
Open

Ear Placement

Jointed Bear's Head
Cut 2
(one reverse)

Open

Open

Fold

Nose end

Open

Jointed Bear's Gusset
Cut 1
(on fold)

All seams allowances are $1/8$".

Patterns for Jointed Teddy Bear

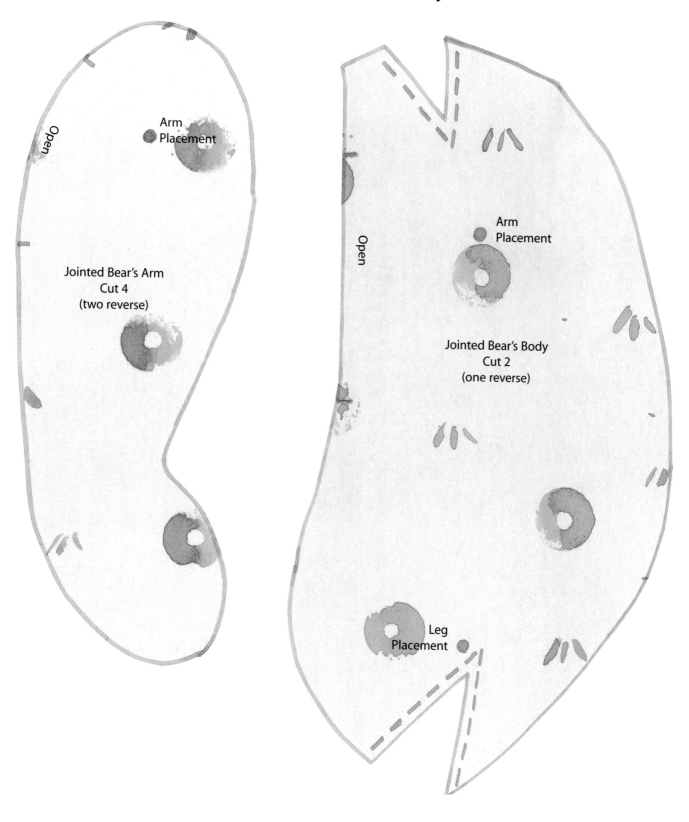

Open

Arm
Placement

Jointed Bear's Arm
Cut 4
(two reverse)

Open

Arm
Placement

Jointed Bear's Body
Cut 2
(one reverse)

Leg
Placement

Patterns for Jointed Teddy Bear

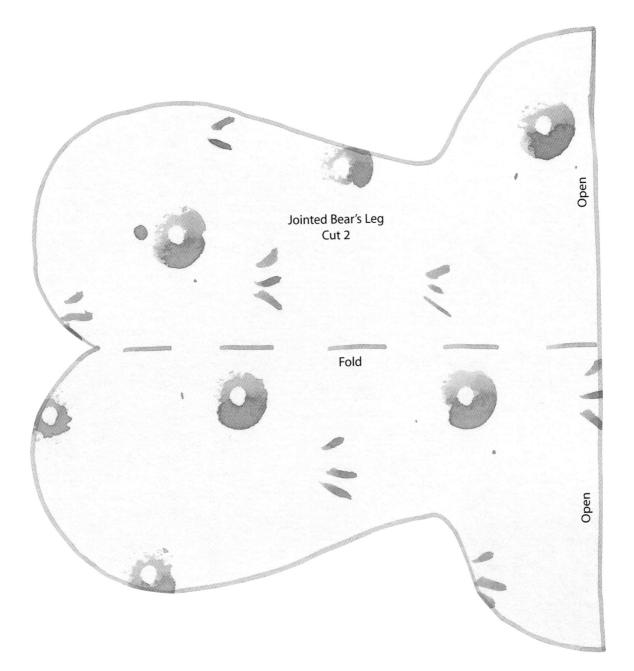

Jointed Bear's Leg
Cut 2

Open

Fold

Open

Lop-Eared Bunny

MATERIALS

¼ yd. synthetic fur or mohair (for arms, ears, body, head, legs, and tail)
Square felt scrap (for nose)
4 medium buttons
Embroidery floss: brown
10 mm glass or safety eyes: black
¾ cup plastic pellets
Small bag polyester filling
Heavy thread for sewing, coordinating color of choice
Cardboard
Fabric marker
Doll needles (5" or longer)
Sewing and embroidery needles
Pins
Craft and fabric scissors
Stuffing stick
Tracing paper

CUTTING & CONSTRUCTION

1. Read Bear Necessities on pages 90-93. Copy pattern pieces on pages 102-103.
2. Place patterns on back of fabric; trace them, and cut out fabric pieces.
3. Sew darts in head. Sew head, ear, arm, and leg pieces, with right sides together, leaving open where marked. Gather-stitch around tail.
4. Sew body pieces, with center seams first. Sew sides and bottoms, with right sides together, leaving open where marked. Check all seams. Turn all sewn pieces right side out.

Note: If using glass eyes, stuff head first. If using safety eyes, insert eyes first and then stuff head.

5. Using stuffing stick, stuff head firmly with polyester filling. Stuff arms, legs, and tail. Fill bottom of body with plastic pellets, then stuff body firmly to the top with polyester filling.
6. Mark eye placement with pins; insert eyes onto face with doll needle and heavy thread.
7. Pin ears onto head as marked on pattern. Sew ears to head with heavy thread and Ladder Stitch. (See page 93.)

Note: Try sewing pipe cleaners inside ears, so that they can bend in different directions.

8. Trace desired nose pattern from page 93 onto tracing paper, creating template. Cut out template and trace onto felt. Cut out felt nose and pin to face.
9. Embroider over felt nose with embroidery floss and Satin Stitch. (See page 93.) Embroider mouth.

10. Gather-stitch around opening on body with heavy thread, leaving slightly open to fit base of head. Sew arms and legs closed.

11. Using doll needle, sew arms and legs onto body with heavy thread and buttons. (See page 93.)

12. Align center seams of head and body; sew head onto body with heavy thread and Ladder Stitch. Sew around head twice for strength. Pull knot and thread ends into head.

13. Pull gathering threads on tail to close. Sew tail onto back of bunny with embroidery floss and Ladder Stitch.

The Lop-Eared Bunny can wear the jacket shown on page 112.

Patterns for Lop-Eared Bunny

Stands 10" high.

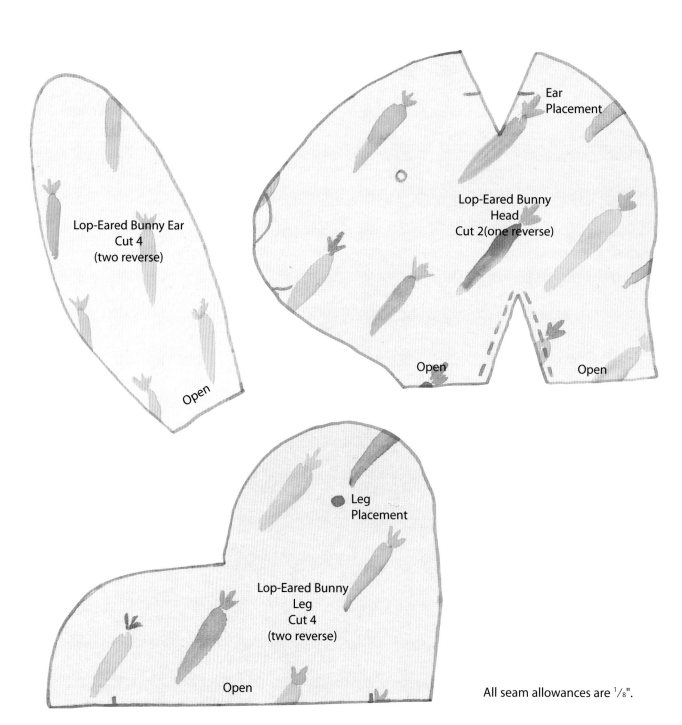

Lop-Eared Bunny Ear
Cut 4
(two reverse)

Open

Ear
Placement

Lop-Eared Bunny
Head
Cut 2(one reverse)

Open

Open

Leg
Placement

Lop-Eared Bunny
Leg
Cut 4
(two reverse)

Open

All seam allowances are $^1/_8$".

Patterns for Lop-Eared Bunny

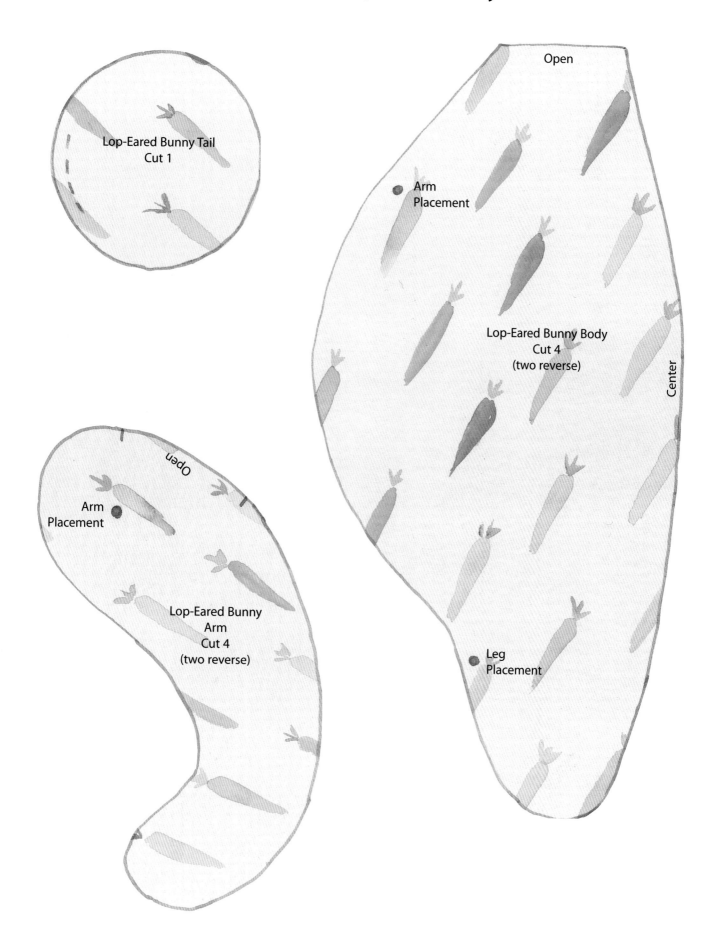

Lop-Eared Bunny Tail
Cut 1

Open

Arm
Placement

Lop-Eared Bunny Body
Cut 4
(two reverse)

Center

Leg
Placement

Open

Arm
Placement

Lop-Eared Bunny
Arm
Cut 4
(two reverse)

Leggedy Bear

MATERIALS

⅓ yd. flannel (for body and legs)
¼ yd. felt or quilted batting (for arms, ears, and head)
Square felt scrap (for nose)
½ yd. flannel for scarf
2 medium buttons (for arm joints)
Heavy thread for sewing, coordinating color of choice
Embroidery floss: brown
8 mm glass or safety eyes: black
1 cup plastic pellets

Small bag polyester filling
Sweater: small baby or medium teddy bear
Hiking boots: child's size 2
Shoelaces: red
Children's socks
1 old ribbed adult sock
Cardboard
Fabric marker
Doll needles (5" or longer)
Sewing and embroidery needles
Pins
Craft and fabric scissors

This bear has long legs, and if you fill his bottom with some plastic pellets, he sits nicely on a shelf with his legs crossed or hanging down. Take your bear shopping for socks and shoes.

CUTTING & CONSTRUCTION

1. Read Bear Necessities on pages 90-93. Copy pattern pieces on page 105-107.
2. Place patterns on back of fabric, trace them, and cut out fabric pieces.
3. Sew darts in head. Sew head, ear, and arm pieces, with right sides together, leaving open where marked.
4. Sew body pieces, with center seams first. Sew sides, with right sides together, leaving open where marked. Match seams, then sew across bottom. Check all seams. Turn all sewn pieces right side out.

Note: If using glass eyes, stuff head first. If using safety eyes, insert eyes first and then stuff head.

5. Stuff head firmly with polyester filling, using stuffing stick. Stuff arms. Fill bottom of body with plastic pellets, then stuff body firmly to the top with polyester filling.
6. Sew head and body closed with embroidery floss and Ladder Stitch. (See page 93.)
7. Mark eye placement with pins. Using doll needle, pull eyes onto face with heavy thread.
8. Pin ears onto head where marked on pattern. Sew ears onto head with heavy thread and Ladder Stitch.
9. Trace desired nose pattern from Bear Necessities on page 93, creating template. Trace template onto felt; cut out felt nose and pin onto face.

10. Embroider over felt nose with embroidery floss and Satin Stitch. Embroider mouth.

11. Gather-stitch around opening on body with heavy thread, leaving slightly open to fit base of head.

12. Sew arms closed and attach to body 2½" from neck edge using doll needle, heavy thread, and buttons.

13. Using stuffing stick, stuff legs to first mark with polyester stuffing. Match up seams and sew across legs. Feet will be facing forward. Repeat process for second mark. Stuff upper legs to 2" from top. Sew across legs, leaving unstuffed section for hem. Fold in hem to insides of legs. Sew legs onto bottom of body.

14. Align center seams of head and body. Sew head onto body with heavy thread and Ladder Stitch. Sew around neck twice for strength.

15. For scarf, cut a 3" x 18" piece of flannel fabric. Using sewing needle, pull threads out along all edges to create fringe. Tie scarf loosely around bear's neck.

16. For hat, cut "hat" from old sock along dotted line. (See Diagram A.) Hand sew raw edges together with sewing thread, closing top of hat. Fold bottom edge up for brim.

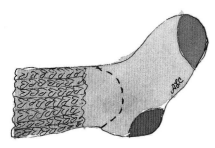

Diagram A

17. Place hat on bear's head; tack to secure with sewing thread, if desired.

Patterns for Leggedy Bear

Stands 20" tall.

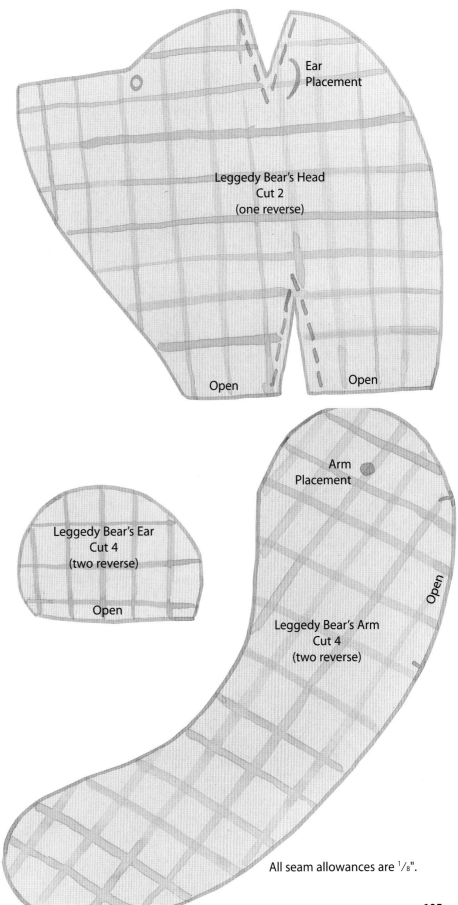

Ear Placement

Leggedy Bear's Head
Cut 2
(one reverse)

Open   Open

Leggedy Bear's Ear
Cut 4
(two reverse)

Open

Arm Placement

Leggedy Bear's Arm
Cut 4
(two reverse)

Open

All seam allowances are ⅛".

Patterns for Leggedy Bear

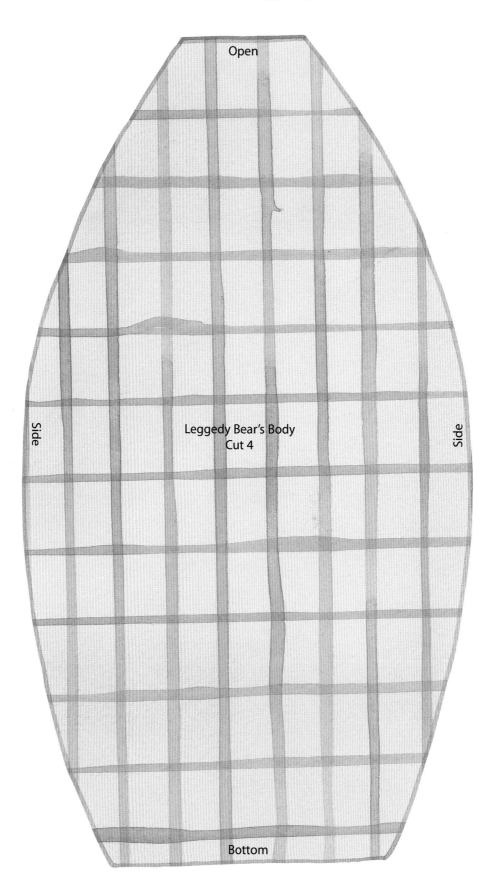

Open

Side

Side

Leggedy Bear's Body
Cut 4

Bottom

Patterns for Leggedy Bear

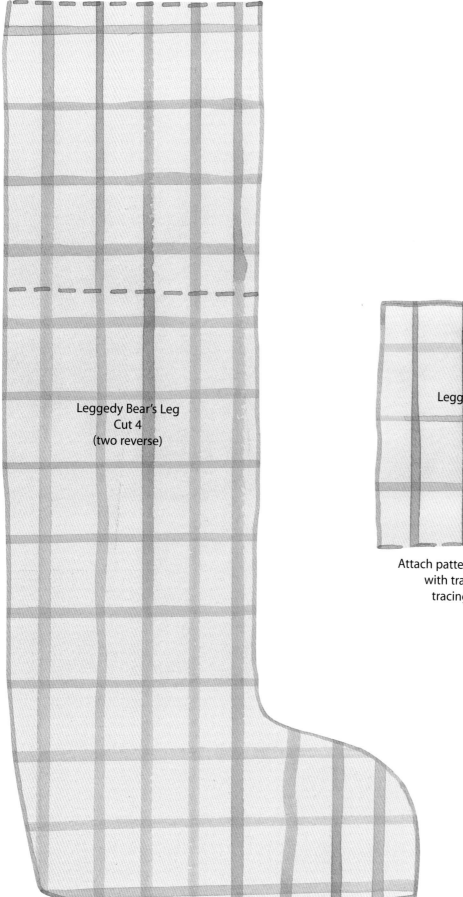

Leggedy Bear's Leg
Cut 4
(two reverse)

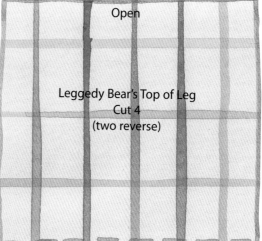

Open

Leggedy Bear's Top of Leg
Cut 4
(two reverse)

Attach pattern to top of pattern on left
with transparent tape before
tracing and cutting fabric.

Measuring a Doll or Bear for Clothes

MATERIALS

Craft scissors
Pencil
Straight pins

Tape measure
Tracing paper
Transparent tape

The patterns that follow have been designed by doll height for 12", 14", 16", and 18" dolls (or stuffed animals). Body dimensions will vary from doll to doll. It is imperative that you measure your doll's body proportions as well as height before starting. A slim 18" doll may have the body proportions of the 14" pattern, while a soft full-bodied 14" doll could have the body proportions of an 18" doll.

Your doll's pattern size may be determined by measuring the following and comparing measurements to corresponding pattern pieces:

1. Neck circumference plus seam allowance
2. Chest circumference under armpit, plus seam allowance
3. Arm length from shoulder to wrist, plus seam allowance and hem
4. Waist circumference, plus 1"
5. Length from waist to ankle, plus hem and waistband, or casing
6. Length from neck to ankle, plus hem

Note: If your doll's measurements fall between two sizes, select the larger size. Do not mix pattern sizes.

If the selected pattern size still requires modification, it is easily adjusted up or down in size if you use the following methods:

1. Using a pencil and tracing paper, trace the selected size pattern. Mark intersecting lines. (See Figures 1a and 1b.) Cut the pattern along intersecting lines.

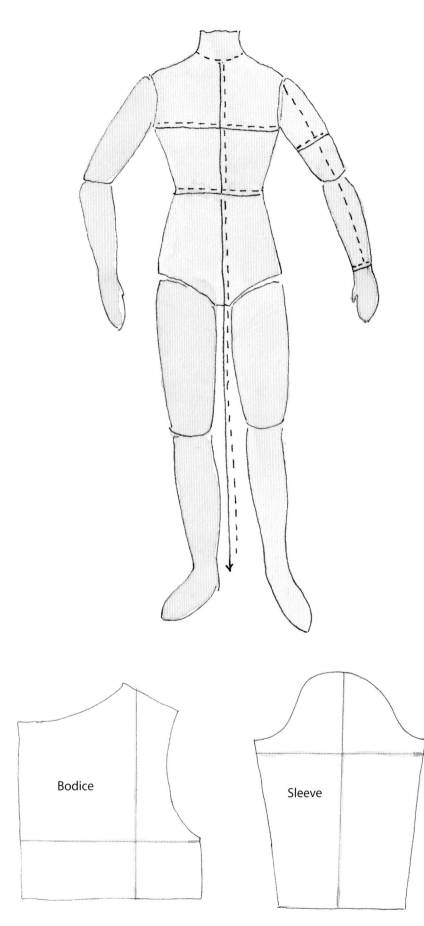

2. Enlarge pattern by spreading pattern pieces apart on sheet of tracing paper to doll's determined dimensions. (See Figure 2.) Tape pieces in place, and trace.

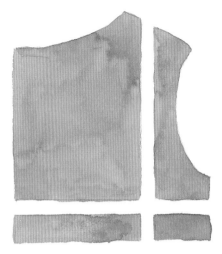

Figure 2

3. Decrease the pattern size by overlapping pattern pieces. Tape or trace resized patterns. (See Figure 3.)

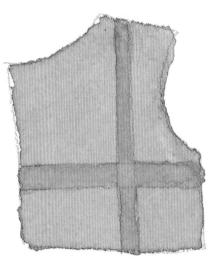

Figure 3

4. Skirts and dresses may be lengthened or shortened by adding or decreasing length when cutting out or when hemming.

Note: Patterns are not included for basic shapes, such as rectangles and strips. In these cases, the cutting dimensions are included.

Bodice

Figure 1a

Sleeve

Figure 1b

Pinafore

MATERIALS

1 yd. lace, 8" to 10" wide
  scalloped-edge
2 yds. satin ribbon, ¼" wide
Optional: Fusible hem tape

Thread
Craft and fabric scissors
Measuring tape
Straight pins
Tracing paper and pencil

This can also be made with a piece of antique eyelet, such as you might salvage from the hem of an old petticoat.

Option: Make a pinafore apron from a pretty printed fabric.

CUTTING & CONSTRUCTION

1. Trace patterns on page 111 onto tracing paper. Place and pin skirt pattern so bottom is on scalloped edge of lace. Place and pin bodice pattern above scalloped edge. Cut out pattern pieces.
2. With right sides together, sew shoulder seams. Press seams open.
3. Fold neck edge in ⅛" and sew hem in place. Press hem. *Optional:* ½" wide lace may be sewn to neck if desired, or the neck may be bound with bias binding. (See pages 10–11.)
4. Fold armholes and center back edges of bodice in ⅛" and press. Fold side edges of all skirt pieces in ⅛" and press. Sew all edges in place.
5. Sew top edge of all skirt pieces with gathering stitch. Pull bobbin thread to gather. Sew skirt back pieces to back bodice. Sew skirt front piece to front bodice. (See Figure 1.)
6. Cut eight 9" pieces of ribbon for ties. Sew ribbon to back, neck, and sides.

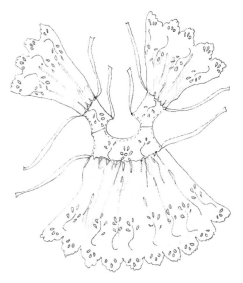

Figure 1

Patterns for Pinafore

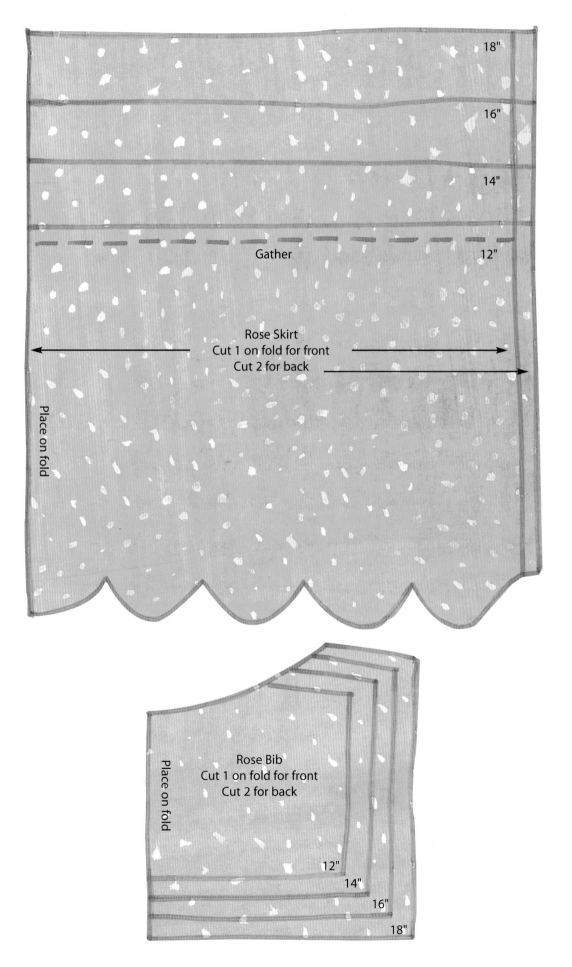

18"

16"

14"

Gather   12"

Rose Skirt
Cut 1 on fold for front
Cut 2 for back

Place on fold

Rose Bib
Cut 1 on fold for front
Cut 2 for back

Place on fold

12"

14"

16"

18"

Jacket

MATERIALS

¼ yd. felt, old blanket, or fabric of
  your choice
Thread in coordinating color
Embroidery floss (for accent
  edging)
3 small buttons

Optional: Velcro® tabs
Sewing and embroidery needles
Pins
Craft and fabric scissors
Measuring tape
Tracing paper and pencil

Both the jointed teddy bear (page
97) and the lop-eared bunny (page
101) can wear this jacket.

CUTTING & CONSTRUCTION

1. Trace patterns on page 113.
   Place and pin jacket sleeve and
   back patterns on fold of fabric.
   Place and pin jacket front on
   doubled fabric, wrong sides
   together, with side seam along
   straight grain of fabric. Cut out
   pattern pieces.
2. Sew shoulder seams of jacket,
   with right sides together. Ease
   sleeves into sleeve openings; pin,
   and sew.
3. Sew jacket closed from wrist
   edge of sleeve to bottom of
   jacket on each side. Finish hem
   and edges with Blanket Stitch.
   (See pages 9 and 93.)
4. Fold lapel back and tack, if necessary.
5. Sew buttons at marks, and make
   buttonholes on other front edge
   of jacket, either machine- or
   hand-bound. (Work Buttonhole
   Stitch as for Blanket Stitch, with
   shorter, tighter stitches.) Or, sew
   Velcro® tabs under buttons to
   close jacket.

Patterns for Jacket

Jacket Sleeve
Cut 2
(on fold)

Fold

Fold for lapel

Jacket Front
Cut 2
(one reverse)

Jacket Back
Cut 1
(on fold)

Fold

Dress and Coat

MATERIALS

½ yd. cotton for dress
½ yd. cotton damask, or fabric of
   choice (for coat)
3 buttons, ½" diameter
7 decorative buttons
Optional: Fusible hem tape

Thread
Velcro® tabs
Craft and fabric scissors
Measuring tape
Sewing needles
Pins
Tracing paper and pencil

CUTTING & CONSTRUCTION

Dress

Bias Dimensions:
12"   5¼" x 1¼"
14"   6¼" x 1¼"
16"   8" x 1½"
18"   9½" x 1½"

Skirt Dimensions:
12"   24¼" x 6¾"
14"   28¼" x 7⅝"
16"   32⅛" x 8½"
18"   36" x 9½"

1. Trace patterns on page 115. Place and pin dress pattern to cotton fabric. Cut sleeve and bodice.

2. See Skirt Dimensions below at left. Cut or tear a rectangle for skirt. See Bias Dimensions below at left. Cut bias strip for neckline. (See pages 10-11 for technique.)

3. Sew shoulder seams, with right sides together. Press seams open.

4. Sew bias strip to neck edge, with right sides together. Fold bias strip in half to inside of neck edge and machine-stitch or hand-stitch in place.

5. Fold wrist end of sleeve in ½" and press. Machine- or hand-stitch in place.

6. Sew running stitch across top of sleeve to help ease sleeve into armhole. Center and pin top of sleeve to shoulder seam, with right sides together. Sew from center out on both sides. Repeat for second sleeve.

7. With right sides together, sew side seams of bodice and sleeves. Press seams open.

8. Sew top of skirt with two rows of gathering stitches. Pull bobbin threads to gather. Center and pin skirt to bodice, with right sides together. Sew in place.

9. Sew center back edges of skirt, with right sides together, stopping 2" below bodice.

10. Fold center back opening in ⅜" and press. Sew or fuse in place.

11. Hand-stitch one ½" button at back neck edge, midway back bodice, and waist.

12. Make corresponding buttonholes or thread loops, or cut six 6" ribbons. Machine- or hand-stitch two ribbons opposite each button on other side of bodice. Tie ribbons around buttons to secure dress.

13. Pin dress to desired length and press. Machine-stitch, hand-stitch, or fuse hem in place.

Patterns for Dress

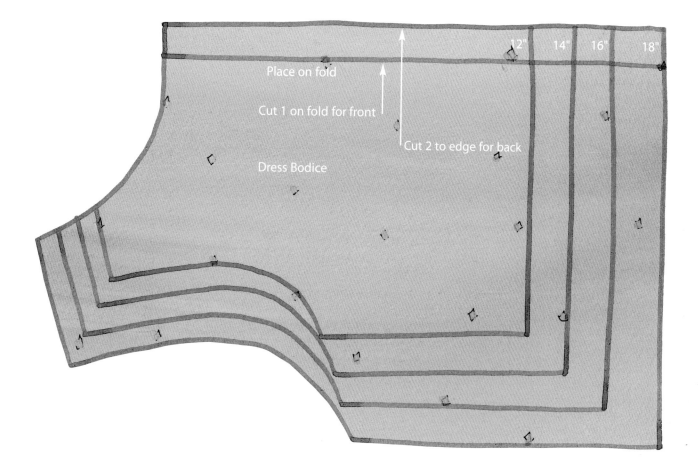

Place on fold

Cut 1 on fold for front

Cut 2 to edge for back

Dress Bodice

12" 14" 16" 18"

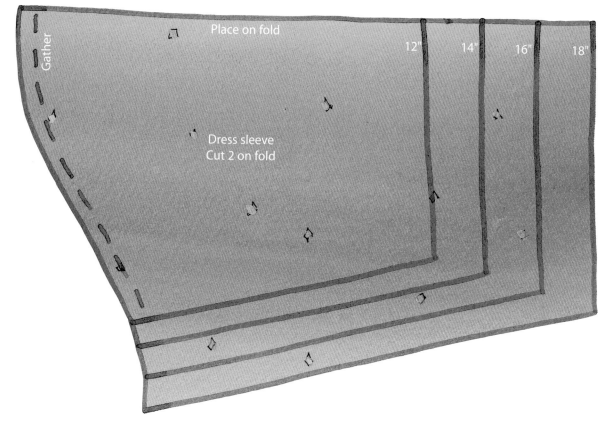

Gather

Place on fold

Dress sleeve
Cut 2 on fold

12" 14" 16" 18"

Coat

Cuff Dimensions:

12"	4" x 1¾"
14"	4½" x 1⅞"
16"	5" x 2"
18"	5½" x 2⅛"

Pocket Dimensions:

12"	2" x 1½"
14"	2⅜" x 1⅝"
16"	2⅝" x 1⅞"
18"	2⅞" x 2"

1. Trace patterns on pages 117–118 onto tracing paper. Place and pin coat pattern to cotton damask fabric. Cut two 2" x 3½" pieces for lapel lining. Cut out pattern pieces.

2. Place and pin jacket lapel lining to jacket front, with right sides together, aligning with front edge. Using sewing machine, sew outside corner of lapel. Trim off excess fabric along neck edge. Turn right side out and press. Repeat for other side. Topstitch ¼" from edge around front opening and neck. Fold lapels back and press.

3. See Pocket Dimensions at left. Cut out two rectangles for pockets.

4. Fold all pocket edges in ⅛" and, using iron, press. Place and pin one pocket on each front section. Sew in place.

5. Sew shoulder seams, with right sides together. Press shoulder seams flat.

6. Place and pin back dart. Sew in place. Fold back neck edge in ⅜". Machine-stitch or hand-stitch in place. *Optional:* Sew lace hem tape to back neck edge and fold in. Machine-stitch or hand-stitch in place.

7. Sew top and wrist end of sleeve with gathering stitch. Pull bobbin threads to gather.

8. See Cuff Dimensions above left. Cut out two rectangles for cuffs. Place and pin cuff to wrist end of sleeve. Sew in place. Fold cuff in half to inside of sleeve. Hand- or machine-stitch in place.

9. Center and pin top of sleeve to shoulder seam, with right sides together. Sew from center out. Repeat for second sleeve.

10. Sew side seams and sleeves of jacket, with right sides together.

11. Sew lace hem tape to coat hem. Turn lace hem tape under and machine-stitch, hand-stitch, or fuse in place.

12. Stitch decorative buttons to one side of coat, and one on each pocket. Make buttonholes, button loops, or attach Velcro® tabs to inside of coat for closure. *Optional:* Cut small square of cotton fabric. Fold and place in pocket; tack in place.

Patterns for Coat

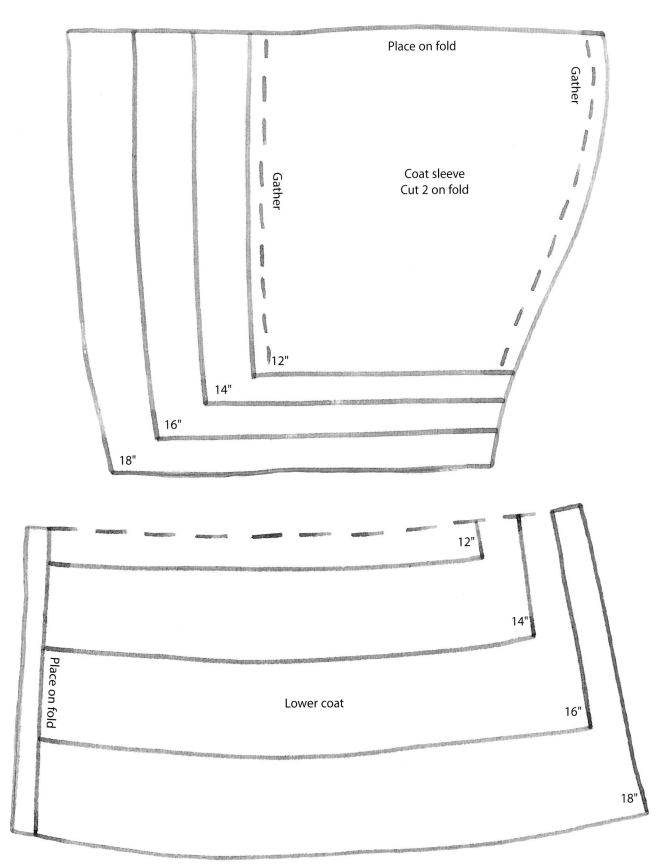

Place on fold

Gather

Coat sleeve
Cut 2 on fold

Gather

12"

14"

16"

18"

12"

14"

16"

18"

Place on fold

Lower coat

Note: Tape lower coat pattern to upper coat pattern before cutting fabric.

Patterns for Coat

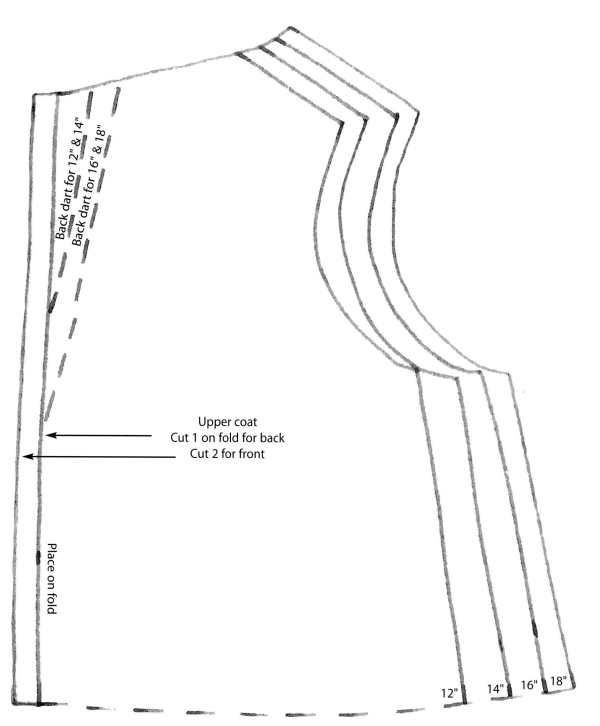

Back dart for 12" & 14"
Back dart for 16" & 18"

Upper coat
Cut 1 on fold for back
Cut 2 for front

Place on fold

12" 14" 16" 18"

Note: Tape upper coat pattern to lower coat pattern before cutting fabric.

Apron Dress & Pantaloons

MATERIALS

¼ yd. each of at least 2 contrasting patterns of cotton, or multi
  scraps (for skirt border)
½ yd. cotton (for pantaloons)
¼ yd. embroidered eyelet
  (for apron)
¼ yd. flannel (for sleeves)
½ yd. flannel, or fabric of choice
  (for bodice and skirt)
½ yd. tape, ribbon, or string, ⅛"
  wide, or ¼" wide elastic
  (for drawstring)
Fusible webbing

Optional: Fusible hem tape
2½ yds. scalloped-edge lace,
  1" wide
Scrap of low-loft quilt batting
  (optional)
⅓ yd. embroidered ribbon,
  ¼" wide
Thread
Velcro® tabs or snap fasterners
Fabric scissors
Measuring tape
Small safety pin
Straight pins
Tracing paper and pencil

Mixing several patterned cotton and flannel fabrics results in an adorable dress and pantaloons with fresh-from-the-country charm. The pattern may be made in any fabric or combination desired.

Skirt Dimensions:
12"   20" x 3"
14"   24" x 3¾"
16"   27" x 5"
18"   36" x 6½"

Patchwork Square Dimensions:
12"   2¼" x 2¼"
14"   2½" x 2½"
16"   2¾" x 2¾"
18"   3" x 3"

Apron Dimensions:
12"   10¼" x 4⅞"
14"   12" x 5⅝"
16"   13½" x 6⅜"
18"   15" x 7"

CUTTING & CONSTRUCTION
Dress

1. Trace patterns on pages 121-
   123. Place and pin bodice
   pattern to ½ yd. of flannel (or
   fabric of choice). Cut bodice.
2. See Skirt Dimensions above. Cut
   or tear a rectangle from same
   fabric as bodice.
3. Place and pin the sleeve pattern
   to the ¼ yd. of contrasting fabric. Cut out sleeves.
4. See Patchwork Square
   Dimensions above. Cut fourteen
   squares for patchwork hem from
   various contrasting fabrics. Sew
   patchwork squares together,
   alternating patterns, to create
   one long strip. (See Figure 1.)
   Press seams flat.

Figure 1

5. Fold one long side of patchwork strip in ½" and press. Machine-stitch, hand-stitch, or fuse with fusible hem tape. Sew lace to inside of hem.

6. Trace Large and Small Heart Patterns on page 122 onto paper side of fusible webbing. Turn hearts over and trace other side, making complete heart. Cut a square around hearts. Following manufacturer's instructions, fuse large heart to same fabric as sleeve trim. Fuse small heart to same fabric as pantaloons. Cut out large and small hearts and remove paper backing. Arrange hearts as desired on bodice front and fuse. *Optional:* Cut quilt batting ⅜" larger than appliqué. Place or pin batting to inside of bodice behind appliqué. Hand-stitch a long running stitch around outside edge of batting. Quilt around outside of appliqué for added dimension and accent. Remove long running stitch.

7. Sew shoulder seams, with right sides together. Press seams open. Fold neck edge in ⅜" and press. Machine-stitch, hand-stitch, or fuse with fusible hem tape. Machine-stitch or hand-stitch lace to inside of neck edge.

Note: Added trim may make sleeve too long for some dolls. Refer to Measuring Your Doll and Adjusting Patterns on pages 108-109.

8. Place and pin sleeve trim piece to wrist end of sleeve, with right sides together. Sew in place. Fold sleeve trim in ½" and press. Machine-stitch or hand-stitch in place. Place and pin lace to underside of sleeve trim. Sew in place. Place and pin ribbon to outside edge of sleeve. Sew in place. Repeat for second sleeve.

9. Sew top of sleeve pieces with gathering stitch. Pull bobbin thread to gather. Center and pin top of sleeve to shoulder seam, with right sides together. Machine-stitch or hand-stitch from center out. Repeat for second sleeve.

10. Sew bodice and sleeve seams, with right sides together.

11. Fold three sides of apron in ¼" and press. Sew in place.

Note: If a scalloped hem is used, only two sides will need to be sewn.

12. Place and pin patchwork strip to one long side of skirt piece, with right sides together. Sew in place. Sew top of skirt and raw edge of apron with two rows of gathering stitch. Pull bobbin threads to gather.

13. Center and pin apron on skirt. Center and pin skirt and apron to bodice, with right sides together. Sew in place. Sew center back edges of skirt, with right sides together, stopping 3" below bodice. Fold center back opening in ½" and press. Sew or fuse in place. Attach Velcro® tabs or snaps for closures.

Pantaloons

1. Sew front seam from A to B with right sides together. Repeat with back seam.

2. Fold in bottom of pants ½" and press. Sew lace to underside edge of hem. Sew second row of lace ½" from hemline to outside of hem.

3. Sew inside leg seam, with right sides together.

4. Fold in top of pants ½" and press. Sew casing ¼" from raw edge around top of pants, leaving 1" opening at back seam for drawstring. Attach safety pin to drawstring and push through casing. Place pants on doll and pull drawstring to fit waist. Tie in bow. *Optional:* Elastic may be inserted into casing in place of drawstring.

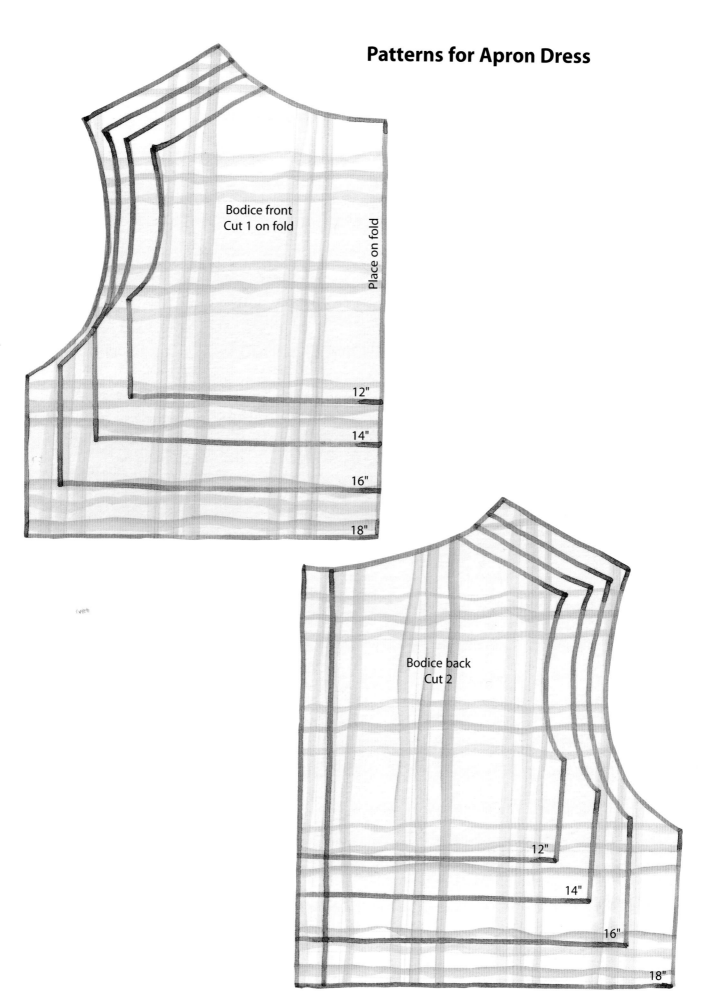

Patterns for Apron Dress

Bodice front
Cut 1 on fold

Place on fold

12"

14"

16"

18"

Bodice back
Cut 2

12"

14"

16"

18"

Patterns for Apron Dress

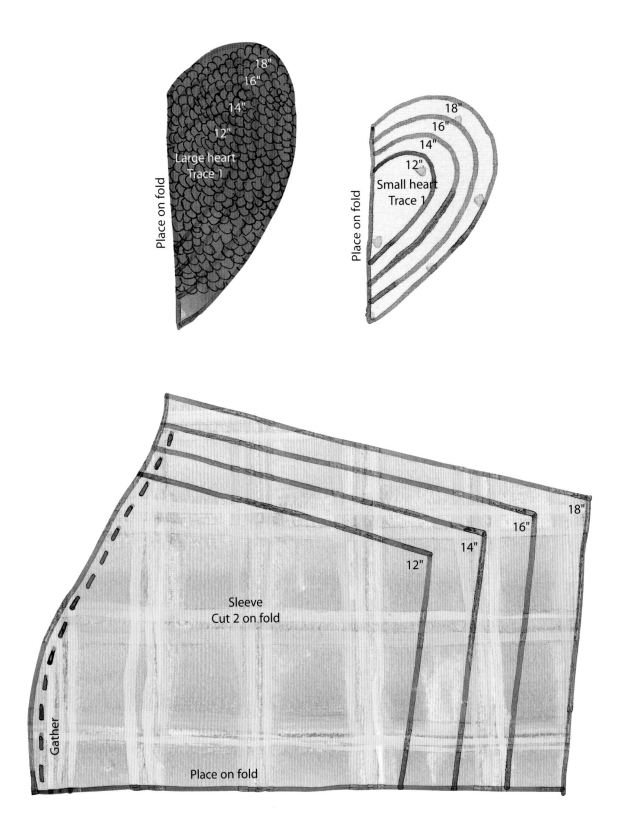

18"
16"
14"
12"
Large heart
Trace 1
Place on fold

18"
16"
14"
12"
Small heart
Trace 1
Place on fold

12"
14"
16"
18"
Sleeve
Cut 2 on fold
Gather
Place on fold

Pattern for Pantaloons

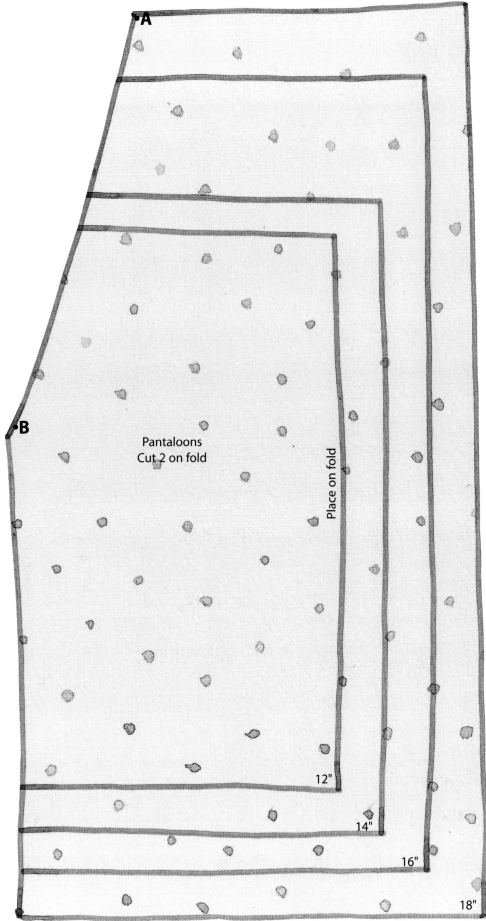

A

B

Pantaloons
Cut 2 on fold

Place on fold

12"

14"

16"

18"

SECTION III

Clothes for Kids

Baby's Sunhat

MATERIALS

1 yd. cotton fabric
½ yd. fusible webbing
Fabric marker or pencil
Straight pins

1¼ yds. cotton string or
  narrow tape
Scissors
Thread in coordinating color

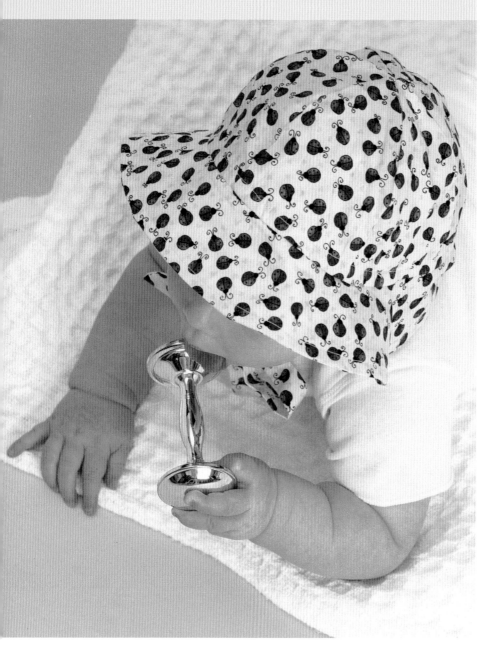

CUTTING & CONSTRUCTION

1. Copy the patterns on page 128, enlarging them to desired size. Cut twelve hat crown pieces, two hat brim pieces, and two pieces, 2" x 18" each, for hat ties.

2. Machine-stitch three top pieces together using a ¼" seam allowance, starting from the point, moving down to the wide bottom side; pressing seams as you go. Repeat with the three remaining top pieces, then stitch the two three-panel top pieces together.

3. Repeat steps 2 and 3 for the remaining six top pieces to create the hat lining (inside top). Press seams.

4. With wrong sides together, pin the hat top to the hat facing, matching the seams. Baste the raw edges together at the wide bottom.

5. Use the brim pattern to cut a brim piece from the fusible webbing, and apply it (following manufacturer's instructions) to the wrong side of top brim piece to reinforce it.

6. Pin center back seams of top and bottom brim pieces, right sides together, and machine-stitch using a ½" seam allowance. Press seams open.

7. Place top and bottom brim pieces right sides together, pin, and stitch around the outside circumference. Trim seams and clip the curves. Turn the brim right side out and press. Baste the raw inside edges together.

8. Machine-topstitch ¼" from the edge around the outside of the brim.

9. Pin the brim to the outside of the top of the hat. Machine-stitch the two parts together using a ½" seam allowance.

10. Fold each 2" x 18" tie piece in half, lengthwise, right sides together over a 20" piece of cotton string or narrow tape, making sure it lies in the fold. The string should protrude at either end. Stitch the long sides using a ¼" seam allowance. Stitch one short end closed, stitching over the string; leave the other end open. Grip the string at unstitched end of tie and pull, working the tube backwards to turn it right side out with your other hand. Clip string off close to stitching on right side end of tie. Press ties.

11. Centering the back seam of the brim, fold hat in half and measure an equal distance from the seam in each direction to the side folds, where you'll place the ties. Put the raw edges of the ties inside the hat, matching them to the raw edges of the brim. Stitch the ties in place. (See photo, below.)

12. Press the raw edges of the brim up into the hat. Stitch ¼" up from the seam all the way around, catching the raw edges and ties.

VARIATIONS

1. For a more finished inside of the hat, omit step 4 and keep the lining piece separate until brim and ties have been attached to the outside top. Turn up and press a ⅝" hem around unfinished edge of lining. With wrong sides together, pin the hat lining inside the hat top, matching the seams. Pin turned-up hem edge of lining to brim edge. Stitch ⅛" up from the brim seam all the way around.

2. Use a contrasting color for the lining, or mix and match colors for the various sections of the hat. Remember that lighter colors reflect sunlight, while darker colors soften glare.

Patterns for Baby's Sunhat

Enlarge to desired size

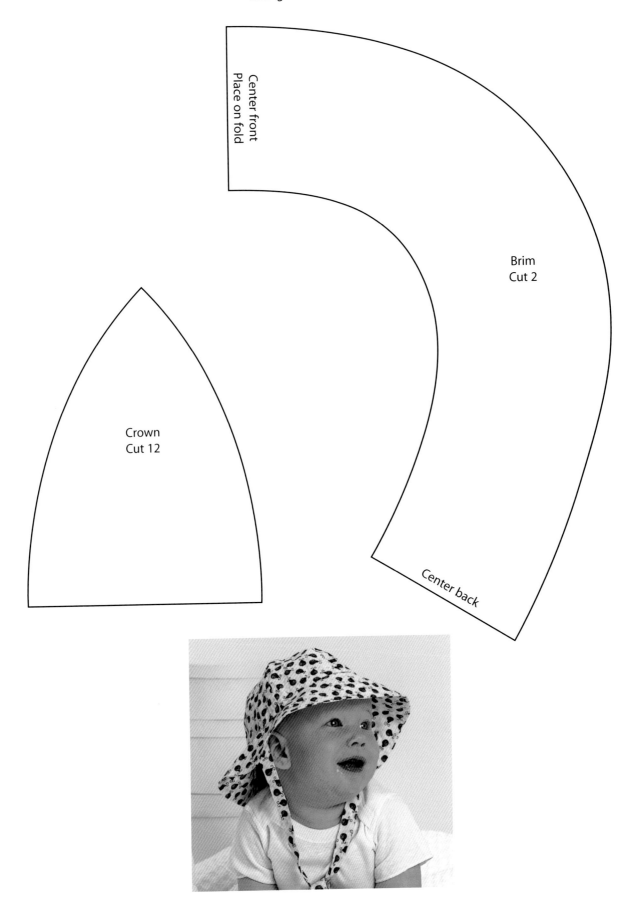

Center front
Place on fold

Brim
Cut 2

Center back

Crown
Cut 12

Baby Bibs and Burp Cloths

MATERIALS FOR BIBS

2 hand towels in contrasting colors
2 yds. purchased bias binding, or ½ yd. fabric to make bias binding
Optional: ⅛ yd. fleece (for animal ears, beak, and tongue)
1" Velcro® tape, or tabs
Thread
Scissors

MATERIALS FOR BURP CLOTHS

Cloth diapers or ⅓ yd. flannel (for burp cloth)
¼ yd. fabric (for binding), or 1⅓ yds. purchased bias binding
Thread

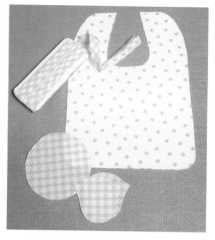

1. Pieces for a bib made from two woven fabrics.

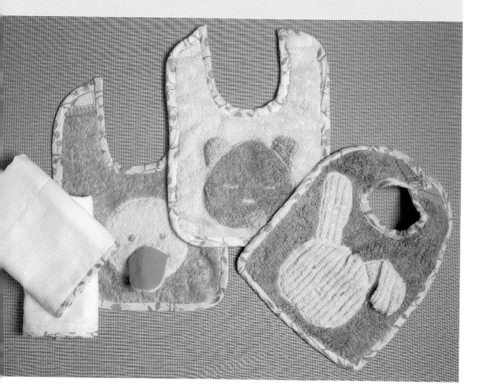

CUTTING & CONSTRUCTION
Bibs

1. Enlarge and copy the patterns on pages 130–132. Using desired pattern, cut the bib shape from a towel. Cut the pieces for an appliqué face (duck, bear, or bunny) from a towel in a contrasting color.
2. Cut out the features (beak, ears, and tongue) from towel scraps and/or fleece.
3. *Option:* Make 2 yds. bias binding from 2" wide bias strips of fabric (to finish at ½" wide). See page 10–11 for instructions on making bias binding.
4. Center the appliqué on the bib and baste in place. Complete by zigzag-stitching along the edge of the appliqué.
5. For the animals parts (ears, tongue, and beak), for each piece—place right sides together and stitch around the edges. Turn right side out and press.
6. Position animal parts on the bib; baste, then zigzag-stitch in place. (See Photo 2.) Some pieces you will want to stitch down and some you will want to stitch only one end to attach it. For example, the duck's bill and the bunny's ear are stitched down at the base so that the part can be dimensional.
7. Stitch eyes using Satin Stitch.
8. Bind the outer edges of the bib with the bias binding.
9. Cut two 1" lengths of Velcro® tape (one female, one male). Place the fuzzy side on the over-lap and the prickly, hooked side on the underlap, so the fuzzy side will face the baby's skin. Stitch around the edges of the strips, attaching them to the bib.

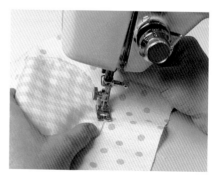

2. Stitching the animal face appliqué.

Burp Cloths

1. Cut two 12" x 12" pieces of cloth diaper or flannel.
2. Pin right sides together and stitch along all edges, leaving 2" open for turning. Turn and press opening to inside.
3. Bind the edges of each piece with bias binding. See pages 10–11 for bias binding instructions.

VARIATION: Use woven fabrics for the bib; make bias binding from the same fabric as the animal face. (See Photo 1.) Cut the bib from one fabric; cut the animal face appliqué from another fabric. Baste the face in place, then zigzag-stitch the edge. (See Photo 2.)

Patterns for Baby Bibs

Enlarge 115% for actual size

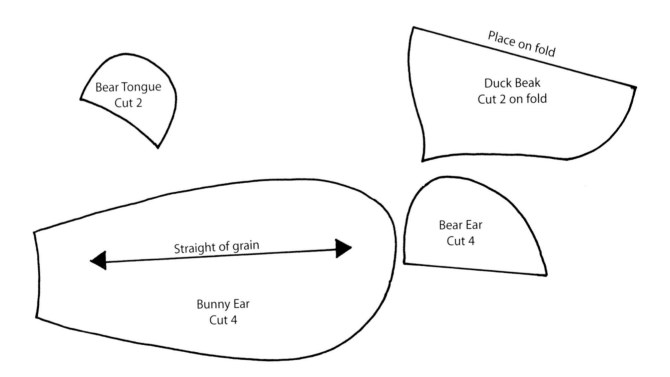

Bear Tongue
Cut 2

Place on fold

Duck Beak
Cut 2 on fold

Bear Ear
Cut 4

Straight of grain

Bunny Ear
Cut 4

Patterns for Baby Bibs

Enlarge 115% for actual size

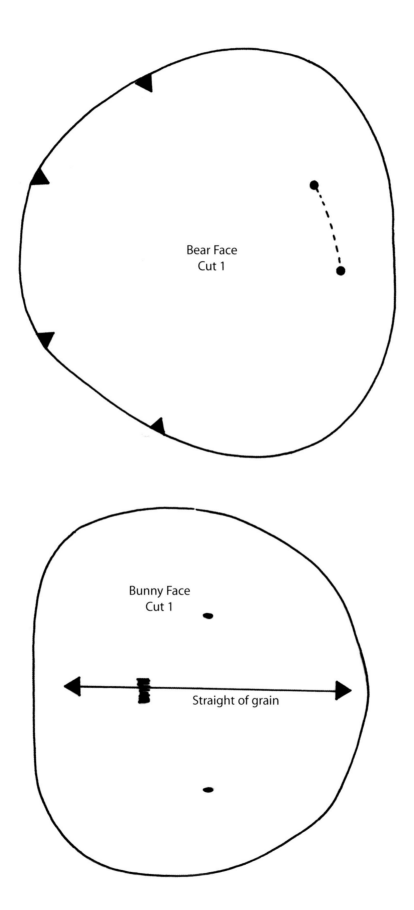

Bear Face
Cut 1

Bunny Face
Cut 1

Straight of grain

Patterns for Baby Bibs

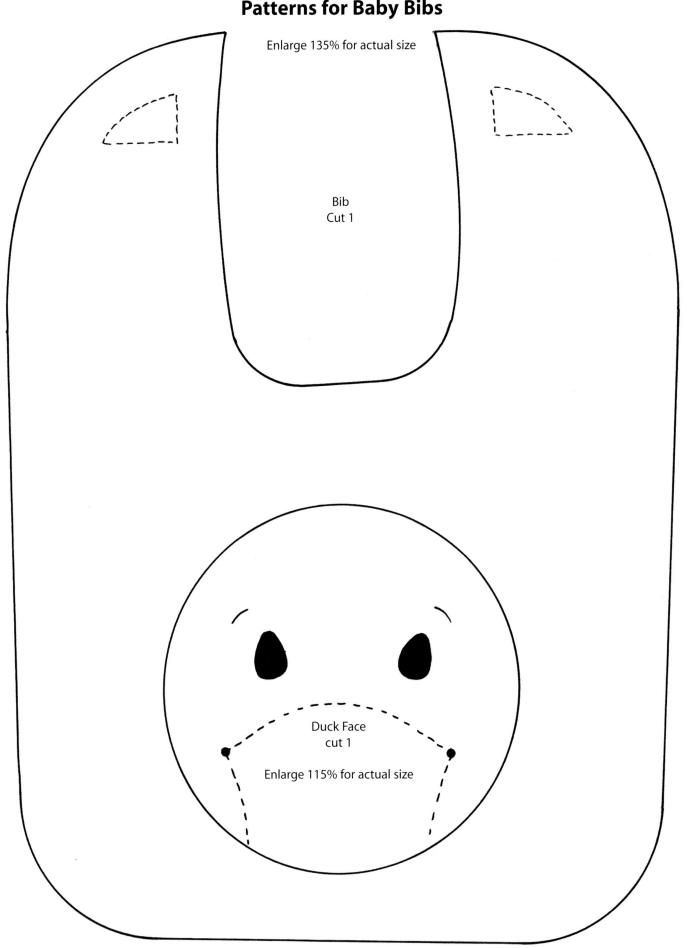

Enlarge 135% for actual size

Bib
Cut 1

Duck Face
cut 1

Enlarge 115% for actual size

Oilcloth Bib

MATERIALS

¼ yd. each of 2 contrasting patterns of oilcloth (for bib and pocket)
Optional: Terry cloth hand towel in coordinating color

½" wide double-fold bias tape
1" x 1" piece of Velcro® tape
Straight pins
Thread
Scissors

These bibs are easy to make from oilcloth, a classic material for tablecloths, and the perfect solution for messy little eaters because it wipes clean.

CUTTING & CONSTRUCTION

1. Copy the Bib Patterns on page 134, enlarging them to desired size. Cut out the copy and trace around it onto the oilcloth. Copy the pocket template, enlarging it until it fits across the bottom of the bib. Repeat the same process for marking; cut out the bib and pocket.

2. Cut a piece of bias tape to fit the length of the top of the pocket piece. Fold the tape over the top of the pocket and machine-stitch it in place.

3. Align the bottom of the pocket with the bottom of the bib and machine-baste in place.

4. Fold a length of bias tape over the edges of the whole bib and machine-stitch in place, easing the tape as you go.

5. Attach a 1" square of Velcro® tape to each side of the neck closure, one on the patterned side and one on the back side of the material. Position with the fuzzy side on the overlap and the prickly side on the underlap.

VARIATIONS

If you can't find oilcloth, you can use vinyl or even a vinyl tablecloth backed with a terry cloth hand towel. It is machine washable, and you can even machine-dry it on low heat.

1. Copy the bib patterns on page 134 and follow the process described in step 1 under Cutting & Construction.

2. Pin the bib shape, wrong-side down, in the center of the hand towel.

3. Machine-baste the bib and hand towel together.

4. Cut the hand towel to match the bib shape.

5. Machine-stitch ½" wide bias tape all the way around the edge of the bib, easing the tape as you go.

6. Attach the Velcro® tape to the neck closure as described in step 5 under Cutting & Construction, with the softer side on the overlap, facing the baby's skin.

Pattern for Oilcloth Bib

Enlarge to desired size

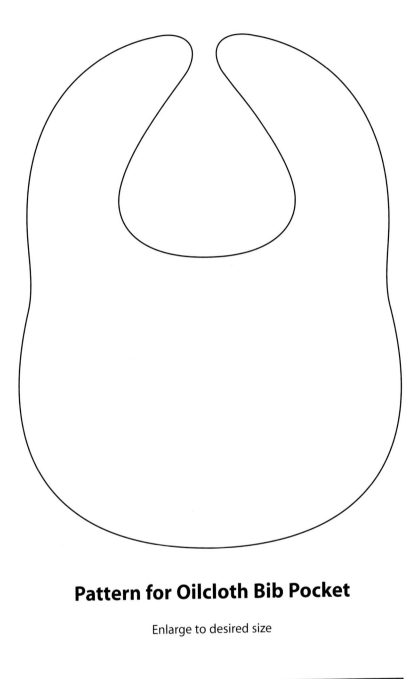

Pattern for Oilcloth Bib Pocket

Enlarge to desired size

Baby Bunting

MATERIALS

1½ yds. fleece fabric
Felt squares in 3 colors (usually sold in 9" x 12" pieces)
Silk embroidery thread or floss in 3 colors
Silver metallic thread
Coordinating thread

Scissors
Straight pins
Large-eye needle
Polymer clay in color of your choice
Rubber stamp or object of your choice for button design
Beads for tassel (optional)

5. Fold under a ¼" hem on side b of the hood and machine-stitch in place. This will be the hood's opening.
6. Fold the rectangle in half and place a pin at the center fold. (See Figure 4.)
7. Center the back seam of the hood over the pin that you positioned in step 6. (See Figure 5.) Sew sides a of the hood to the rectangle.
8. Blanket-stitch (see page 9) all the way around the edge of the rectangle using silk embroidery thread.

Decorative Panels

1. Cut two pieces of colored felt in one color, each about 4" x 6".
2. Cut another two pieces of felt in another color, each about 3" x 4".
3. Cut two hearts out of a third color of felt, sizing them to fit inside the smaller rectangle.
4. Machine-stitch one small rectangle to a larger one using silver thread and a zigzag stitch. Repeat for the additional rectangles.
5. Machine-stitch a heart shape to the center of the smaller rectangle using the silver metallic thread and a zigzag stitch. Repeat for the additional heart and rectangle.

CUTTUNG & CONSTRUCTION

1. Cut a 27" x 32" rectangle from the fleece. (See Figure 1.)
2. Fold under a ¼" hem all around the rectangle; machine-stitch in place.

3. Cut two pieces of fleece to the dimensions shown in Figure 2. These pieces will become the hood.
4. Sew the hood together, side c to c and d to d. (See Figure 3.)

Figure 1

B
A
27"
32"

Figure 2

10"
6"
9"
6"

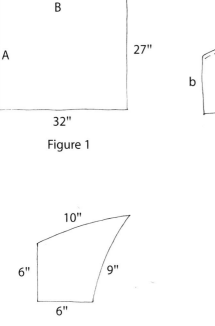

Figure 3

c
b
d
a
c
b
d
a

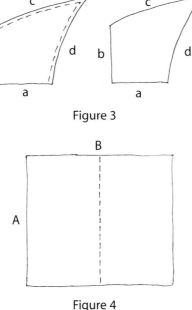

Figure 4

B
A

Figure 5

a   a
A
B

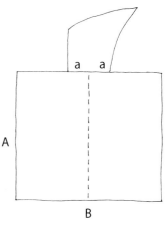

Figure 6

6. Fold the bunting as shown in the diagram. (See Figure 6.) Place the felt rectangles on the front of the bunting in whatever position you'd like. Remember to leave room for the buttons on the top edge near the hood. Hand-sew the rectangles onto the bunting with the embroidery thread.

Make the Buttons

1. Form two small circles from polymer clay and flatten until they are about 2½" in diameter.
2. Find a textured design you like, such as a rubber stamp or a piece of jewelry. Press the texture into the clay circle to leave a clear impression.

Note: You can always reflatten and start over again if your first pressing doesn't work.

3. Use a straight pin or needle to create two neat holes in the circle through which to sew on the button. Make sure the holes are not too close to the edge and that the hole is wide enough to accommodate a needle threaded with embroidery thread.
4. Bake the buttons in an oven according to the clay manufacturer's instructions.
5. The buttons will be on the back side of the rectangle when it's opened out. Fold the left side of the rectangle inward, and cross over the right side. The buttons will be on the underside flap, and the buttonholes will be on the outside flap. (See Figure 7.) Position buttons on the fleece where you want them, approximately 2" in from the edge and 1" down.
6. To make the buttonholes, cut a slit to the same diameter as the button. Machine- or hand-sew an overstitch around the slit to keep it from getting wider.

Figure 7

Make a Tassel for the Hood

1. Cut off about 27½" of embroidery thread. Fold this bundle in half. Unravel about 1 yd. of embroidery thread, but don't cut it. Wrap this piece around the top of the bundle you folded in the previous step. Save a little extra at the end to form a tight knot and a small loop. (See Figure 8.)
2. Cut the bottom of the tassel to make the threads line up. Add beads for interest if desired, then sew the tassel securely to the tip of the hood.

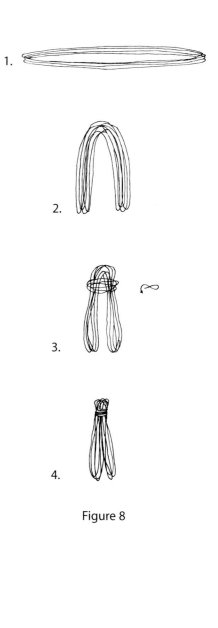

Figure 8

Fleecy Baby Jumper

MATERIALS

½ yd. fleece fabric
¼ yd. contrasting cotton fabric
Straight pins
Scissors

2 yds. (approximately) bias tape, ½" wide
Threads
Sewing needle
2 buttons
Pattern paper or graph paper

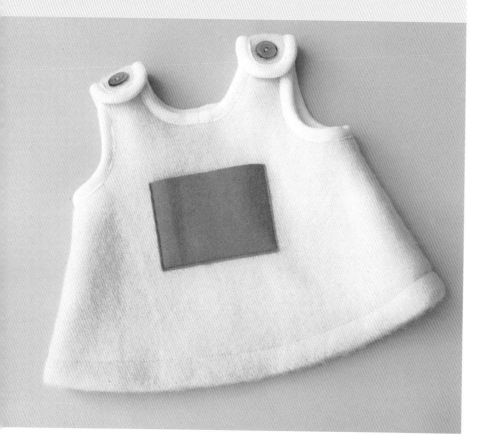

CUTTING & CONSTRUCTION

1. Copy the patterns on page 138. Enlarge to desired size and copy onto pattern or graph paper. Cut out the patterns.

2. Fold the ½ yd. of fleece selvedge to selvedge.

3. Pin the front and back patterns to the fold line. Cut out both pieces.

4. Cut out a 5" x 5" pocket from the contrasting fabric. Fold over and press down 1" of fabric on one side, then fold that piece under ½" to create a hem for the top of the pocket. Press the other three sides of the pocket under ½".

5. On the front piece of the jumper, center and pin the pocket and machine-stitch in place on the two sides and bottom (the sides you pressed under in step 4).

6. Place the front and back pieces of the jumper right sides facing and machine-stitch the side seams together using a ½" seam allowance. Press seams open.

7. Starting at the center back of the neckline, pin on a strip of bias tape and fold over the edge. Pin the bias tape all the way around the neck and arm openings. Machine-stitch in place, joining ends together.

8. With the jumper wrong side out, fold and press a hem of 1½", then fold under ½" and press. Machine-stitch in place.

9. Hand-stitch the buttons in place on the front shoulders.

10. Machine-stitch corresponding buttonholes on the back shoulders.

Pattern for Fleecy Baby Jumper

Enlarge as desired

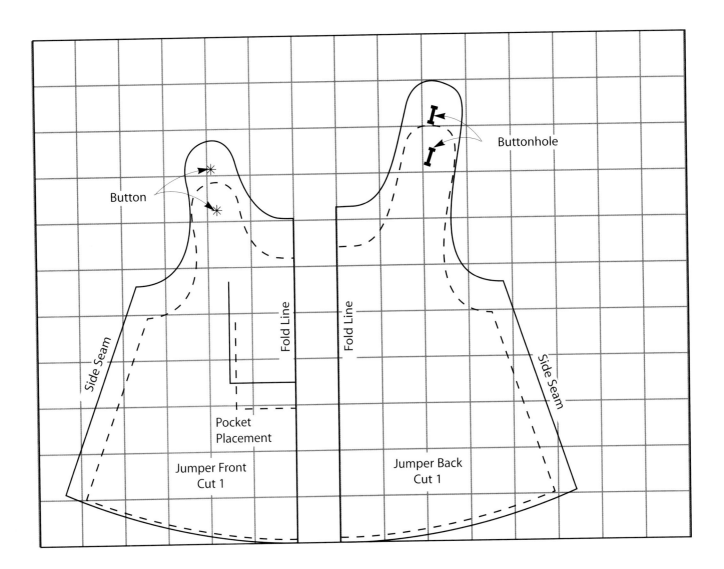

Buttonhole

Button

Side Seam

Fold Line

Fold Line

Side Seam

Pocket
Placement

Jumper Front
Cut 1

Jumper Back
Cut 1

Fleecy Baby Pants

MATERIALS

½ yd. fleece fabric
¼ yd. contrasting cotton fabric
2 knit cuffs
1 yd. elastic, ½" wide
Thread

Straight pins
Sewing needle
Scissors
Ruler or measuring tape
Pattern paper or graph paper
Pencil

10. With right sides facing, pin the front and back pieces together. Machine-stitch the side seams and inseam using a ½" seam allowance. Press seams open.

11. Machine-baste the bottom of the leg openings. Pull the thread, gathering the leg opening to fit the cuffs.

12. With the pants wrong side out, pin the cuffs and the raw edges of the leg openings together. Machine-stitch the cuffs to the openings.

13. Turn under a 1" waistband and press a ¼" hem under it. Machine-stitch around the waist, leaving a 3" opening in the back.

14. Thread the elastic through the waistband. At the place where the ends meet, machine-stitch together. Hand-stitch the 3" opening closed.

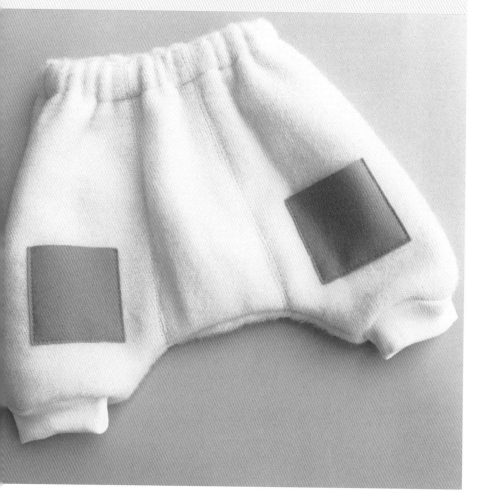

CUTTING & CONSTRUCTION

1. Copy the patterns on page 140. Enlarge to desired size and copy onto pattern or graph paper. Cut out the patterns.

2. Fold the piece of fleece in half, selvedge to selvedge.

3. Pin the pattern to the fabric and cut it out.

Note: You'll need two front pieces, two back pieces, and two gussets (the short edge of the gusset that has no seamline is placed on the fold line).

4. Pin one gusset piece along the center line of the left front, right sides together. Stitch together using a ½" seam allowance.

5. Repeat for the right front side of the pants.

6. Repeat for the left and right back side of the pants and the second gusset piece.

7. Cut two pocket pieces from the cotton fabric, each 4½" x 4½".

8. Press a ½" hem under on three sides of each pocket piece. Press 1" over on the remaining side, then fold ½" under again and hem. Repeat for the remaining pocket piece.

9. Place the pockets in position on the front of the pants. Machine-stitch in place along three sides, leaving the top open.

Pattern for Fleecy Baby Pants

Enlarge as desired

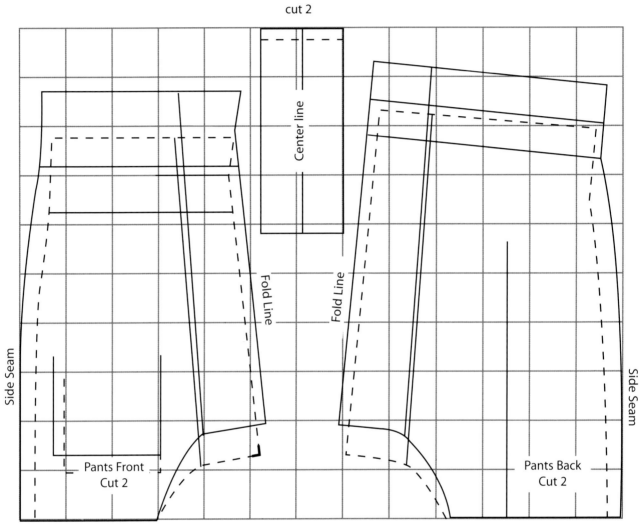

Toddler Jacket and Hat

MATERIALS

Cutter quilt (see note, at right)
Medium-weight lining fabric
Ribbon, in a matching color
3 vintage buttons

Vogue Pattern 7628; use pieces for:
Jacket (front, back, collar, and sleeve)
Hat (brim, crown, flap, and top)

Working with Damaged Quilts

Note: Never cut a vintage quilt in good condition; it should be preserved. But you can always find damaged quilts (called cutter quilts) and work with the portions of them that are still in good shape. To use a cutter quilt, open it and place the pattern where the design looks appealing. If the area of the quilt you like has just one bad spot, you can sometimes repair it by stitching with a zigzag stitch. You can also replace badly damaged spots with fabric pieces from another place on the quilt; again, use a zigzag stitch and simply stitch the replacement fabric piece on top of the bad spots. If you don't want the stitches to show, use invisible thread.

PATTERN ALTERATIONS

Make these changes to the instructions in the pattern envelope:

Front Facing: Rather than face the front, use the decorative edging on the quilt for the front edges.

Note: You can also do this for the hem of a jacket or sleeve. If the facing or hem is part of the pattern piece and you don't want or need it, cut it off the pattern piece; or lay the facing line along the decorative edge.

Cuffs: Omit the cuffs.

CUTTING & CONSTRUCTION

1. Fold the quilt and place the jacket front, sleeve, collar, and back, and hat top, flap, brim, and crown pieces. (See Figure 1.) Cut out the pieces.
2. Cut the flap, brim, and collar linings from the folded lining fabric.
3. Follow the pattern's instructions for construction, noting the alterations listed above.

Pattern courtesy of The McCall Pattern Company: Vogue Pattern 7628

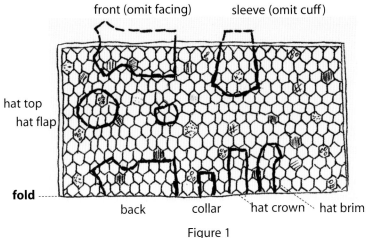

front (omit facing)   sleeve (omit cuff)

hat top
hat flap

fold

back   collar   hat crown   hat brim

Figure 1

Variation
Scalloped-Edge Jacket

MATERIALS

Cutter quilt with decorative edging (see Note on page 141)
Lining fabric
1 vintage button

Vogue Pattern 7628;
use pieces for:
Jacket front, back, and sleeve
Custom front and back neck facing

CUTTING & CONSTRUCTION

1. Follow the layout for the toddler jacket. (See Figure 1 on page 141.) Omit the hat pieces and the collar. Cut the neck facing pieces from lining fabric. Place the front on the edge and don't incorporate the facing portion of the front pattern piece.

2. Follow the pattern's instructions for construction, noting the alterations listed. Add the facing at the collar step. Stitch the front and back facings together, right sides facing, and then finish the raw edge. Stitch the facing to the neck edge, right sides together, trim the seam, and clip the curves. Turn the facing to the inside and tack in place.

3. Hand-sew the button and make a corresponding buttonhole or loop for the closure.

Pattern courtesy of The McCall Pattern Company: Vogue Pattern 7628

PATTERN ALTERATIONS

Make these changes to the instructions in the pattern envelope:

Front Facing: Rather than face the front, use the decorative edging on the quilts for the front edges. If the facing is part of the pattern piece and you don't want or need it, cut it off the pattern piece, or lay the facing line along the decorative edge.

Cuffs: Omit the cuffs. Use quilt edge if desired.

Collar and Neck Facing: Omit the collar and apply a neck facing. You don't need the entire front facing since you're using the decorative edge of the quilt for the front edge. But you do need to make a separate neck facing, using the neck portion of the front facing and the neckline of the back. (See Figures 1 and 2, below.) Simply draw in a facing on these pieces, transferring it to paper if necessary, and cut out. The facing you make for the back should be cut on the fold.

Figure 1   Figure 2

Lavender Floral Dress

MATERIALS
Tablecloth with floral motifs
1 vintage button
Ribbon, in a matching color
Extrafine thread
Safety pin

The Children's Corner Patterns:
Hillary; use pieces for:
Skirt front, skirt back, yoke
front, yoke back, sleeve B

*Note: Use extrafine thread and ¼"
seam allowances throughout, unless
directed otherwise.*

PATTERN ALTERATION
Make this change while following
the instructions in the pattern
envelope:

Back Closure: Omit the tie in
the back of each of these dresses
and use a button closure instead.

CUTTING & CONSTRUCTION
1. Fold the tablecloth. Place the
   skirt front and the skirt back so
   large bouquets of flowers are
   centered across them. If your
   tablecloth has a colorful overcast
   edging like this one, or has any
   other decorative treatment you
   want to highlight, use it for the
   hem of the dress, adding some
   extra length to allow for the
   growth of the child.
2. Place the yoke front, yoke back,
   and sleeve so smaller bouquets
   of flowers are centered on these
   pieces. (See Figure 1.) Cut the
   facings and linings now, too.
3. Follow the pattern's instructions
   for construction, noting the
   back closure change listed
   above. You may also add a decorative bow, as pictured.

*Note: Pin decorative bows onto the
dress from the inside, so they can be
removed for washing or replaced later
with fresh ribbon.*

*Pattern courtesy of The Children's
Corner Patterns: Hillary*

Figure 1

Variation
Handkerchief Yoke Dress

*Note: Use extrafine thread and ¼"
seam allowances throughout, unless
directed otherwise.*

MATERIALS

Vintage handkerchief(s)
Lace doily
Bridge cloth (36" square
    tablecloth) with cutwork
    and decorative edging
Imitation batiste
1 ¼ yd. vintage tatting or antique
    lace

Extrafine thread
1 vintage button
The Children's Corner Patterns:
    Hillary; use pieces for:
    Skirt front, skirt back, yoke
        front, yoke back, sleeve B

CUTTING & CONSTRUCTION

1. If the dress is a small size, you
   should be able to cut the yoke
   front and yoke back out of one
   vintage handkerchief. Fold the
   handkerchief and place the yoke
   pattern pieces, being sure to put
   the yoke front on the fold. (See
   Figure 1.) Cut these pieces and
   the lining for them.

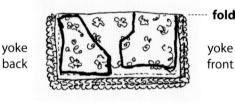

Figure 1

2. For the sleeves, fold the lace
   doily and cut the sleeves. (See
   Figure 2.)

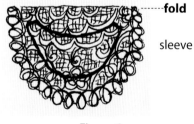

Figure 2

3. Fold the imitation batiste and
   cut the skirt front, skirt back,
   and yoke and sleeve lining
   pieces.
4. Follow the pattern's instructions
   for construction, noting the
   back closure alteration described
   on page 143.

5. To add the decorative hem edging, first cut off 7" from opposite ends of the bridge cloth. (See Figure 3.) Each piece should be 7" x 36". (See Figure 4.) Since the pattern for the skirt is just a little wider than 72", you can solve this problem by making an adjustment in the skirt—take up the side seams until the skirt is 72" around the bottom.

Figure 3

Figure 4

6. Finish the raw edge of each piece of the bridge cloth. Make a 1" machine hem on the dress, and mark a seamline all the way around the dress that is 6" from the bottom. Pin the bridge cloth edging to the dress, wrong side of the edging to the right side of the skirt front at the marked seamline. Pin the other piece of bridge cloth edging to the Skirt back. Zigzag-stitch along the seamline. Stitch the edging down at the side seams.

7. Hand-sew the tatting or antique lace along the bottom edges of the yoke front and yoke back.

Note: These directions are for a very small dress size, so both of the yoke pieces could be cut from one handkerchief. If you're making a larger size, you may need to use more than one handkerchief and piece the yoke.

SLEEVE VARIATION

1. This variation features sleeves with appliquéd handkerchiefs. Cut four sleeves from the imitation batiste (two as base for the appliqué, two as lining).

2. To make the handkerchief appliqué for the sleeve, fold the handkerchief diagonally. Place the sleeve pattern over a decorative corner of the handkerchief. (See Figure 5.) Cut this piece out. Pin the handkerchief piece onto the sleeve, wrong side of the handkerchief piece to the right side of the sleeve. (See Figure 6.) Stitch to each sleeve using tight zigzag stitch. Line the sleeve as directed in the pattern instructions.

Pattern courtesy of The Children's Corner Patterns: Hillary

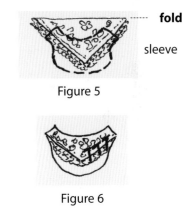

Figure 5

Figure 6

Tulip Yoke Dress

MATERIALS:

100 percent cotton sheet

1 or 2 linens with embroidery
and/or appliqué (a tablecloth
and table runner were used in
the project pictured)

3 vintage buttons

The Children's Corner Patterns:
Louise; use pieces for:
Skirt front, skirt back, back
yoke, back yoke lining, front
yoke, front yoke lining

CUTTING & CONSTRUCTION

1. Cut out all the pattern pieces
   from the folded cotton sheet
   except the back yoke.
2. Open the front yoke and place
   it on top of the appliquéd tablecloth. Make sure the appliqué is
   straight. Draw the outline of the
   front yoke onto the linen, using
   a water-soluble marker. Draw a
   simple patch pocket around the
   other appliqué. (See Figure 1.)
   Cut out these pieces.

Figure 1

3. Pin the appliqué to the front
   yoke, wrong side of the appliqué
   on the right side of the front
   yoke, and stitch it on all edges,
   making it part of the front yoke.
4. Lay the table runner flat and
   separately cut out each side of
   the back yoke from the embroidered ends. (See Figure 2.)
5. Follow the pattern's instructions
   for construction.

*Note: This dress is a good example of
how to use your imagination and think
in terms of elements when designing with
vintage linens. You can use just about any
size or shape linen. You can even add an
extra piece, like the pocket on this dress.*

back yoke   back yoke

Figure 2

Variation
Bordered
Tablecloth Dress

MATERIALS:
Tablecloth with a large border
Lining fabric
3 vintage buttons

The Children's Corner Patterns:
Louise: use pieces for:
  Skirt front, skirt back, back
  yoke, back yoke lining, front
  yoke, front yoke lining

PATTERN ALTERATION
For this variation only, make the following change to the instructions for the pattern:

Pleats: Omit the pleats in this dress. To remove the pleats, fold the pattern piece in at the pleat mark before you cut.

CUTTING & CONSTRUCTION
1. Fold the tablecloth and place the skirt front and skirt back pieces on the fold, with the bottom of the skirt falling on the border.

Note: Place the pattern pieces on separate ends of the cloth to do this. (See Figure 1.) Be sure the borders match up at the side seams before you cut.

2. After cutting out the skirt pieces, fold the leftover cloth to cut the yokes, placing the front yoke on the fold. (See Figure 2.) This allows you to take advantage of the design on the border, so be sure to carefully position the yokes on the tablecloth.
3. Cut the front yoke lining and the back yoke lining from the lining material.
4. Follow the pattern's instructions for construction, noting the pleat alteration listed above.

Note: Omitting the pleats not only allows you to use less material, but it also lets you emphasize a pretty border or edging, like the one in this project. If you made pleats in this border, it would ruin the symmetry of the design motif.

Pattern courtesy of The Children's Corner Patterns: Louise

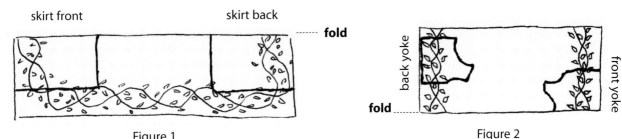

Figure 1

Figure 2

SECTION IV

Clothes for Women

Chenille Jacket

MATERIALS

Chenille bedspread
4 buttons, vintage or novelty
Thread in coordinating color
Straight pins
Scissors

Cutting Line Designs Pattern:
By Popular Demand 60565;
use pieces for:
Jacket front, back, back yoke,
    collar, upper sleeve, under
    sleeve

PATTERN ALTERATION

Omit pockets and tabs for this
project.

CUTTING & CONSTRUCTION

1. Fold the chenille bedspread and
   carefully place the pattern pieces
   to take full advantage of the
   bedspread's design. (See Figure
   1.) In the sample project, the
   horizontal stripes of chenille at
   the hem create the illusion of a
   band, and some features of the
   design have been matched to
   good effect on either side of the
   front pieces.
2. Follow the pattern's instructions.
   Other jacket patterns with simple lines may be used in this
   manner as well.

*Pattern courtesy of Cutting Line
Designs: By Popular Demand 60565*

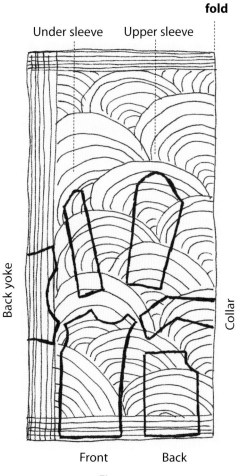

fold

Under sleeve   Upper sleeve

Back yoke

Collar

Front   Back

Figure 1

Embroidered Blouse

MATERIALS

Linen table runner with
   embroidered ends
Linen bridge cloth with
   embroidered corners
Optional: Lace to complement the
   embroidery
Optional: Shoulder pads
4 vintage buttons
Thread in coordinating color

Straight pins
Scissors
Cutting Line Designs Pattern:
   By Popular Demand 60565;
   use pieces for:
   Blouse front, back, sleeve front,
     sleeve back, front facing

CUTTING & CONSTRUCTION

1. Lay the table runner flat so the embroidery is at the ends. Place the front and front facing pattern pieces on the table runner; the embroidery should fall at the bottom of the front pieces, as shown. (See Figure 1.) Cut out each piece separately.

2. Fold the bridge cloth and cut the sleeve front, sleeve back, and back. Study the construction of this raglan sleeve; if you have an embroidered item, make sure its orientation is correct before you cut. This piece had butterflies embroidered on all four corners, so both sleeve pieces (front and back) were cut on these corners. The back was cut on the fold from the undecorated portion of the linen. (See Figure 2.)

3. Follow the instructions in the pattern envelope for construction. Add lace edging to the sleeves, if desired.

Note: The embroidered blouse demonstrates how you can easily use small linens in an adult garment by taking advantage of the blouse's design. The two-piece raglan sleeve presents a great opportunity to incorporate a napkin, a handkerchief, or a special piece of embroidery like these butterflies.

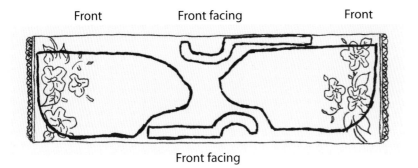

Front   Front facing   Front

Front facing

Figure 1

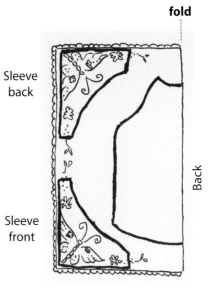

fold

Sleeve back

Sleeve front

Back

Figure 2

Variation
White Blouse with Drawnwork

MATERIALS

Round white tablecloth
   embroidered with lace
White tablecloth with
   drawnwork
100 percent cotton sheet or
   lining fabric
4 large snaps
Shoulder pads (optional)
Thread in coordinating color

Straight pins
Scissors
Cutting Line Designs Pattern:
   By Popular Demand 60565;
   use pieces for:
   Blouse front, back, sleeve front,
   sleeve back, front facing

CUTTING & CONSTRUCTION

1. Cut the front from the folded
   round linen tablecloth. (See
   Figure 1.) If your tablecloth has
   lace, save it to apply to the
   sleeves.
2. Cut the back, sleeve front, and
   sleeve back from the tablecloth
   with drawnwork. (See Figure 2.)
   Place the back so the bottom
   displays the drawnwork. In this
   project, the drawnwork on the
   sleeves cascades down the shoulders from the neckline.
3. Place the front facing on the
   folded cotton sheet or lining
   material and cut out the pieces.
4. Follow the instructions in the
   pattern envelope for construction, adding to the sleeves the
   lace that you saved in step 1.
   Snaps are substituted for buttons
   in this variation.

*Pattern courtesy of Cutting Line
Designs: By Popular Demand 60565*

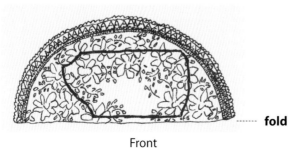

Front

Figure 1

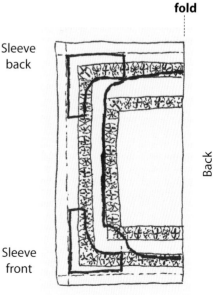

Sleeve back

fold

Back

Sleeve front

Figure 2

152

Vintage Miniskirt

MATERIALS

Large vintage patterned
   tablecloth
Zipper in coordinating color, 7"
Thread in coordinating color

McCalls Pattern 3501;
   use pieces for:
Skirt front, back, front facing,
   back facing
Optional: Custom ruffle

CUTTING & CONSTRUCTION

1. Study the design of your table-cloth and decide how you can best incorporate it into the skirt. For the sample project, the tablecloth was folded and the back and the front were placed in opposite directions so the stripes would match at the side seams. (See Figure 1.) Place the front facing, back facing, and optional ruffle patterns, and cut out the pieces.

2. Follow the pattern's instructions for skirt construction. Check the length of the skirt. If you are omitting the ruffle, pin and hem the skirt to the desired length. If you are applying the ruffle, make adjustments for the added 2" of length before you attach the ruffle to the skirt.

3. To make the ruffle, cut strips from the tablecloth that are 2½" wide and sew them together to the needed length. The length of the ruffle should be twice the circumference of the bottom of the skirt. Serge or zigzag-stitch one edge of the ruffle, turn it under ¼", and stitch. (See Figure 2.) Gather the top edge of the ruffle with two lines of long Running Stitches.

4. Sew the ruffle to the bottom edge of the skirt using a ¼" seam allowance, starting and ending at a side seam. Topstitch ⅛" up from skirt edge above ruffle, catching in seam allowance.

Pattern courtesy of The McCall Pattern Company: McCalls 3501

Ruffle strips

Back

Front

Back facing   Front facing

- - - - - **fold**

Figure 1

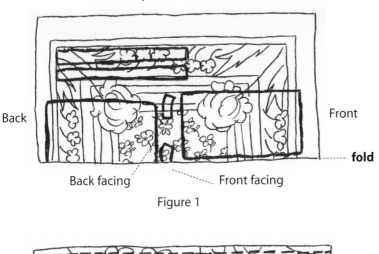

Figure 2

Terrific Tablecloth Shirt

MATERIALS

Large striped tablecloth
6 vintage buttons
Thread in coordinating color
Straight pins
Scissors

Vogue Pattern 1813;
use pieces for:
Shirt front, back, yoke back,
sleeve D, collar D, pocket

PATTERN ALTERATION

Make this change while following the instructions in the pattern envelope:

Hem: The hemline on the front and back of the sample project was altered to make a shirt-tail hem. To get a curved hemline, draw a curve at the side corners of the front and back pattern pieces, as shown below. Allow ½" to turn the hem under.

CUTTING & CONSTRUCTION

1. Fold the tablecloth and arrange the pieces to take advantage of the stripes. (See Figure 1.) In this project, the stripes fall along the sleeve, pocket, and collar, as well as the hem. Notice how the intersection of the stripes accents the front as shown in the photo at left. The pattern front was positioned with a stripe at the centerline, so that when the facing piece was folded back it gave the look of a placket. Cut out the pieces.

2. Follow the pattern's instructions for construction, incorporating the hem alteration, if desired.

Note: If you don't have enough tablecloth fabric to cut out the whole sleeve, as was the case for the sample project, it may be pieced together to get the look you want. If you look closely, you can see the seam. Feel free to alter the pattern pieces to meet your fabric needs.

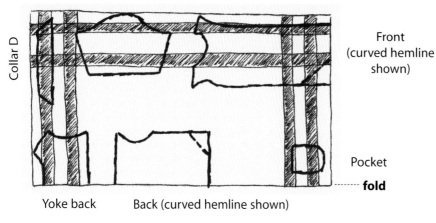

Sleeve D

Collar D

Front
(curved hemline
shown)

Pocket

fold

Yoke back   Back (curved hemline shown)

Figure 1

Variation
Blue Checked Tablecloth Shirt

MATERIALS

Large checked tablecloth
4 vintage buttons
Thread in coordinating color
Straight pins
Scissors

Vogue Pattern 1813;
 use pieces for:
 Shirt front, back, yoke back,
  sleeve D, collar D

PATTERN ALTERATION

Note the hem change explained on page 154.

CUTTING & CONSTRUCTION

1. Fold the tablecloth and place the front, sleeve, and collar on the straight grain; put the back and yoke back on the fold. Be sure to match the stripes at the side seams.

2. Follow the pattern's instructions for construction, noting the shirt-tail hem alteration explained on the opposite page. The pocket has been omitted in this sample variation.

Note: Another way you can be creative with your garments is to vary the number of buttons you use. In this checked variation, only four buttons were used, while six were added to the striped shirt. If you happen to have only four great vintage buttons, but the pattern calls for six, simply adjust the spacing of the buttonholes.

Pattern courtesy of The McCall Pattern Company: Vogue Pattern 1813

Reversible Wrap Skirt

MATERIALS

2 large tablecloths, 1 with striped
   border
2 vintage buttons

Dos de Tejas Patterns: The
Ultimate Wrap Skirt 5032;
use pieces for:
Skirt front, front overlay, back
tie, custom right tie

PATTERN ALTERATIONS

Make these changes while following the instructions in the pattern
envelope:

Tie: For this sample, the right tie
was made as a separate piece
because it hindered the placement
of the skirt pieces on the vintage
fabric. To change your pattern, too,
cut the tie off of the front overlay.
(See Figure 1.) Cut it out as a separate piece, adding a ½" seam
allowance along the edge where
you cut it from the front overlay.
Add a corresponding ½" seam
allowance to the skirt. After you've
cut out both pieces, stitch the right
tie to the front overlay, right sides
together.

Front overlay—cut off tie

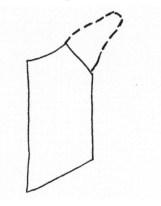

Figure 1

Finishing: To place the buttonhole closure, first try on the skirt and tie it. Use a water–soluble marker to mark the buttonhole location on the opposite side of the front overlay from the tie, near the side seam. (See Figure 2.) Reverse the skirt, tie it again, and check the placement of the buttonhole. Now, make the buttonhole and sew a button on the inside and the outside of the front at the marked spot, so you can button it closed no matter which side you wear on the outside.

CUTTING & CONSTRUCTION

1. Lay the tablecloth flat. Place the front, front overlay, tie, and right tie as shown. (See Figure 3.) Remember to add a ½" seam allowance to the right tie and the front overlay where the pieces were cut from one another. Cut out each piece separately.
2. Fold the remaining tablecloth and cut out the back on the fold. (See Figure 4.)
3. Cut the second skirt (the reversible skirt lining) out of another tablecloth, following the directions at left.
4. Follow the pattern's instructions for construction, noting the alterations given on page 156.

Pattern courtesy of Dos de Tejas Patterns, Designer L. Karen Odam: The Ultimate Wrap Skirt 5032

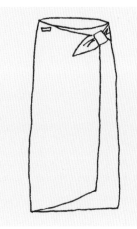

Figure 2

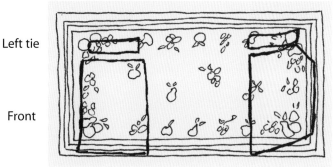

Left tie

Front

Right tie (cut from front overlay)

Front overlay

Figure 3

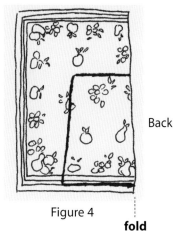

Back

Figure 4

fold

Vest Wardrobe A

Kraft or tracing paper of choice
Felt-tip marking pen
Pencil

Craft scissors
Fabric marking pen or chalk
Straight pins

Transferring markings from pattern to fabric

Five very different styles can be made from this one basic pattern shape.

1. Enlarge and copy pattern pieces on pages 160-163.
2. Place patterns on fabric and cut out pieces for the desired variation. Transfer all markings from pattern to vest pieces. (See photo above.)

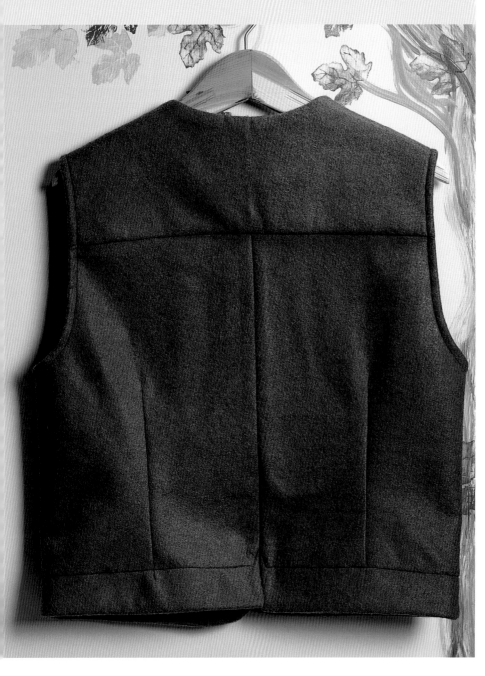

Vest Wardrobe A
Variations

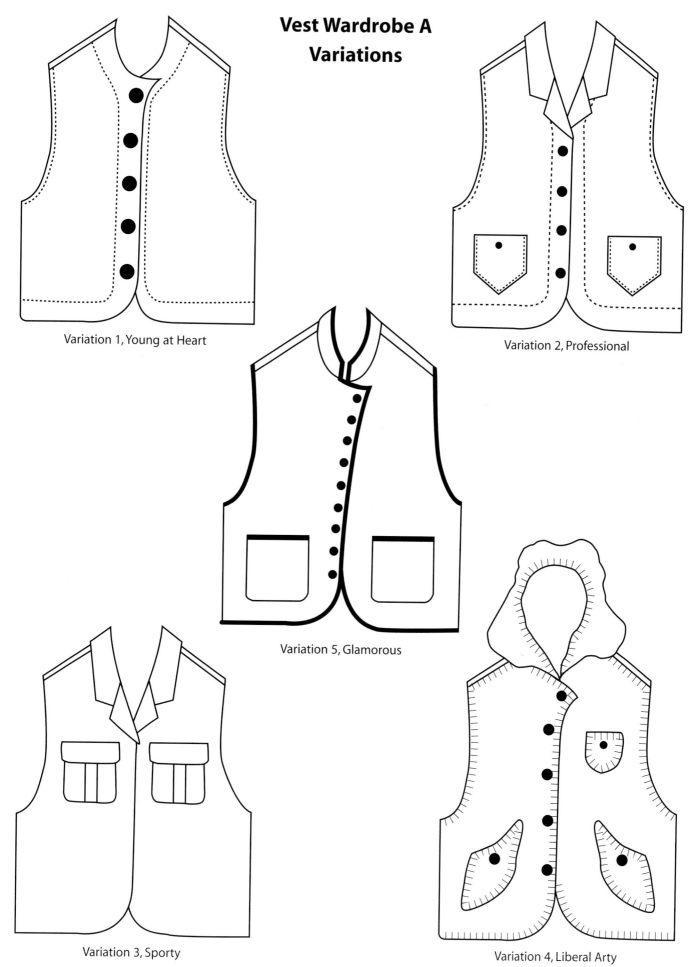

Variation 1, Young at Heart

Variation 2, Professional

Variation 5, Glamorous

Variation 3, Sporty

Variation 4, Liberal Arty

Patterns for Vest Wardrobe A

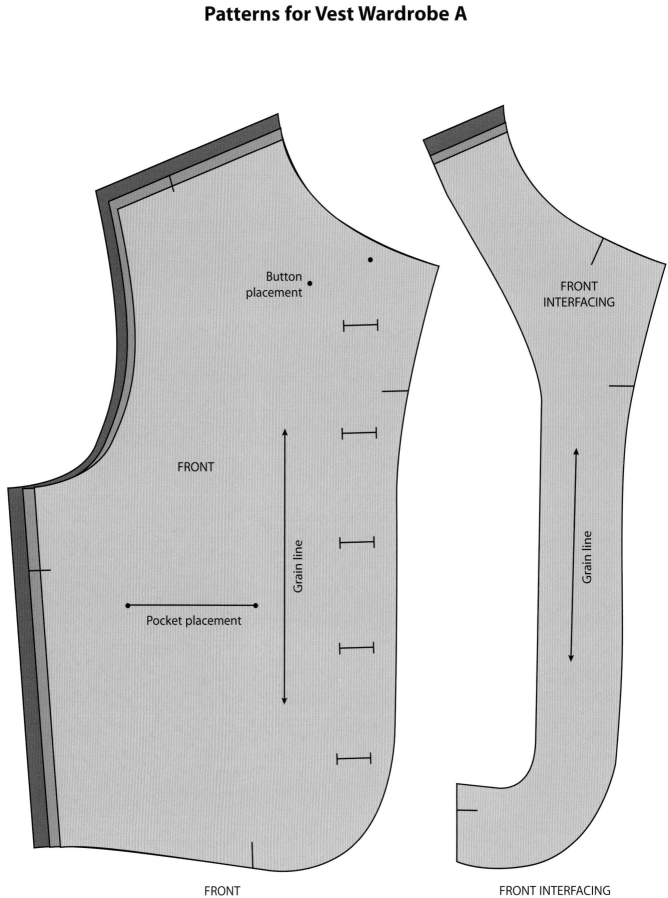

Button
placement

FRONT

Grain line

Pocket placement

FRONT INTERFACING

Grain line

FRONT
Cut 2 from fabric one, 2 from lining, and 2 from interfacing

FRONT INTERFACING
Cut 2 from interfacing

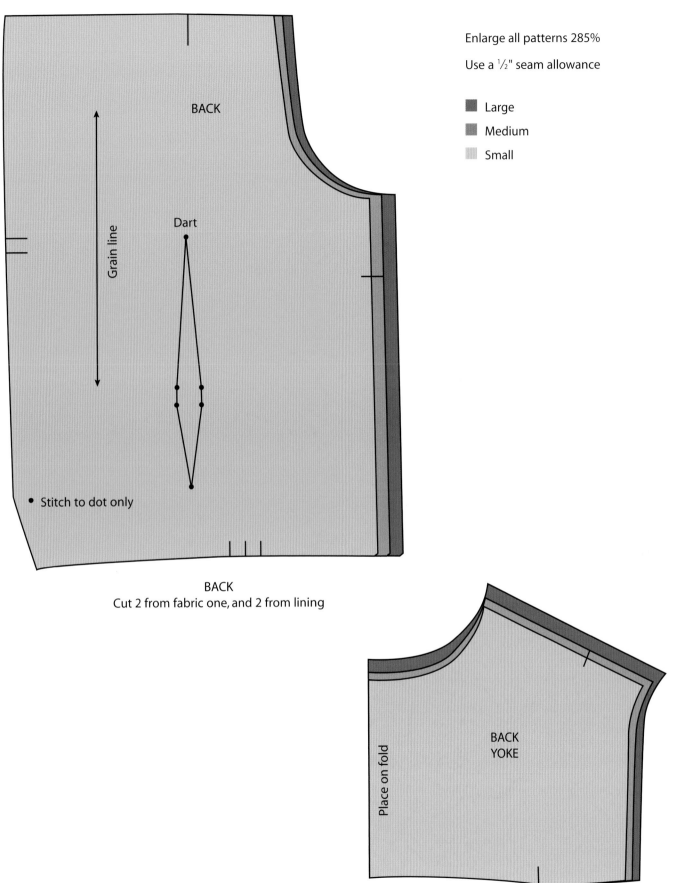

BACK

Grain line

Dart

Enlarge all patterns 285%

Use a $\frac{1}{2}$" seam allowance

Large
Medium
Small

• Stitch to dot only

BACK
Cut 2 from fabric one, and 2 from lining

Place on fold

BACK
YOKE

BACK YOKE
cut 2 along fold from fabric one

Patterns for Vest Wardrobe A

Enlarge all patterns 285%

■ Large
■ Medium
■ Small

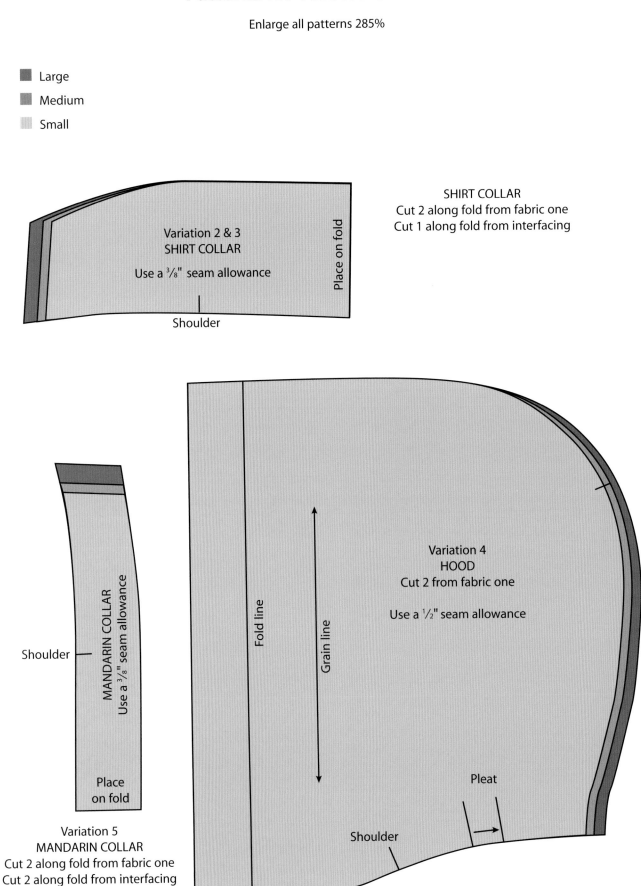

Variation 2 & 3
SHIRT COLLAR

Use a ³⁄₈" seam allowance

Place on fold

Shoulder

SHIRT COLLAR
Cut 2 along fold from fabric one
Cut 1 along fold from interfacing

MANDARIN COLLAR
Use a ³⁄₈" seam allowance

Shoulder

Place
on fold

Variation 5
MANDARIN COLLAR
Cut 2 along fold from fabric one
Cut 2 along fold from interfacing

Fold line

Grain line

Variation 4
HOOD
Cut 2 from fabric one

Use a ¹⁄₂" seam allowance

Pleat

Shoulder

Patterns for Vest Wardrobe A Pockets

Enlarge all patterns 285%

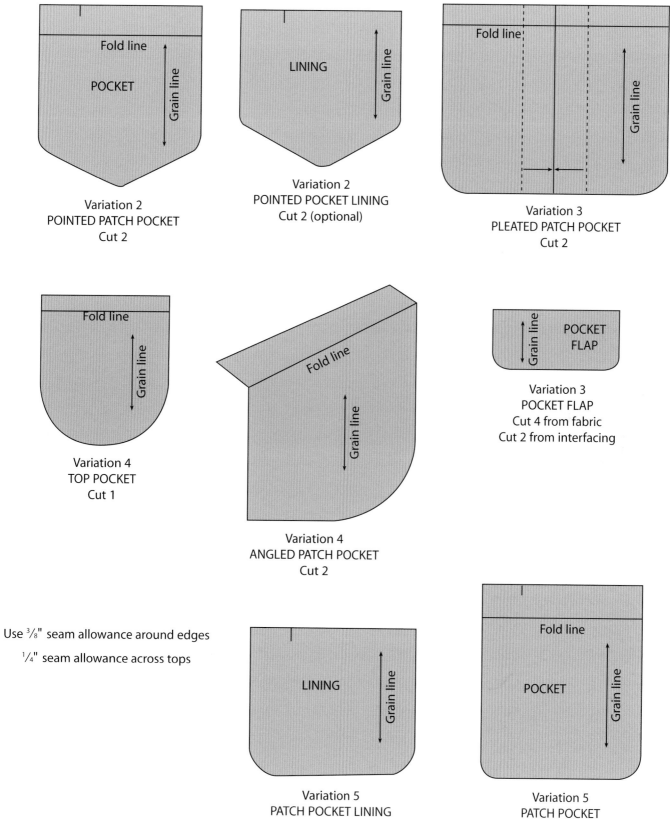

Fold line

POCKET

Grain line

Variation 2
POINTED PATCH POCKET
Cut 2

LINING

Grain line

Variation 2
POINTED POCKET LINING
Cut 2 (optional)

Fold line

Grain line

Variation 3
PLEATED PATCH POCKET
Cut 2

Fold line

Grain line

Variation 4
TOP POCKET
Cut 1

Fold line

Grain line

Variation 4
ANGLED PATCH POCKET
Cut 2

Grain line

POCKET
FLAP

Variation 3
POCKET FLAP
Cut 4 from fabric
Cut 2 from interfacing

Use ³⁄₈" seam allowance around edges

¹⁄₄" seam allowance across tops

LINING

Grain line

Variation 5
PATCH POCKET LINING
Cut 2 (optional)

Fold line

POCKET

Grain line

Variation 5
PATCH POCKET
Cut 2

Variation 1
Young at Heart

MATERIALS

1 yd. fabric, 44" to 60" wide
⅞ yd. lining fabric, 44" wide, or
   ¾ yd. lining fabric, 54" to
   60" wide

⅔ yd. fusible interfacing, 18" wide
5 buttons in various sizes/shapes
Thread in coordinating color

Note: Yardages have been calculated for making the basic vest in a medium size. Adjust yardage amounts accordingly for collars, pockets, and variations in size or fabric usage.

Do not seam fusible interfacing bias pieces.

CUTTING & CONSTRUCTION

The sample vest was made from the following: Main fabric—royal blue felt; lining—royal blue felt; decorative buttons—porcelain

Fabric: Front, cut 2; back, cut 2; back yoke, cut 2

Lining: Front, cut 2; back, cut 2

Fusible interfacing: Front interfacing, cut 2; bias strips, 1" wide by 36" long

1. Hand-baste fusible front interfacing to vest front, and trim edge of interfacing pieces down to ⅛" seam allowance on all edges except the inward edge. Fuse interfacing to front edge. Place bias interfacing strips around remaining bottom edges of vest fronts and backs, placing interfacing ⅜" in from cut edges and seam edges. Fuse bias interfacing strips to bottom edges.
2. Stitch dart in fabric back and lining back. Press darts toward center back.

3. Stitch fabric center back seam and lining center back seam to dot. Press center back seams open. Stitch fabric back yoke to top edge of back, matching center back and notches. Press seam toward yoke. Topstitch back yoke ¼" from the seam. Stitch lining back yoke to top edge of lining back in the same manner. Press yoke seam open.

4. Stitch fronts to back at shoulder seams and stitch lining at shoulder seams. Press fabric at shoulder seams toward back yoke. Topstitch ¼" from seams. Press lining seams open.

5. Pin lining to vest, right sides together, matching front edge notch, shoulder and center back neck seams and armhole edges. Stitch back neck, vest front edges, and armhole edges using a ½" seam allowance. Cut bulk from corners, grade seam allowances, and clip curves. Edge-press all seams. Turn right side out, pulling the front through the shoulders toward the back.

6. Pin and stitch front to back at side seams, matching notches and armhole seams, using a ½" seam allowance. In a continuous seam from outer fabric, pin and stitch lining front to back at side seams, matching notches. At one lining side seam, leave a 4½" opening. Press side seams open.

7. Pin and stitch lower edges of vest to vest lining, right sides together, matching seams, using a ½" seam allowance and breaking stitches at the dot. Do not catch center back seam to itself when stitching to dot. Cut bulk from corners, grade seam allowances, and clip curves. Edge-press lower vest seam. Turn right side out through lining side seam opening. Press thoroughly. Slipstitch lining side seam closed.

8. Mark and stitch five buttonholes on right front. Stitch five buttons in place on left front. If desired, on right front, make a 1" long chain-stitched thread loop at right front top edge. On left front, stitch a button where indicated on pattern.

Variation 2
Professional

MATERIALS

1 yd. fabric, 44" to 60" wide

¼ yd. contrast fabric, any width,
    (for collar)

⅞ yd. lining/facing fabric,
    44" wide; or ¾ yd. lining/fac-
    ing fabric, 54" to 60" wide

⅔ yd. fusible interfacing, 18" wide

Bias strips or packaged bias bind-
    ing in coordinating color

4 buttons, ⅞"; 2 buttons, ⅝"
    (matching style)

Thread in coordinating color

Note: Yardages have been calculated for making the basic vest in a medium size. Adjust yardage amounts accordingly.

Do not seam fusible interfacing bias pieces.

The sample vest was made from the following materials:

Fabric: Textured linen weave, brown

Facings: Textured linen weave, brown

Collar: Linen weave, black

Pocket lining: Cotton broad-cloth, black

Decorative buttons: Black/gold, ⅞" (4); ⅝" (2)

The vest is transformed by adding a shirt collar and patch pockets. To allow space for the collar, only four buttons are used, and buttons have been added to the patch pockets. The sample vest was made without a full lining. (See photo below.) Only the yoke has been lined, and facings cut of the same fabric as vest. Topstitching accentuates the simple lines and secures the facing around the edges.

CUTTING & CONSTRUCTION

1. To make facings instead of lining, lay the interfacing pattern over the front pattern, aligning the front edges. Trace a line around the inner edge onto the front pattern, extending the band at the bottom edge all the way to the side seam. Draw a band the same depth across the bottom of the back pattern. Copy both front and back facings that you have drawn onto tracing paper, transferring markings and adding ½" along the inner edge for a hem allowance. Pin and cut out facings and all other pieces.

2. Hand-baste front interfacing to vest front, and trim edge of interfacing pieces so there is a ⅛" seam allowance on all edges except the inward edge. Fuse interfacing to front edge. Place bias interfacing strips around bottom edges of vest, placing interfacing ⅜" in from cut edges and seam edges. Fuse bias interfacing strips to remaining bottom edges of front and to bottom edges of back. Fuse optional interfacing to the wrong side of the pocket pieces, if desired.

3. Stitch pocket linings to pockets, right sides together and matching notched edges. Press seam open. Fold pockets over on foldline,

right sides together. Stitch sides and lower edges, using a ⅜" seam allowance. Do not stitch across folded edge. Trim bulk from corners and clip curves. (See photo below, left.) Edge-press the seams. Cut a slit in the pocket linings near the bottom edge to pull pocket right side out through the opening. Press pockets flat. Fuse a small piece of interfacing over the slits in the linings. If desired, make buttonholes in center tops of pockets. Pin pockets in place on vest fronts and topstitch.

4. Stitch dart in fabric back and press darts toward center back. Stitch fabric center back seam to dot. Press center back seams open. Stitch fabric back yoke to top edge of back, matching center back and notches. Press seam toward yoke. Stitch fronts to back at shoulder seams. Press fabric at shoulder seams toward back yoke.

5. Stitch facing backs to facing fronts at side seams. Stitch facing backs together above dot at center back seam (this will be a very short seam). Turn in and stitch a ¼" hem on inner edge of facings. Press seams and hem. Stitch remaining fabric back yoke to front facing at shoulders, right sides together. Press seam allowances toward yoke.

6. Trim shirt collar interfacing piece so there is a ⅛" seam allowance on all edges. Trim the interfacing flush to the corner point seamline. Fuse the interfacing to the top collar piece.

7. Trim ⅛" from the outer (unnotched) edges of the undercollar piece. Pin top and undercollar together, right sides together. Stitch, using a ⅜" seam allowance, easing undercollar to fit top collar. Take one or two stitches across collar points to reinforce the corners, and/or double-stitch about 1" on either side of point. Do not stitch neck edge.

8. Trim bulk from points, grade seam allowances, and clip curves if applicable. Edge-press as much of collar as possible before turning. Coax out collar point using a pointer or pin. Press collar from underside. Align and baste-stitch neck edges together. Pin assembled collar to front and back neck edges, matching notches and shoulder marks.

9. Pin facing to vest, right sides together with collar between, matching front edge notch, shoulder and center back neck seams and armhole edges. Stitch back neck, vest front edges, and around bottom of back, using a ½" seam allowance. Do not catch center back seam to itself when stitching to dot. Cut bulk from corners, grade seam allowances, and clip curves. Edge-press all seams. Turn facing and back yoke lining to inside.

10. Pin under seam allowance at base of back yoke lining and at shoulders. Topstitch ⅛" to ¼" from yoke seam edges, both across back and at shoulders.

11. Pin and stitch front to back at side seams in a continuous seam, matching notches, armhole, and facing edges, using a ½" seam allowance. Press seams open, turn facing up and press.

12. Pin or baste facing in place all around vest edge. Measure and mark outside of vest front and back for topstitching placement and stitch through all thicknesses on marks.

13. Stitch bias binding around armhole edges. Clip seams and curves and press binding to the inside. Topstitch armhole edges ¼" from seam.

14. Mark and stitch four buttonholes on right front. Stitch buttons in place on left front and to correspond to pocket buttonholes.

Variation 3
Sporty

MATERIALS

1 yd. fabric, 44" to 60" wide
⅞ yd. lining fabric, 44" wide, or
    ¾ yd. lining fabric, 54" to 60"
    wide

⅔ yd. fusible interfacing, 18" wide
5 buttons in various sizes/shapes
Thread in coordinating color

Note: Yardages have been calculated for making the basic vest in a medium size. Adjust yardage amounts accordingly for collars, pockets, and variations in size or fabric usage.

Do not seam fusible interfacing bias pieces.

For the look for the outdoors lover, add a shirt collar and a pair of pleated breast pockets. In the sample, no buttons are used, but, depending on the style of fabric used for this vest, buttons may be added and it can be made into a "safari"-type vest and/or topstitching can be added around the vest and pockets.

CUTTING & CONSTRUCTION

To make vest with facings instead of lining, follow steps on page 167.

To line vest completely, see instructions on pages 164–165.

Pleated Patch Pockets

1. Fuse a strip of ¾" wide bias cut interfacing to the underside of the pleated pocket, ⅛" above the foldline.

2. To create the pocket hem, press under ¼" along the top edge of the pleated pocket. Fold the top of the pleated pocket over on the foldline to the right side of the fabric. Beginning at fold, stitch one end of hem and continue stitching around pocket raw edges, using a ⅜" seam allowance, ending at fold on opposite side of pocket. (See photo below, left.) Trim corners and clip curves. Turn the top fold right side out, and press. Press under the pocket seam allowance along the stitching.

3. On the wrong side of the pleated pocket, fold and press the fabric along the left foldline. Fold the pressed edge to the center of pleated pocket. Press, forming half of an inverted box pleat. On the wrong side, fold and press the fabric along the right foldline. Fold the pressed edge to the center of pleated pocket. (See photo below, right.) Press, forming the remainder of the inverted box pleat. Pin in place. Topstitch close to the top and bottom edges of the pocket hem. Stitch the pocket to the vest.

Pocket Flap

1. Trim pocket flap interfacing to have a ⅛" seam allowance. Fuse trimmed interfacing to wrong sides of pocket flaps.

2. Pin and stitch pocket flap linings to pocket flaps. Trim bulk from corners, clip curves, edge-press, turn, and press flaps.

3. Pin flaps to vest fronts, pointing upwards, aligning the raw edges above the pleated pockets. Stitch straight across, ⅜" above raw edges. Trim seam allowance, turn, and press flaps down. Topstitch across the top of the flaps, ¼" below fold.

4. Press vest thoroughly.

Variation 4
Liberal Arty

MATERIALS

1 yd. fabric, 44" to 60" wide

⅞ yd. lining fabric, 44" wide, or
⅞ yd. lining fabric, 54" to 60" wide

⅔ yd. fusible interfacing, 18" wide

7 buttons, ⅞"; 1 button, ⅝"
Thread in coordinating color
Sock yarn or embroidery floss
in contrasting color
Tapestry needle

Note: Yardages have been calculated for making the basic vest in a medium size. Adjust yardage amounts accordingly.

Do not seam fusible interfacing bias pieces.

Sewing a hood onto any vest will add a functional element—the hood can be worn up for warmth or down the back in a casual manner. Angled patch pockets have been added on each side and a small patch pocket as a top pocket. Five buttons close the front and buttons adorn the angled pockets. A slightly smaller button is used on the top pocket. Blanket-stitching is worked around all outside edges, including the hood and pocket edges.

CUTTING & CONSTRUCTION

To make vest with facings instead of lining, follow steps on page 167.

To line vest completely, see instructions on page 164–165.

Pockets

1. To create pocket hems, press under ¼" along the top edge of the pocket. Fold the top of the pocket over on the foldline, wrong sides together, to the inside of the fabric. Stitch hems in place.
2. Using a ⅜" seam allowance, machine-baste around the lower three sides of the pockets. Clip curves and press seam allowance in to the wrong side. (See photo below.)
3. Pin and stitch pockets to vest fronts, carefully aligning placements.

Hood

1. To add the hood, stitch the notched edge of the hood, using a ½" seam allowance. Press seam open and run topstitching ¼" on either side of seam. Trim close to stitching. (If using a fabric that frays easily, turn under the seam edges before stitching.)
2. Fold the straight edge of the hood down along the foldline. Turn raw edge under ¼" and stitch hem in place. Fold and pleat the hood at neck edge where indicated and baste-stitch in place.
3. Pin hood into neckline, right sides together, and machine-baste using a ½" seam allowance.
4. Pin lining or facing to vest and continue construction as given on page 165 or 167.

Finishing

1. Mark and stitch five buttonholes on right front. Stitch buttons in place on left front and on pockets.
2. Work Blanket Stitch (see page 9) around pocket edges, armholes, and all outer edges of vest and hood.

Variation 5
Glamorous

MATERIALS

1 yd. fabric, 44" to 60" wide
⅞ yd. lining fabric, 44" wide, or
    ¾ yd. lining fabric, 54" to 60"
    wide

⅔ yd. fusible interfacing, 18" wide
9 buttons, ⅝"
Decorative braid in contrasting
    color
Thread in coordinating color

Note: Yardages have been calculated for making the basic vest in a medium size. Adjust yardage amounts accordingly.

Do not seam fusible interfacing bias pieces.

A mandarin collar, combined with the dropped shoulders of the basic vest, gives a clean look to be dressed up or down. Patch pockets have been placed on each side. To add a glamorous touch with Asian flair, nine buttons are used and braid applied to all edges.

CUTTING & CONSTRUCTION

To make vest with facings instead of lining, follow steps on page 167.

To line vest completely see instructions on page 164–165.

Pockets

1. Stitch pocket linings to pockets, right sides together and matching notched edges. Press seam open. Fold pockets over on foldline, right sides together. Stitch sides and lower edges, using a ⅜" seam allowance. Do not stitch across folded edge. Trim bulk from corners and clip curves. Edge-press the seams. Cut a slit in the pocket linings near the bottom edge to pull pocket right side out through the opening.

2. Press pockets flat. Fuse a small piece of interfacing over the slits in the linings. (See photo below.) Slipstitch braid around edges of pockets.
3. Pin pockets in place on vest fronts and slipstitch or topstitch in place, being careful to align placements.

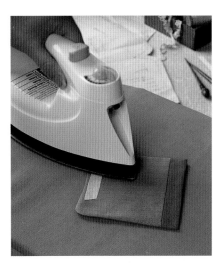

Mandarin Collar

1. Trim Mandarin collar interfacing piece so there is a ⅛" seam allowance on all edges. Fuse the interfacing to the outer collar piece.
2. Trim ⅛" from the un-notched edges of the inner, or lining, collar piece. Pin outer and inner collar together, right sides together. Stitch, using a ⅜" seam allowance, easing inner collar to fit top collar. Take one or two stitches across collar points to reinforce the corners, and/or double-stitch about 1" on either side of point. Do not stitch neck edge.

3. Trim bulk at corners and clip curves. Grade seam allowances and edge press as much of collar as possible before turning. Coax out collar points using a pointer or pin. Press collar from underside. Align and baste neck edges together. Pin assembled collar to front and back neck edges, matching notches and shoulder marks.
4. Continue construction as given on page 165 or 167, depending whether you are lining or facing the vest.

Finishing

1. Mark and stitch nine buttonholes on right front, following curve of overlap. Stitch nine buttons in place on left front.
2. Slipstitch braid to edges, as desired.

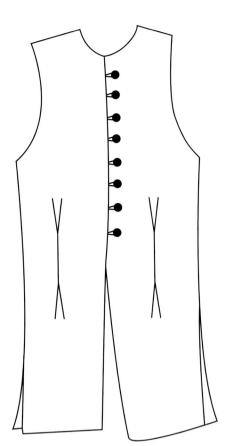

Variation 1, Festive

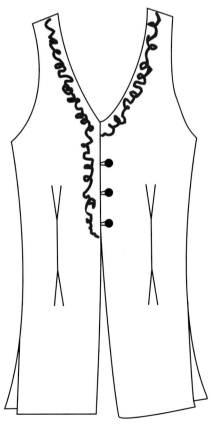

Variation 2, Elegant

Vest Wardrobe B
Variations

This long, streamlined vest has slits in the bottom of the side seams to prevent restriction of movement.

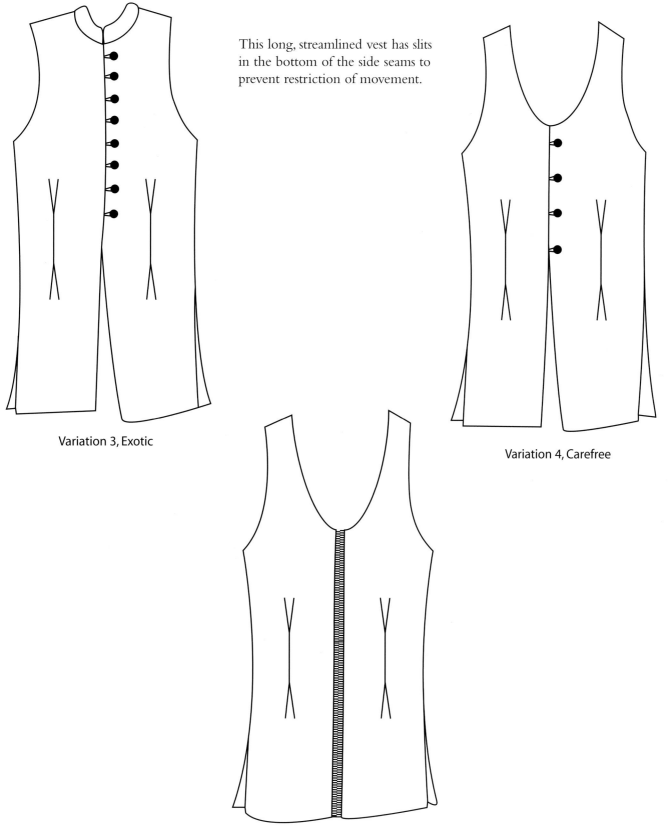

Variation 3, Exotic

Variation 4, Carefree

Variation 5, Streamlined

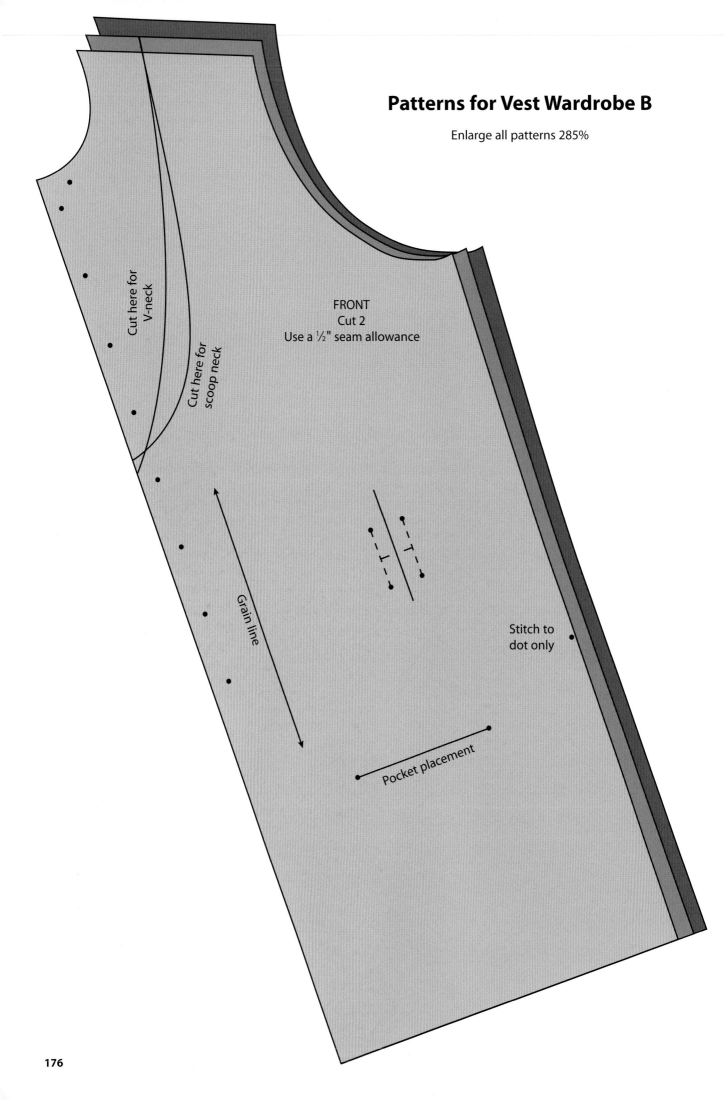

Patterns for Vest Wardrobe B

Enlarge all patterns 285%

Cut here for V-neck

Cut here for scoop neck

FRONT
Cut 2
Use a ½" seam allowance

Grain line

Stitch to dot only

Pocket placement

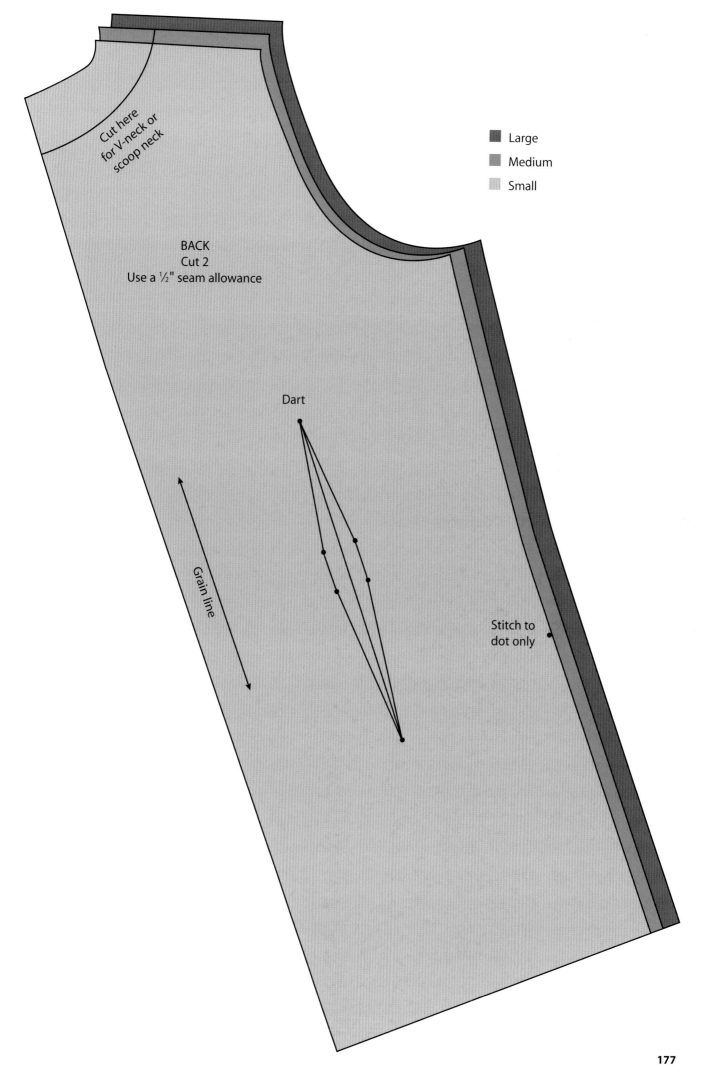

Cut here
for V-neck or
scoop neck

BACK
Cut 2
Use a ½" seam allowance

Large
Medium
Small

Dart

Grain line

Stitch to
dot only

Patterns for Vest Wardrobe B

Enlarge all patterns 285%

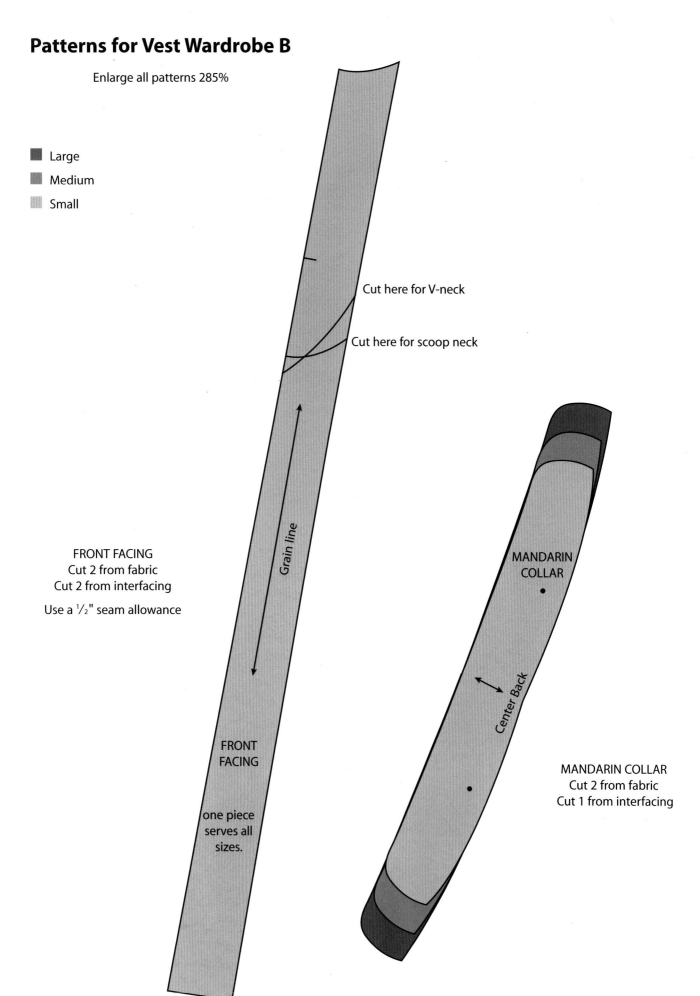

■ Large
■ Medium
■ Small

Cut here for V-neck

Cut here for scoop neck

Grain line

FRONT FACING
Cut 2 from fabric
Cut 2 from interfacing

Use a ½" seam allowance

FRONT
FACING

one piece
serves all
sizes.

MANDARIN
COLLAR

Center Back

MANDARIN COLLAR
Cut 2 from fabric
Cut 1 from interfacing

Variation 1
Festive

MATERIALS

1½ yds. fabric, 44" wide, or 1 yd. fabric 54" to 60" wide

⅞ yd. fusible interfacing, 18" wide

8 decorative buttons, ½"

Thread in coordinating color

Note: Yardages have been calculated for making the basic vest in a medium size. Adjust yardage amounts accordingly.

The sample vest was made from the following materials:

Fabric: Cotton/polyester blend, Christmas print

Decorative buttons: Metal poinsettias

CUTTING & CONSTRUCTION

1. Cut front vest pieces with the high, jewel-neckline variation. Cut 1" wide bias strips, 20" long, from fabric.
2. Trim front facing interfacing pieces so there is a ⅛" seam allowance on all edges. Fuse interfacing to front facing pieces.
3. Stitch back darts. Press darts toward center back. Stitch front tucks and press toward the center. Stitch back seam, right sides together, using a ½" seam allowance. For a clean finish, stitch back seam as a French seam. (See page 12 to review technique.) Press the French seam toward the right back.
4. Press the back hem up ¾" to the wrong side. Turn the raw edge under ¼" and stitch the hem in place. Press.
5. For fabric button loops, fold 1" wide bias strip in half, matching long edges. Stitch ⅛" in from folded edge, widening stitches to ¼" at the end of the strip. Insert a loop turner through loop opening, exiting turner at wider end. Latch the turner to fabric and turn fabric inside out through the tube, creating "spaghetti."
6. Baste "spaghetti" trim to the right front edge on button loop placement lines. Make loops ⅝" deep.

7. Turn under ¼", press, and stitch the long, unnotched edge of the front facing. Stitch front facing to the neck, front, and hem edge of front, using a ½" seam allowance. At hem edge, use a ¾" seam allowance. Trim seam along front edge and clip bulk from corners. Trim seam allowance on facings only at neck and hem edges. Press front edge seam allowances toward the facings.

8. Press the remaining front hem up ¾" to the wrong side. Turn raw edge under ¼" and stitch hem in place, stitching through the front facings as well. Press.

9. Stitch front to back at shoulder seams, right sides together, using a ½" seam allowance. Press seams open, or, for a clean finish, stitch French seams. Press French seams toward back. Stitch sides, right sides together, using a ½" seam allowance and ending at the dots. Press seam open.

10. Roll slit side seams under ⅛" and stitch close to the folded edge for a clean finish. Machine-stitch a narrow hem at neck and armhole edges. Press thoroughly. An alternative would be to fully line the vest. (See photo below.)

11. Stitch buttons in place on left front, corresponding to button loops.

Variation 2
Elegant

MATERIALS

1½ yds. fabric, 44" wide, or
   1 yd. fabric, 54" to 60" wide
   (for base fabric)
1½ yds. lace, 44" wide or
   1 yd. lace, 54" to 60" wide
   (for overlay fabric)

⅞ yd. fusible interfacing, 18" wide
3 yds. silk ribbon, 7mm wide
1½ yds. picot edge trim
3 decorative buttons, ⅝"
Thread in coordinating color

This version is made of two fabrics worked as one. A slight curve has been given to the V-neck, and ribbon trim added around the neckline and partially down the front of the vest. There are fewer buttons, and the vest has an elegant, dressy effect.

The sample vest was made from the following materials:

Fabric one (base): Taupe moiré

Fabric two (overlay): Chantilly lace, lavender/gray

Trim: Silk ribbon, gray; picot-edge trim, gray

Decorative buttons: Mauve glass (3)

CUTTING & CONSTRUCTION

1. Cut front vest pieces with the V-neckline. Overlay lace pieces onto the matching base cloth fabric pieces. Pin and baste-stitch in place, then proceed with construction as with one cloth.
2. Trim front interfacing pieces down to a ⅛" seam allowance on all edges. Fuse interfacing to front facing pieces.
3. Stitch back darts. Press darts toward center back. Stitch front tucks and press toward the center. Stitch back seam, as a French seam, right sides together, using a ½" seam allowance. (See page 12 to review technique.) Press the French seam toward the right back.
4. Press the back hem up ¾" to the wrong side. Turn the raw edge under ¼" and stitch the hem in place. Press.
5. For button loops, baste-stitch picot edging trim to the right front edge at the button loop placement lines. Make loops ⅝" deep.

6. Turn under ¼", press, and stitch the long, un-notched edge of the front facing. Stitch front facing to the neck, front, and hem edge of front, using a ½" seam allowance. At hem edge, use a ¾" seam allowance. Trim seam along front edge and clip bulk from corners. Trim seam allowance on facings only at neck and hem edges. Press front edge seam allowances toward the facings.

7. Press the remaining front hem up ¾" to the wrong side. Turn raw edge under ¼" and stitch hem in place, stitching through the front facings as well. Press.

8. Stitch front to back at shoulders, right sides together, using a ½" seam allowance. Stitch the seams as French seams, and press French seams toward back. Stitch sides, right sides together, using a ½" seam allowance and ending at the dots. Press seam open.

9. Roll the slit side seams under ⅛" and stitch close to the folded edge for a clean finish. Narrowly hem remaining side seams and press. Narrowly machine-hem neck edge and armhole edges. Press thoroughly.

Finishing

1. Hand-stitch picot trim to front and back at neck edge.

2. Cut 7 mm gray ribbon into two equal lengths. Fray the fibers from an end of one length of ribbon, and pull a center fiber to gather the ribbon. Position and pin the gathered ribbon in a random manner to left front neck edge. Hand-stitch the ribbon in place. Repeat with the remaining ribbon length on the right front neck edge. (See photo below for detail.) Steam lightly.

3. Sew buttons on left front to correspond with picot loops.

Variation 3
Exotic

MATERIALS

1½ yds. fabric, 44" wide, or
   1 yd. fabric, 54" to 60" wide
⅞ yd. fusible interfacing, 18" wide

8 decorative buttons, ½"
Thread in coordinating color

A mandarin collar makes a whole new look, and the slit in the bottom of the side seams can be raised for an even more exotic effect.

CUTTING & CONSTRUCTION

1. Cut front vest pieces with the high, round neckline. Cut 1" wide bias strips, 20" long, from the fabric.

2. Proceed as for *Variation 1*, steps 2 through 6, on page 179.

3. Stitch front to back at shoulder seams, right sides together, using a ½" seam allowance. Press seams open, or, for a clean finish, stitch French seams. Press French seams toward back. Stitch sides, right sides together, using a ½" seam allowance and ending at, or as much above, the dots as desired. Press seams open.

4. Trim Mandarin collar interfacing so there is a ⅛" seam allowance on all edges. Fuse interfacing to the wrong side of outer collar piece. Trim ⅛" from un-notched edges of inside collar. Pin and stitch inside collar, right sides together, to outside collar, easing to fit. Trim bulk, clip curves, edge-press, and turn Mandarin collar. Press collar.

5. Using a ½" seam allowance, stitch outer collar only to neck edge; match notches, shoulder marks, and center back. Press seam toward collar.

6. On the long, un-notched edge of the front facing, turn under, press, and stitch a ¼" hem. Stitch curved neck edge of front facing to the bottom edge of the inner collar, then down vest front, using a ½" seam allowance. At hem edge, use a ¾" seam allowance. Trim seam along front edge and clip bulk from corners. Trim seam allowance on facings only at neck and hem edges. Press front edge seam allowances toward the facings.

7. Clip inner collar to seam at front facing. Turn under remaining inner collar edge ½" and pin in place to encase back neck edge. Stitch close to seam.

8. Press remaining front hem up ¾", turn raw edge under ¼", and stitch. Roll slit side seams under ⅛" and stitch close to the folded edge. Machine-stitch narrow armhole edge hems. Press thoroughly. An alternative would be to fully line the vest.

9. Sew buttons on left front to correspond with button loops.

MATERIALS

1½ yds. fabric, 44" wide, or 1 yd.
   fabric, 54" to 60" wide
⅞ yd. fusible interfacing, 18" wide

4 buttons, ⅝"
Thread in coordinating color

The scoop neck on this vest reveals a little more of the chest area. Fewer buttons have been used to make the vest a little more casual. Button loops or regular button-holes may be used.

CUTTING & CONSTRUCTION

1. Cut front vest pieces with the scoop neckline variation. Cut 1" wide bias strips, 20" long, from the fabric.

2. Trim front interfacing pieces down to a ⅛" seam allowance on all edges. Fuse interfacing to front facing pieces.

3. Stitch back darts. Press darts toward center back. Stitch front tucks and press toward the center. Stitch back seam, right sides together, using a ½" seam allowance. For a clean finish, stitch back seam as a French seam. (See page 12 to review technique.) Press the French seam toward the right back.

4. Press the back hem up ¾" to the wrong side. Turn the raw edge under ¼" and stitch the hem in place. Press.

5. For fabric button loops, fold 1" wide bias strip in half, matching long edges. Stitch ⅛" in from folded edge, widening stitches to ¼" at the end of the strip. Insert a loop turner through loop opening, exiting turner at wider end. Latch the turner to fabric and turn fabric inside out through the tube, creating "spaghetti" trim.

6. Baste "spaghetti" trim to the right front edge on button loop placement lines. Make loops ⅝" deep.

7. Turn under ¼", press, and stitch the long, un-notched edge of the front facing. Stitch front facing to the neck, front, and hem edge of front, using a ½" seam allowance. At hem edge, use a ¾" seam allowance. Trim seam along front edge and clip bulk from corners. Trim seam allowance on facings only at neck and hem edges. Press front edge seam allowances toward the facings.

8. Press the remaining front hem up ¾" to the wrong side. Turn raw edge under ¼" and stitch hem in place, stitching through the front facings as well. Press.

9. Stitch front to back at shoulder seams, right sides together, using a ½" seam allowance. Press seams open, or, for a clean finish, stitch French seams. Press French seams toward back. Stitch sides, right sides together, using a ½" seam allowance and ending at the dots. Press seam open.

10. Roll slit side seams under ⅛" and stitch close to the folded edge for a clean finish. Machine-stitch a narrow hem at neck and armhole edges. Press thoroughly. An alternative would be to fully line the vest.

Variation 5
Streamlined

MATERIALS

1½ yds. fabric, 44" wide, or
   1 yd. fabric, 54" to 60" wide
⅞ yd. fusible interfacing, 18" wide

Separating zipper, length as
   desired
Thread in coordinating color

The neckline on this vest allows it to be worn very nicely without anything underneath. A zipper up the front replaces the buttons.

CUTTING & CONSTRUCTION

1. Cut front vest pieces along the V-neckline variation, then follow steps 2 through 4 of *Variation 1* on page 179.

2. Set a separating zipper into front, making sure left and right sides align. The zipper base may be flush with the bottom of the front, as pictured, or placed some inches above hem, if desired.

3. On the long, un-notched edge of the front facing, turn under, press, and stitch a ¼" hem. Stitch front facing to the neck, front, and hem edge of front, using a ½" seam allowance. At hem edge, use a ¾" seam allowance. Trim seam along front edge and clip bulk from corners. Trim seam allowance on facings, only at neck and hem edges. Press front edge seam allowances toward the facings.

4. Press the remaining front hem up ¾" to the wrong side. Turn raw edge under ¼" and stitch hem in place, stitching through the front facings as well. Press.

5. Stitch front to back at shoulder seams, right sides together, using a ½" seam allowance. Press seams open, or, for a clean finish, stitch French seams. Press French seams toward back. Stitch sides, right sides together, using a ½" seam allowance and ending at the dots. Press seam open.

6. Roll slit side seams under ⅛" and stitch close to the folded edge for a clean finish. Narrowly hem remaining side seams and press. Machine-stitch a narrow hem at neck and armhole edges. Press thoroughly. An alternative would be to fully line the vest.

Glossary

Braid trim A narrow, banded trim that can range in width from ⅛" to 5" and beyond and includes embroidered, sequinned, or fringed bands and ribbon.

Breaking the stitch Stopping the stitching process in a seam line. The process will include the ¼" backstitch, repositioning the needle, and beginning again with a ¼" backstitch at the new location.

Center back A mark or line that indicates where a garment will fall at the center back of the body or at the center back of an accessory.

Center front A mark or line that indicates where a garment will fall at the center front of the body or at the center front of an accessory.

Clipping bulk Trimming fabric from the seam allowance of a corner by cutting diagonally across the corner, leaving a ⅛"–¼" seam allowance. Trim some excess from the seam allowance near the corner as well.

Clipping curves On an inward curve, make cuts into the seam allowance at ½"–2" intervals. On an outward curve, cut small wedges into the seam allowance at ½"–2" intervals. Allows a seam to lie flat when pressed, eliminating tension or pull.

Crosswise grain The direction of threads that run from selvege to selvege, at right angles to the lengthwise grain threads. Crosswise grain generally has a slight amount of give. Also known as Weft.

Dart A V-shaped seam that shapes a garment to the curves of the body. Darts are a basic method of shaping flat fabric into contoured shapes.

Dart legs Two stitching lines that meet at a point and are matched up and joined as two sides of a dart.

Easing Slightly gathering to reduce the slack in one layer to fit another.

Edge-pressing A preliminary pressing step that exposes the seam line when turned right side out. It is used when it is not possible to press a seam allowance open.

Fashion Ruler™ A transparent plastic ruler that is a combination of French curve (see below), hip curve, and straight edge.

Finished edge The edge of the fabric after it is seamed, hemmed, or otherwise finished.

Fitting ease Extra fabric allowed over and above the body measurements to ensure comfort, ease of movement, and smoothness in a garment.

Flexible ruler Flexible, transparent plastic ruler, marked with a ⅛" grid, which simplifies the drawing of parallel lines, such as cutting lines. Its flexibility enables it, when placed on its side, to follow a curved seamline for measuring.

Fold line A marking that indicates where fabric is to be folded for construction purposes, such as for pleats and tucks.

French curve ruler A pattern-maker's tool made of transparent plastic; the edges are curved to serve as templates for drawing smooth curves.

Fuse To adhere a product such as fusible interfacing to a fabric surface, using iron heat.

Fusible web A non-woven web of adhesive fabric, usually packaged with one smooth side (or sometimes with paper on one side) that melts and adheres to fabric when heat and steam are applied. Will bond two surfaces together.

Grain The lengthwise or crosswise direction of threads, which compose the fabric. See True bias, Crosswise grain, Lengthwise grain.

Grain line The direction of the lengthwise threads running parallel to the selvage. Place all grain line arrows on patterns along the lengthwise grain.

Gusset A fabric piece inserted into a seam that provides ease, flair, or space.

Interfacing A fabric, woven or nonwoven, that is primarily used to shape detail areas. It adds body to garment edges, cuffs, collars, and pockets, and keeps the shape of necklines and buttonholes. Interfacings are categorized by their type of application, such as sew-in or fusible.

Lengthwise grain The vertical, more sturdy threads which the crosswise threads are worked over and under. Also known as Warp.

Lining A nearly duplicate copy of a garment or accessory that is sewn to the inside and completely covers seam and construction details.

Lose thread ends In hand-sewing, stitching the needle into a fold of the fabric next to an ending knot, and then out again about 1" away. The thread is trimmed at the exit point and the thread end is hidden within the space.

Marking The transfer of construction details from a pattern to the fabric, using any of several different fabric-marking pens, pencils, chalks, or transfer papers. Marking is done immediately after a project has been cut out.

Nap The hairy, downy, or tufted surface of a fabric such as velvet or corduroy. When you stroke the nap it is smooth and lies down in one direction and resistant and stands up in the opposite direction. All pieces of a pattern must be cut with the nap going either up or down. If nap is going down the fabric appears lighter, if it is going up, the color is deeper and richer.

Narrow hem A fine hem finish, ⅛"–¼" wide, suitable for sheers and when weight is not needed for a hem. It is achieved with a basic fold-over sewing technique or by using a roll-hemmer foot.

Notches Wedge-shaped pattern marking along cutting lines primarily found in commercial patterns, to be matched up for accuracy in aligning seams.

Overcast stitch See Whipstitch.

Pattern cutting/sewing guide A detailed guide found inside commercial pattern envelopes, along with full-sized patterns. The guide includes general sewing instructions, pattern marking interpretations, special instructions for the specific designs in the envelope, an encapsulated cutting guide for each design, and detailed sewing instructions for each design.

Pattern-making papers Tissue paper is too fragile to stand up to the repeated use of a pattern. Durable options for pattern-making are: **Alphabet paper,** on 45" wide rolls, is pre-marked with a grid to aid in transferring measurements and

markings. It is about the weight of bond typing paper. **Brown paper bags** are sturdy and a good size for most pattern pieces when cut open and spread out. **Newsprint** can be purchased in large sheets from art suppliers or as end roles from newspaper printers. **Oak tag or manila** is an ideal substance to hold up to repeated usage, and is easy to trace around. **Tracing paper** or **architectural trash paper,** used by architects and artists to overlay and/or protect drawings, comes in 36" wide rolls and is available from art, drafting, or architectural supply stores or through the internet.

Place-on-fold A pattern marking that indicates that the center line of the pattern is to be placed on the folded edge of the fabric. When cut, a left and right side of the pattern piece will automatically be cut from the fabric.

Pleat A fold in the fabric made by doubling the fabric over on itself in various ways that provides controlled fullness or is used as a decorative application.

Pellets (plastic or poly) A product used for stuffing dolls, toy parts, or pillows that adds weight and flexibility to the area being filled. Can be used along with polyester stuffing or alone.

Preshrunk Fabric that has been washed and dried prior to its pattern pieces being cut out. This eliminates the concern that the finished item will shrink when washed. Before preshrinking, check the washing instructions, as some fabrics may only be dry-cleaned.

Press Using an iron and ironing board to flatten seams and seam allowances and any construction aspect done concurrently with assembly and after assembly.

Press under Pressing the designated amount along a raw edge over on itself, wrong sides together, creating a finished edge on the right side of the fabric.

Raw edge The unfinished, cut edge of a piece of fabric.

Right sides together Placing two layers of fabric so the right sides are facing each other.

Seam A joining of two pieces of fabric with a line of stitches.

Seam allowance Amount of fabric allowed beyond the seamline or stitching line for joining garment sections.

Seam line A broken line on a commercial pattern indicating where a garment or accessory is to be stitched.

Self lining A lining that is of, or is an extension of, the same material as the garment or accessory.

Selvege The finished woven border that results along both lengthwise edges of fabric in the weaving process.

Staystitching Stitching around the edge of the fabric to secure two or more layers together and/or to prevent fabric from stretching or becoming misshapen.

True Bias The diagonal intersection of the lengthwise and crosswise threads. True bias exists at the 45° angle when lengthwise and crosswise grains are perpendicular. Fabric cut on the bias has a great amount of give, similar to the stretch of a knit, but without the elasticity of a knit.

Wrong sides together Placing fabrics so the wrong, or unfinished, sides are facing each other.

Metric Conversions

MM-MILLIMETRES   CM-CENTIMETRES

INCHES TO MILLIMETRES AND CENTIMETRES

INCHES	MM	CM	INCHES	CM	INCHES	CM
⅛	3	0.3	9	22.9	30	76.2
¼	6	0.6	10	25.4	31	78.7
⅜	10	1.0	11	27.9	32	81.3
½	13	1.3	12	30.5	33	83.8
⅝	16	1.6	13	33.0	34	86.4
¾	19	1.9	14	35.6	35	88.9
⅞	22	2.2	15	38.1	36	91.4
1	25	2.5	16	40.6	37	94.0
1 ¼	32	3.2	17	43.2	38	96.5
1 ½	38	3.8	18	45.7	39	99.1
1 ¾	44	4.4	19	48.3	40	101.6
2	51	5.1	20	50.8	41	104.1
2 ½	64	6.4	21	53.3	42	106.7
3	76	7.6	22	55.9	43	109.2
3 ½	89	8.9	23	58.4	44	111.8
4	102	10.2	24	61.0	45	114.3
4 ½	114	11.4	25	63.5	46	116.8
5	127	12.7	26	66.0	47	119.4
6	152	15.2	27	68.6	48	121.9
7	178	17.8	28	71.1	49	124.5
8	203	20.3	29	73.7	50	127.0

YARDS TO METRES

YARDS	METRES	YARDS	METRES	YARDS	METRES	YARDS	METRES	YARDS	METRES
⅛	0.11	2 ⅛	1.94	4 ⅛	3.77	6 ⅛	5.60	8 ⅛	7.43
¼	0.23	2 ¼	2.06	4 ¼	3.89	6 ¼	5.72	8 ¼	7.54
⅜	0.34	2 ⅜	2.17	4 ⅜	4.00	6 ⅜	5.83	8 ⅜	7.66
½	0.46	2 ½	2.29	4 ½	4.11	6 ½	5.94	8 ½	7.77
⅝	0.57	2 ⅝	2.40	4 ⅝	4.23	6 ⅝	6.06	8 ⅝	7.89
¾	0.69	2 ¾	2.51	4 ¾	4.34	6 ¾	6.17	8 ¾	8.00
⅞	0.80	2 ⅞	2.63	4 ⅞	4.46	6 ⅞	6.29	8 ⅞	8.12
1	0.91	3	2.74	5	4.57	7	6.40	9	8.23
1 ⅛	1.03	3 ⅛	2.86	5 ⅛	4.69	7 ⅛	6.52	9 ⅛	8.34
1 ¼	1.14	3 ¼	2.97	5 ¼	4.80	7 ¼	6.63	9 ¼	8.46
1 ⅜	1.26	3 ⅜	3.09	5 ⅜	4.91	7 ⅜	6.74	9 ⅜	8.57
1 ½	1.37	3 ½	3.20	5 ½	5.03	7 ½	6.86	9 ½	8.69
1 ⅝	1.49	3 ⅝	3.31	5 ⅝	5.14	7 ⅝	6.97	9 ⅝	8.80
1 ¾	1.60	3 ¾	3.43	5 ¾	5.26	7 ¾	7.09	9 ¾	8.92
1 ⅞	1.71	3 ⅞	3.54	5 ⅞	5.37	7 ⅞	7.20	9 ⅞	9.03
2	1.83	4	3.66	6	5.49	8	7.32	10	9.14

Baby Sizes & Pattern Company Contacts

Plan to make clothes a little larger than you think they ought to be. If what you make doesn't fit the baby now, it soon will. Use the chart below as guide to help you size.

STANDARD BABY SIZES

	Weight	Length	Chest	Head	Thigh
0 to 3 months	Up to 12 lbs. (5.4 k)	22" – 25" (55.9 – 63.5 cm)	16" (40.6 cm)	14" (35.6 cm)	5" – 10" (12.7 – 25.4 cm)
3 to 6 months	12 –17 lbs. (5.4 – 7.7 k)	25" – 28" (63.5 – 71.1 cm)	17" (43.2 cm)	15" (38.1 cm)	10" – 13" (25.4 – 33 cm)
6 to 12 months	18 – 22 lbs. (8.1 – 9.9 k)	28" – 31" (71.1 – 78.74 cm)	19" (48.3 cm)	16" (35.6 cm)	11" – 14" (27.9 – 35.6 cm)

PATTERN COMPANIES

The Children's Corner Patterns
3814 Cleghorn Avenue
P.O. Box 150161
Nashville, Tennessee 37215
800-543-6915
www.childrenscornerfabric.com
Hillary (pages 143-145)
Louise (pages 146-147)

Cutting Line Designs
900 South Orlando Avenue
Winter Park, Florida 32789
877-734-5818
www.fabriccollections.com
By Popular Demand: 60565 (pages 150-152)

Dos de Tejas Patterns
P.O. Box 1636
Sherman, Texas 75091
800-883-5278
www.dosdetejas.com
The Ultimate Wrap Skirt: 5032 (page 156-157)

The McCall Pattern Company
P.O. Box 3755
Manhattan, Kansas 66505-3755
United States: 800-766-3619, extension 488
International: 785-776-4041, extension 488

Some projects are made with McCall and Vogue patterns. For a complete selection of their patterns, please visit your local retail fabric store or visit their Web site: www.mccallpattern.com

McCall: 3501 (page 153)

Vogue: 1813 (pages 154-155)

Vogue: 7628 (pages 141-142)

Index

Projects designed by the following people appear in this book on the pages given below:

Anita Louise Crane:
Breadloaf Bunny or Bear, 94-96; Jointed Teddy Bear, 97-100; Lop-Eared Bunny, 101-103; Leggedy Bear, 104-107;
Doll Pinafore, 110-111; Bear's Jacket, 112-113; Doll/Bear's Dress and Coat, 114-118; Doll's Apron Dress and Pantaloons, 119-123

Arden Franklin:
Designed the usage of vintage materials for: Toddler Hat and Jacket, 141-142; Lavender Floral Dress, 143; Handkerchief Yoke Dress, 144-145;
Tulip Yoke Dress, 146; Bordered Tablecloth Dress, 147; Chenille Dress, 150; Embroidered Blouse, 151; White Blouse with Drawnwork, 152;
Vintage Miniskirt, 153; Terrific Tablecloth Shirt, 154; Blue Checked Tablecloth Shirt, 155; Reversible Wrap Skirt, 156-157

Mary Jo Hiney:
Pajama Bag, 51-53; Fancy Felt Pincushion, 54-57; Monogrammed Memory Album, 58-61; Hanging Organizer, 62-64;
Zippered Pouch, 70-71; Vest Wardrobe A, 158-173; Vest Wardrobe B, 174-185

Renee Holland:
Baby Bibs & Burp Cloths, 129-132

Jennifer Jacob:
Neck Pillow and Sleep Mask, 45-48; Tooth Fairy Pillow, 49-50; Cinch Knapsack, 72-73;

Joan Morris:
Stuffed Scottie Dog, 84-85; Baby's Sunhat, 126-128

L. Karen Odam:
Pattern for Reversible Wrap Skirt, 156-157

Joanne O'Sullivan:
Color-Slice Felt Rattle, 82-83; Fuzzy Ducky, 86-87; Snuggle Bunny, 88-89; Fleecy Baby Jumper and Pants, 137-140;

Emma Pearson:
Baby Bunting, 135-136

Allison Smith:
Nursing and Play Pillow, 78-79, Soft Blocks and Ball, 80-81, Oilcloth Bib, 133-134

Diana L. Thomas:
Eyeglasses Case, 42-44

Cindy Lou Who:
Flower Pot Purse, 65-69; Duvet Cover, 74-75